# CROSS, CRESCENT, AND SWORD

Recent Titles in
Contributions to the Study of Religion

# CROSS, CRESCENT, AND SWORD

The Justification and Limitation of War in Western and Islamic Tradition

Edited by *James Turner Johnson* and *John Kelsay*

Contributions to the Study of Religion, Number 27
Henry Warner Bowden, Series Editor

GREENWOOD PRESS
NEW YORK • WESTPORT, CONNECTICUT • LONDON

**Library of Congress Cataloging-in-Publication Data**

Cross, crescent, and sword : the justification and limitation of war in
    Western and Islamic tradition / edited by James Turner Johnson and
    John Kelsay.
        p.      cm.—(Contributions to the study of religion, ISSN 0196–7053 ; no. 27)
    Papers presented at four conferences held at Rutgers University in
the winter and spring of 1988–1989.
    Includes bibliographical references.
    ISBN 0–313–27348–0 (lib. bdg. : alk. paper)
    1. War (International law)   2. War—Religious aspects—Islam.
    3. War—Religious aspects—Christianity.   4. Terrorism.
    I. Johnson, James Turner.   II. Kelsay, John.   III. Series.
    JX4511.C76   1990
    291.5′6242—dc20          90–3159

British Library Cataloguing in Publication Data is available.

Library of Congress Catalog Card Number: 90–3159
ISBN: 0–313–27348–0
ISSN: 0196–7053

First published in 1990

Greenwood Press, 88 Post Road West, Westport, CT   06881
An imprint of Greenwood Publishing Group, Inc.

Printed in the United States of America

The paper used in this book complies with the
Permanent Paper Standard issued by the National
Information Standards Organization (Z39.48–1984).

10 9 8 7 6 5 4 3 2 1

# Contents

**Part II: Irregular Warfare and Terrorism**

**Part III: Combatancy, Noncombatancy, and Noncombatant Immunity**

# Foreword

*Henry Warner Bowden*

Since the rise of OPEC, the Iraqi-Iranian war, Soviet involvement in Afghanistan, and saber rattling from Libya, perhaps no portion of the globe has attracted more attention than the Middle East. Most observers admit now as never before that their knowledge of Islam, the traditional faith of people in the Middle East as well as elsewhere, is woefully inadequate. This volume comprises a significant effort to rectify such ignorance. Alongside chapters on Islam are ones on various aspects of the Christian tradition too. These studies by nine specialists are coordinated around important questions about religion and its impact on human experience in war, peace, and politics.

A glance at the table of contents and a perusal of the editors' introductory comments will easily direct readers to specific topics in this book's cogent format. It is unnecessary for the series editor to paraphrase the obvious. But as a way of highlighting notable features of the chapters contained herein, a few evaluative comments may provide additional orientation. Jeffrey Stout provides a succinct overview of current positions in Protestantism and Catholicism regarding pacifism and just war theory. Ranging from Augustine to Aquinas and including contemporary voices in a critical analysis, he expounds one religious tradition's remarkable conceptual diversity. Abdulaziz Sachedina gives a thoughtful explanation of the way *jihad*, or defensive war, is grounded in the Qur'an. He also shows how Sunni jurists legitimize warfare as a means of requiring human submission to God and how Shi'i jurists even justify offensive war when a designated authority can assure participants of its divine sanction.

How can people wage a limited war after participants affirm that a just one has begun? Stephen Lammers surveys criteria used by twentieth-century thinkers in the West who try to deal realistically and rationally with this problem. Whereas early and medieval theorists concentrated on approaches to war, more recent spokespersons—including Christian theologians—have stressed the need for discrimination and proportionality as keys to limiting combat. By the same token Charles Butterworth focuses on one medieval Islamic philosopher, al-Fârâbî, to explain how warfare can be characterized as just and how it fits into the overall conception of a well-ordered regime. Al-Fârâbî's view includes a great reluctance to declaring any war just, even by appealing to *jihad* as a defense of Islam. While he makes the ability to wage war one of the qualities of those fit to rule the virtuous city, al-Fârâbî ultimately concludes that the exceptional moral qualities of such a ruler will eschew such violence.

Openly declared hostilities and formal confrontation are one thing; irregular outbursts and terrorist attacks are another. Considering questions of moral responsibility in this amorphous area, Courtney Campbell argues for maintaining traditional standards as a device with which to measure guerrilla tactics. Though just war theory may need broadening to include sanction for a people's war, the collectively binding criteria of authorization, intentionality, and responsibility need to be reaffirmed, lest insurgency be too easily justified. Tamara Sonn tackles the tough question of why Islamic literature almost uniformly condemns irregular warfare and yet terrorism is so frequent in the Islamic world. She finds that extremist activities appear at the flash points of radical socio-economic and political change, even though they contravene the letter and spirit of Islam. Along similar lines, Khaled Abou El Fadl focuses on irregular warfare from the perspective of classical Islam. Medieval jurists incorporated concepts of proportionality and discrimination in their thinking, he notes, but it remains for modern Muslims to resolve ambiguities in those general legal injunctions.

Robert Phillips addresses the thorny problem of determining who is a combatant and who is entitled to noncombatant immunity from violence. In a tenacious analysis, he grapples with what is justifiable killing and what is simply calculated murder. There are no final answers to questions like these, and John Kelsay pursues the topic further, probing the relationship between categorical prohibitions of murder and noncombatant immunity. Using contemporary events in Muslim countries, he points out that the content of "justice" and "injustice," of "guilt" and "innocence," are specified by nonmoral factors—religious, military, and political—and that the Islamic contribution to rules about the conduct of modern war is still emerging from concrete political experience.

All these chapters deal with crucial questions in today's world. Each

is thoughtful, restrained, and couched in a knowledge of classical traditions as well as contemporary events. They exist on the growing edge
of creative scholarship and, by their efforts, push that edge forward.

# Introduction

*James Turner Johnson*

In the winter and spring of 1988–89 four conferences were held at Rutgers University, supported by a grant from the United States Institute of Peace, on the theme of the relationship between Western and Islamic religious and cultural traditions on war, peace, and the conduct of state-craft. This book, together with a companion volume,[1] represents the outcome of the interdisciplinary and cross-cultural dialogue these conferences sought to create.

Such a project as this is needed because of the significant expansion of the role within the international community that is played by nations and political movements with Islamic religious and cultural traditions. Scholarly analysis and interpretation of Islamic traditions and of areas of relationship and commonality between these traditions and those of the West have lagged behind the rapid, energetic resurgence of Islamic religion and the associated cultural and political changes. Despite the urgency of the moral problems examined in the present project, they have never before been treated collaboratively by scholars of religion and culture intent on bridging the gap of knowledge and understanding between study of the West and study of Islam. Indeed, apart from the occasion of these conferences and the resultant books, these two groups of scholars would normally not engage in dialogue regarding their respective fields.

Students of the religious and other aspects of the historical development of Western culture have typically paid no attention to Islam, except at the edges of their field of view—as, for example, in acknowledging the influence of Muslim philosophers on medieval Christian scholastic theology and philosophy. For its part, scholarship on Islam has been hampered by a legacy from a previous age of comparative study that represented the religion and culture of the Islamic world as inferior to that of the West. Contemporary Islamicists, concerned about avoiding such condescension, have bracketed the West out of their own field of concern and have focused their study on one or another individual, movement, or historical period within the development of Islamic traditions. The result has been that the two groups of scholars—those focused on the Western world and those focused on the world of Islam—have plied their respective trades without interaction with each other.

The problem of dialogue is compounded by the asymmetry of the two fields of study. Nowhere is this lack of correspondence more apparent than in the case of the religious and cultural traditions addressed in this book: those concerned with defining when war is justifiable and what limits ought to be observed in justified warfare. Whereas the just war tradition of the West has been the focus of much concentrated attention devoted to identifying and analyzing its sources, its historical development, and its implications for contemporary war, nothing comparable as yet exists in the field of Islamic studies.

Despite the importance in the present context of the concept of *jihad*, for example, there is no longitudinal study of this idea from its appearance in the Qur'an, to its treatment by various sorts of commentators over history, and to its association with various nationalist and revolutionary political movements in the present. Nor has there been sustained attention to the interaction between religious and nonreligious forces in the shaping of the tradition on justification and limitation of war in the Islamic world. To be sure, excellent individual works exist on specific subjects related to war and its conduct within the historical development of Islamic tradition, such as Majid Khadduri's *The Islamic Law of Nations*, which translates the medieval Muslim jurist al-Shaybani's *Kitab al-Siyar*.[2] Though important, however, such works are but single limited windows on a large, rich, and varied tradition, whose extent is much broader in both time and place. Much work of investigation, analysis, and—not least—translation remains to be done for the Islamic tradition on war before a general judgment as to its nature, content, and implications is possible.

The present volume, within its own restricted space, seeks to provide a beginning both for cross-disciplinary and cross-cultural dialogue between students of Western and of Islamic religion and culture and for more intensive and systematic study of Islamic traditions related to war, its justification, and the limitations attached to its conduct. For scholars of the major Western religious and cultural tradition on these topics, that centered on the idea of just war, it responds to a need to know and understand more about the tradition of *jihad* and the constellation of ideas and attitudes on war, peace, and politics that are normative in

Islamic religion and present in the cultures of Islamic lands. For scholars of Islamic religion and culture, it addresses a need to engage in systematic study of these same ideas and attitudes, to appraise their development and influence over history in ways similar to the appraisal that has been made of the evolution of the just war tradition, and to assess how these ideas and attitudes should be placed in relationship to those of Western culture.

In general terms, the format of this book is the same as that of the four conferences mentioned above: two groups of scholars, one whose field of work is the just war tradition of Western culture and one whose subject of study is Islamic religion and culture, examine from their different perspectives a number of important issues relating to the justification and limitation of war. Four chapters examine the general problem of when war is justified and what restraints ought to be observed in the conduct of war; then two other groups of chapters address specific issues that have become especially pressing in the present historical context: the judgment on irregular warfare and terrorism in the two traditions and the definition of noncombatancy and the provision for protection of noncombatants during armed hostilities. The chapters range broadly over the historical development of the two traditions, seeking individually and collectively to open up the unfamiliar and to bring elements of the two traditions to bear on contemporary moral problems of armed violence and war.

Over the last thirty years a spirited debate over the ethical issues raised by modern war has been the catalyst for scholarly reexamination and rethinking of the just war tradition of Western culture. That debate is mirrored in the chapters in this volume.[3] It is important, though, to sketch in general terms the origins, nature, and pattern of development of this tradition as background for the discussions in the chapters. This is especially important since to better serve the purpose of comparative dialogue the categories of analysis employed here have been derived from those of just war thought. At the same time, however, Islamic tradition has produced its own ways of thinking and a distinct terminology, and some of the more important of these are sketched below by way of introduction to the debate in this volume.

Just war tradition, broadly understood, includes elements from Christian theological reflection and canon law, professional military experience and codes of conduct, international law and the practice of politics among nations. Though its deepest roots are found in ideas from classical Greece and Rome and the world of the Old Testament, the actual coalescence of this tradition as a recognizably coherent body of thought and practice concerning the justification and limitation of war was an accomplishment of western European society in the Middle Ages. There, especially during the twelfth through fourteenth centuries, chivalric and churchly interests gradually merged, and in merging were mutually transformed into a cultural consensus defining the just use of force, the right of access to force, the protection of the innocent, and much more. This consensus was in place by the era of the Hundred Years War, and early modern theorists, like Franciscus de Victoria (mid-sixteenth century), and Hugo Grotius (early seventeenth century), generally recognized as progenitors of international law, knew just war tradition in the form of a number of major categories or criteria for judgment that have remained substantially the same ever since, with the specific form of their contents evolving to reflect the contingencies of history.

These categories are generally divided into two parts, one having to do with when it is justified to resort to war (the *jus ad bellum*, in the traditional Latin terminology) and the other concerning the limits to be observed in a just war (the *jus in bello*). The *jus ad bellum* included three principal requirements—just cause, recognized authority to make war, and right intention or purpose—together with the further stipulations that the use of force should be a last resort, should be proportionate to the evil remedied, and should contribute to establishing a new state of peace. The *jus in bello* added two further requirements: that the conduct of a justified war should seek to protect noncombatants from harm (the principle of discrimination or noncombatant immunity) and that the means of war should not be grossly destructive compared to the goals sought (the principle of proportionality).

Commentators early in the modern period, identifying these ideas as expressions of the natural law, stressed what they saw to be the universal character of these ideas. Theorists of international law wove the inherited just war tradition into their reasoning without questioning this conception, and the development of positive international law followed suit. Accordingly, international law has been one of the major carriers of just war tradition in the modern era, and the law of armed conflict in contemporary international law stands as one of the major signs of the continuing impact of this tradition not only within Western culture but in the relations among states regardless of cultural background. At the same time, internal to Western culture, just war tradition also remains as a focus for theological and philosophical moral reflection on war and violence and, in the professional military sphere, continues to be visible in codes of conduct and rules of engagement.

In the case of Islam the situation is both similar and different. Classical Islam developed its own "just war doctrine" as early as the first and second centuries A.H.—the seventh and eighth centuries C.E.—that is, before the just war tradition of the West began to coalesce into its classical form. Building on the Qur'an and the *hadith* (traditions reporting Muhammad's words and deeds) jurists like al-Shaybani developed a sophisticated concept of the law of nations that included rules for justified fighting and was in theory to govern the relations between the Islamic state and all other. Like the later Western theory of international law based on natural law, the Muslim law of nations was in principle universal, that is, accessible to all peoples and binding on them all. Here, though, the universal claims were explicitly tied to religious ones, for the classical Muslim jurists assumed the division made in the Qur'an between the "territory of submission [to God]" (dar al-Islam) and the "territory of war" (dar al-harb), where disorderliness and strife are endemic. Spread of the rule of law thus implied spread of the dar al-Islam, and this therefore became both a temporal and an eschatological goal.[4]

The success of Islamic temporal power led to the establishment of a settled, stable society from the Middle East to Spain, whose intellectual life was the product not only of the Qur'an but also of Greek and Hellenistic philosophy. By the tenth century C.E./fourth century A.H., Muslim philosophers were producing synthetic works reconciling insights of the classical philosophers with the Qur'an and traditions regarding the Prophet. Preeminent among those writing on statecraft and the use of power by the good ruler was al-Fârâbî, whose Aphorisms of the Statesman and The Virtuous City laid down principles for the place of military force in government as a response to the practical needs of virtuous rule. His concern was with harb (war) rather than the more theologically laden concept of jihad (struggle, effort), which through most of Muslim history has been taken as having to do in the first place with the inner struggle of each individual to follow the path of God.[5]

For classical Muslim thought on the concept of jihad as connected to harb (war) and qital (fighting), the most authoritative source is a contemporary of al-Fârâbî, the jurist al-Tabari. For this commentator, jihad by military means is justified by the Qur'an itself, which imposes on Muslims an obligation to make the world aware of the need to obey the divine will. It is thus a response not only to lack of right belief but to the discord and disorder that obtains in the world outside the dar al-Islam. The call to faith (al da'wa) sets the context for jihad by military as well as nonmilitary means, the former being justified when the latter fail or are not allowed to proceed by the unfaithful.[6] The ultimate justification for war in the sense of jihad is thus the need to establish the divine rule in all the earth. The contact point with the harb that, following al-Fârâbî, a virtuous ruler may wage is the common goal of punishing evil and securing good. Yet there is a substantive difference. Jihad, with its root sense of the inner struggle to establish obedience to God in the heart, is a category of the right ordering of the moral life, an ordering that, when universalized within the political community, will bring an end to discord and strife; by contrast the harb waged by the virtuous ruler is a category of how to impose a right order within the political life of a community in which the proper interior disposition of obedience to God has not yet become universal. *Jihad*, because of its fundamentally religious nature, requires religious authorization; *harb* is a category of practical politics and requires only political authorization and direction.

As Abdulaziz Sachedina notes in his chapter, the two major branches of Islam, the Sunni and the Shi'i, differ sharply for doctrinal reasons on the authority necessary to wage war in the sense of *jihad*. The position established by the Sunni jurists was that both offensive and defensive *jihad* could be waged by any Muslim authority against the *dar al-harb*. The Shi'i position, on the other hand, has been that a divinely appointed person, the just *Imam*, who would unite political and religious sovereignty, is necessary for any *jihad* that is not defensive. Only such a person can guarantee that the resulting fighting is in accord with the goals of Islam. Yet in the world as it now is, there is no just *Imam*, and only war to protect true religion and the territory in which it is practiced is justified.

In their classic forms both the traditions of the Islamic world and those of Western culture share concerns that can be classified within the categories of the just war tradition: just cause, right authority, right intention, and so forth. For both traditions in their early stages, religious interests intermingled with those of the political order, and no effort was made to separate them from each other. In the West, though, the growing trend of secularization led first to the rejection of the right of religious authorities to undertake war (a settled fact by the end of the thirteenth century) and then to rejection of the right to propagate religion by force of arms (established in theory by the sixteenth century and in fact at the end of the wars of religion following the Reformation). The just war tradition of the West, accordingly, has developed so as to reflect the needs of a political order defined in terms of secular interests, and religious claims must compete with those of other ideologies within that framework. How these claims can compete effectively has been a principal concern in the contributions to recent just war debate by religious theorists.

Within the Islamic world, by contrast, no concept of the fully secular state, divided from religion in both theory and practice, ever became established. Even the vast Ottoman Empire mixed sacerdotal with secular elements in its pattern of rule. The result, as Tamara Sonn argues in her chapter, is that contemporary political theory within the culture of Islam is experiencing considerable stress in the presence of an international order that includes numerous states claiming to be Islamic societies yet acknowledging no universal common authority and often engaging in conflict with one another. Present-day application of Islamic tradition on justification and limitation of war is similarly stressed by the disparity between current political realities and those of the historical context during the centuries when the classic definition of that tradition was accomplished.

What can be concluded about the contemporary relevance of these two traditions? So far as just war tradition is concerned, there is a considerable and growing body of literature based in one or another aspect of this perspective and focused on the particular moral problems of contemporary warfare. Such a literature remains to be generated from within the perspective of Islamic tradition, and the essays in the present volume represent a step in that direction. On the specific topics of irregular warfare, terrorism, and provision for mitigation of harm to noncombatants, this book establishes a firm basis both for critical assessment of actions within the framework of Islamic culture and for cross-cultural comparative dialogue between the Islamic tradition and the just war tradition of the West.

Many people deserve gratitude for their contributions to this project. First, John Kelsay and I wish to express our appreciation and thanks to all the members of the core seminar on Western and Islamic traditions: besides those who prepared chapters published in the present volume, this includes those whose work will appear in a companion volume: Frederick Donner of the University of Chicago; John Langan, S. J., of Georgetown University; Bruce Lawrence of Duke University; David Little, formerly of the University of Virginia but now a scholar in residence at the United States Institute of Peace; Richard Martin of Arizona State University; Ann Elizabeth Mayer of the University of Pennsylvania; and William V. O'Brien of Georgetown University. Our thanks also to others who have assisted us ably and tirelessly: at Rutgers, Mrs. Henriette Cohen, who with a meticulous eye for detail arranged travel and accommodations for the four seminars, and Mrs. Connie Burke, who assisted in the above and who prepared the composite select bibliography that appears in this volume; at Florida State, Mrs. Maureen Jackson, who typed final versions of several of the chapters. Finally, we wish to thank the United States Institute of Peace for the grant that made this project possible and Rutgers University for hosting the conference series from which this volume has come.

## NOTES

1. John Kelsay and James Turner Johnson, eds., *Just War and Jihad: Historical and Theoretical Perspectives on War and Peace in Western and Islamic Traditions* (Westport, CT: Greenwood Press, 1991).

2. Majid Khadduri, *The Islamic Law of Nations* (Baltimore: Johns Hopkins University Press, 1966). See further the discussion in the chapter by John Kelsay in this volume.

3. See the chapters by Jeffrey Stout, Stephen Lammers, Courtney Campbell, and Robert Phillips. On the historical development of the just war tradition see further James Turner Johnson's chapter in Kelsay and Johnson, *Just War and Jihad*.

4. See further the chapter by John Kelsay in this volume.

5. See further the chapter by Charles Butterworth in this volume.

6. On matters treated in this paragraph and the next see the chapter by Abdulaziz Sachedina in this volume.

# I

## When Is War Justified? What Are Its Limits?

# 1

## Justice and Resort to War: A Sampling of Christian Ethical Thinking

*Jeffrey Stout*

If Christian thinking about resort to war were as simple as leading spokespersons for the tradition would have us believe, summarizing its most salient features for comparative purposes would be easy.[1] But traditions get complicated as they go along. And church officials and theologians are often engaging in disguised polemics when they make pronouncements about the essence or structure of their tradition's teachings. Thus there is reason to treat any simple account, above all an official one, with suspicion. It is a mistake to suppose that some such account must be accepted and that the problem is merely to decide which account to accept. Rather, doing justice to the diversity of a venerable moral tradition means coming to terms with competition among the various patterns of reasoning within it, each of which may present itself as *the* traditional pattern. So it is with Christian thought on resort to war.

It does not matter much which sample of Christian thinking we consider first, as long as we are prepared to see it as one among others. If I had the space to tell a long evolutionary story, I would begin at the beginning, with the days when Christians anxiously awaited the apocalypse at the margins of the Roman Empire, convinced that God himself was about to perform whatever violent acts necessary to establish his kingdom forever. But given the limits of space, I will instead begin with several conflicting accounts of the tradition currently in circulation. I will resist the temptation to declare one of these accounts the correct historical view and will strive instead for a broader view of the tradition in which each account can receive its due as a *partial* truth—partial because incomplete: no simple account brings the full history of its predecessors and competitors into view; and partial because motivated by

particular normative concerns: each account considered here is designed
to portray one pattern of reasoning as either the authentically Christian,
the logically necessary, or the morally preferable pattern.

## A CATHOLIC PASTORAL LETTER

Consider how the Catholic bishops of the United States characterized
Christian thinking about resort to war a few years ago in two passages
from their widely disseminated pastoral letter, *The Challenge of Peace*:

The church's teaching on war and peace establishes a strong presumption against
war which is binding on all; it then examines when this presumption may be
overridden, precisely in the name of preserving the kind of peace which protects
human dignity and human rights.[2]

The moral theory of the "just-war" or "limited war" doctrine begins with the
presumption which binds all Christians: We should do no harm to our neighbors;
how we treat our enemy is the key test of whether we love our neighbor; and
the possibility of taking even one human life is a prospect we should consider
in fear and trembling. How is it possible to move from these presumptions to
the idea of a justifiable use of lethal force?[3]

The bishops ask not whether this movement is possible but rather how
it is. They remain convinced that resort to war is sometimes necessary.
Yet they convey the impression that there is something paradoxical in the
idea. Why? Because they assume—and here they echo what has recently
become a scholarly commonplace—that Christian reasoning about resort
to war begins with a presumption against doing harm, using force, committing violent acts, or killing. Waging war unquestionably involves all
of these things. So if there is a presumption against doing any of these
things, there is also a presumption against resorting to war. The question
is under what circumstances and in the pursuit of what ends, if any, can
the presumption be overcome. As the bishops present the matter, Christians differ over how this question should be answered, not over whether
Christian reasoning about resort to war should proceed from a presumption against violence or doing harm.

The bishops imply that Christians have given two basic answers to
the one basic question about resort to war. Pacifists answer the question
by saying that the presumption is never overcome. They therefore adopt
an exceptionless rule prohibiting war, and they try to show that this
rule is too weighty to be overridden by other considerations. Nonpa-
cifists argue that the presumption can be overcome, and then defend
exceptions to the rule or propose considerations capable of overriding
it. Arguing in this second way is to adhere to "the moral theory" of the
just war.[4] This theory specifies the "criteria" that must be satisfied before

resort to war may be deemed justified.[5] The criteria indicate when the presumption against war is overridden. Both Christian pacifists and just war theorists, according to the pastoral letter, begin their reasoning about resort to war from a single starting point—a presumption against war or violence. The two groups part ways only at a subsequent point: that at which the weight and stringency of the presumption must be decided.

It is worth keeping in mind that when the bishops accepted this picture of resort-to-war reasoning, they were not leaving unchanged the standard language of previous Catholic pronouncements on the doctrine of *jus ad bellum*. They were making a new gesture of ecumenical tolerance to Christian pacifists, offering as warrant the call for "a completely fresh reappraisal of war" issued by Vatican II. The bishops were trying to show more respect than their predecessors had shown for Christian pacifism as an authentically Christian stance. They wanted to affirm that pacifist opponents of war and principled advocates of just war can assume "a complementary relationship" in service of the common good, each employing its own means in the quest for peace and the protection of the innocent, each appealing to the same basic idea.[6] "They diverge on some specific conclusions, but they share a common presumption against the use of force as a means of settling disputes."[7]

A close reading of *The Challenge of Peace* shows why some pacifists were quick to refuse the complementary position the bishops had offered them. The bishops wished to recognize a measure of diversity in Christian ethics without abandoning the idea, central to their own position, that states are sometimes obliged to resort to war in defense of the common good. So they opened up room for pacifism as an acceptable option for Christian *individuals* who conscientiously object to participation in war, but they insisted nonetheless that any *state* committed to pacifism would be incapable of exercising the full scope of its responsibilities. Pacifists who propose unilateral disarmament as an option for states, or who see Christian witness and discipleship as antithetical to the business of the state, are implicitly condemned by the bishops. It was to only some kinds of pacifists, in fact, that the bishops' offer had been extended: to someone like Erasmus, who became convinced that war was too destructive and corrupting to foster either peace or justice, or to someone like Martin Luther King, Jr., who advocated nonviolent resistance to evil. In contrast, pacifists like Tolstoy and the sectarians he most admired are implicitly condemned for favoring nonresistance to evil and noncooperation with state violence. They fare no better than another group that bishops and theologians rarely mention these days: Christian crusaders, like Bernard of Clairvaux, who believed they had been called not to peace but to war against the infidels.

## VARIETIES OF CHRISTIAN PACIFISM

I shall restrict myself in this section to addressing several forms of absolute pacifism, the view that resort to war is never morally permissible. One argument for this view has been associated with an outlook sometimes called Christian liberalism or idealism. Christian liberalism holds that Christian love means doing unto others as you would have them do unto you and that you should, therefore, act in ways that would produce the best overall result if everyone acted likewise. Clearly the world would be a better place if no one ever used force or committed injustices against others. And if no one ever used force or committed injustices, there would be no need to use force in order to preserve and protect the common good. Hence, according to this view, you should never use force against others.

In contrast, Christian "realists" argue that because we do not live in a world in which everyone actually behaves lovingly, we have no clear reason for permanently eschewing the use of force ourselves.[8] In our world, following the dictates of pacifism—the policies that would lead to the best overall result if everyone followed them—would not actually lead to the best result, given that not everyone will follow those policies even if we do. Practical wisdom requires that we act as if things are the way they are, not some other way we wish they were. Similar arguments have also been brought against the idea, found in Kant and elsewhere, that you ought always to act as if you were a member of a kingdom of ends in which everyone always did the right thing.[9] Since in our world people often do the wrong thing, the Christian realist argues, it is unrealistic and unreasonable to act as if they did not. Absolute pacifism would be justified if everybody did the right thing all the time, because then nobody would ever have to be repelled by force in order to protect the common good, but this hardly tells us why we, in our world, have reason to be pacifists.

The liberal or idealist varieties of Christian pacifism just mentioned might plausibly be said to reason from a presumption against violence. Another variety of pacifism, the eschatological pacifism often ascribed to the early Jesus movement, would be much harder to interpret in terms of the bishops' presumption. Eschatological pacifism does not ask us to act as if some counterfactual statement were true. Nor does it ask us to suppose that Christian nonviolent action is capable, by itself, of transforming the real world into a domain of perpetual peace and justice. It holds instead that the world is not what it seems to be. It is not what it seems to be, because the impending end (or eschaton) of the present age is at hand. "The time is fulfilled, and the kingdom of God is at hand; repent and believe the gospel" (Mark 1:15). If the kingdom of God is at hand, if "there are some standing here who would not taste death before they see the kingdom of God come with power" (Mark 9:1), then it will be unvarnished realism to follow the ideal rules—the rules that would be best to follow if everybody followed them—and to act as if we are members of a kingdom of ends in which everybody always does the right thing. For, presumably, the kingdom of God will not need political force as a check against human evil, that having been dealt with decisively by God on the day of judgment. Behave in a way appropriate to the coming of the kingdom: do not be anxious; care not about tomorrow; let the dead bury the dead; do good to those who hate you; above all, discontinue business as usual, including the business of using force to secure justice, and repent. Behave as if the kingdom of God is at hand, but only because it is.

Christian pacifism achieves somewhat different emphases when it is said that the kingdom has already come, that we live in "a period in which two ages overlap,"[10] one of which "points backwards to human history outside of (before) Christ," the other "forward to the fullness of the kingdom of God."[11] The calling of the church, in this view, is to witness to God's action in bringing about the kingdom, to imitate Jesus, and thus to follow his example of nonresistant love. The true church's nonresistant love involves a willingness to suffer in the face of worldly evil and a refusal to deal with evil as the world does, through violence. As Menno Simons put it his "Reply to False Accusations":

Such exceeding grace of God has appeared unto us poor, miserable sinners that we who were formerly no people at all and who knew of no peace are now called to be such a glorious people of God, a church, kingdom, inheritance, body, and possession of peace. Therefore we desire not to break this peace, but by His great power by which He has called us to this peace and portion, to walk in this grace and peace, unchangeably and unwaveringly unto death.[12]

This is a pacifism of vocation and discipleship, and so far as I can tell, it has little to do with what the Catholic bishops call a presumption against violence.

## RAMSEY'S AUGUSTINIAN REALISM

If the bishops, despite initial appearances, have made little room in their account for certain varieties of Christian pacifism, have they not done better in characterizing the thought of their fellow "realistic" defenders of just war? In his posthumously published book, *Speak Up for Just War or Pacifism*, Paul Ramsey, a distinguished contemporary representative of just war thinking, insisted that they had not.[13] The imperative disjunction Ramsey chose as his title was meant to signal the need for a clean choice between just war theory and pacifism, and thus to resist any conciliatory reinterpretation of the tradition like the one the bishops had proposed. To make this implication of his argument still more prominent, Ramsey invited Stanley Hauerwas, a Christian pacifist of the witness-and-discipleship sort, to contribute an epilogue.[14] By joining forces in this manner, Ramsey and Hauerwas aimed to catch their common opponents in a crossfire of criticism and to show, by the integrity and irreducibility of their own arguments, that Christian ethical tradition has distinct strands that deserve to be respected.

Given Ramsey's stature as a figure within just war tradition and as an interpreter of it, his objections may fairly be said to establish a presumption against the "presumption against violence" view of just war thought.[15] According to Ramsey, just war theory does recognize a presumption against violence in the following two senses: that because love does not value destruction and disorder, it employs violent means toward its ends only when nonviolent means are to no avail; and that the burden of proof falls upon any state declaring war to show that violent means are actually necessary and proportionate under the circumstances in the pursuit of just ends. The criterion of last resort properly expresses the first idea. The second, which Ramsey termed "quasi-legal," can be expressed as a corollary of the criterion of upright intention: a state going to war must not only have upright ends, it must also be prepared to declare them publicly and accept a burden of proof in defending them. But there is a third idea that some thinkers endorse and Ramsey firmly rejects: that avoiding or minimizing destruction and disorder is the primary or ultimate end of statecraft. Ramsey was sharply critical of authors who conflate these three ideas, and he saw the resulting confusion as partly responsible for "the erroneous conviction that pacifism and just war have in common the *same* presumption against violence."[16] But his main concern was to deny that just war thinking begins with a presumption against violence, either in these senses or in any other significant sense.

Where does just war thinking begin, according to Ramsey? If it begins with any presumption, it is "the presumption ... to restrain evil and protect the innocent," or "the presumption against injustice."[17] This presumption derives, in turn, from the requirements of Christian love in a fallen world: "The original just-war assumption is that social charity comes to the aid of the oppressed."[18] This sentence echoes the primacy accorded to agape in Ramsey's first book,[19] as well as in the opening chapter of his first book on war, in which he described his understanding of Christian morality as "faith effective through in-principled love."[20]

The starting point of Ramsey's ethical reasoning was always Christian love, and in his thoughts about war he moved directly from that starting point to the conclusion that Christians must at times resort to war when the innocent suffer injustice. Anyone who rules out war altogether violates the presumption against injustice, a requirement of love properly conceived. In a world marked by sin, agape involves forcible restraint of injustice, including use of arms in protection of the oppressed. Far from reifying a presumption against violence, Ramsey sought to foster conditions in which just war would remain possible as an instrument of love. It was his mission to make the world safe for just war, in the hope that Christians would not be without recourse whenever nonviolent means for opposing grave injustice had been exhausted.

In the early 1960s, Ramsey was not writing out of a relatively continuous tradition of just war thinking. He was recovering and reinventing the tradition in the hope that Protestants like himself might be able to claim it as their own. In the process, he took over ideas and fragments of arguments from Augustine and Aquinas, Luther and Calvin, Reinhold Niebuhr, and twentieth-century Catholic natural law, putting all the pieces together into an eclectic pattern that was distinctively Protestant and uniquely his own. In this pattern, *agape* is the central moral notion, and Augustine, interpreted through the eyes of the Reformation, is the central authority. All other notions and all other thinkers are made to seem subsidiary or marginal. The concept of natural law and associated concepts of justice are to be used whenever they prove helpful, but they always remain radically in need of transformation by Christian love.

For an Augustinian of Ramsey's stripe, true justice is possible only in the heavenly city, where God receives the love he is due and the ravages of sin have already been corrected by God's grace. A just war undertaken by an earthly community is thus, strictly speaking, an impossibility. Even a group that has just cause for war will, this side of God's kingdom, fall far short of true justice in whatever war it chooses to wage. In someone else's hands, this thought might be taken in a pacifist direction: if there are no truly just wars, then resort to war is impermissible. But in Ramsey's hands, the same thought becomes a reason for self-scrutiny and humility in waging the wars we must wage: when we come to the aid of the oppressed in the name of Christian love, we must not suppose ourselves free of guilt. The phrase "just war" must therefore be made to mean not a war that is, strictly speaking, just, but rather a war fought in conformity with love's demand that we protect the innocent from especially grave injustices at the hands of states. Accordingly, the phrase "just war tradition" comes to mean the tradition, fathered by Augustine, in which Christian love elaborated the principles it needed to determine when resort to war is justified in a fallen world.

Once this definition of the tradition is in place, most of Ramsey's historical claims about the tradition's major figures, basic assumptions, and working criteria fall into place as well. Ramsey would be the first to admit the normative theological bias built into the definition. He had no interest in posing as a neutral historian and was prepared to argue for his choice of definitions on theological grounds. When he spoke of *Christian* just war reasoning, he meant a pattern of thinking he could endorse, in good conscience, as genuinely in keeping with biblical sources as he understood them—which is to say, by Augustinian lights. When he lamented the transition from Augustine to Aquinas for its "increasing emphasis upon the natural-law concept of justice in analysis of the cause that justifies participation in war," he did not hesitate to add that the latter "is what is usually meant by the doctrine of the just war." His open rejection of this emphasis, "in the belief that Augustine was more correct and realistic," allowed Ramsey to define a tradition with which he could more easily identify.[21]

Ramsey's definition is too narrow to adopt for my purposes. First of all, as a secular moral philosopher I seek to renew appreciation for the classical conception of justice Aquinas inherited from Aristotle, later versions of which appeared in modern Catholicism; Anglican thinking such as that of Jeremy Taylor; and assorted forms of civic republicanism. It is therefore morally important for me to keep this conception from being squeezed out of the just war story, whether by Ramsey's Augustinian devaluation or by the bishops' desire to make peace with pacifists. Second, I am not trying to determine which, if any, form of just war reasoning is authentically Christian from some theological point of view, but rather to survey various styles of reasoning employed by people who have called themselves Christians. So a definition like Ramsey's comes into play here only as further evidence of diversity. Those who call themselves Christian differ not only on the issue of resort to war and on the issue of what role the concept of justice should have in ethics,[22] but also on the issue of who or what ought to be called Christian. The tradition is constituted in part by debate—among Catholic bishops, Protestant theologians, and many others—over where the boundaries of Christian tradition should be located.[23] And it is possible to value the tradition less for its occasional emphasis on love than for its role in keeping classical patterns of thought alive—as it were, to value not the Christianity but the ethics in Christian ethics.

Ramsey's former student, James Turner Johnson, has done more than anyone else to show how Ramsey's work would have to be amended for the purposes of broadly historical inquiry into the evolution of just war thinking in Christendom. From Johnson's more inclusive point of view, Ramsey's account exaggerates the influence of theologians in general and Augustine in particular, at the expense of canon lawyers, chivalrous knights, international lawyers, and many others.[24] Once we construe the tradition as broadly as Johnson does, which is plainly the wise course to take here, it seems that any talk of *the* moral theory or *the* central idea of just war reasoning is bound to be unconvincing.

## THE METHOD OF CASUISTRY: THE THOMISM OF
## ELIZABETH ANSCOMBE

I shall now try to give this conclusion further support by examining the pattern of *jus ad bellum* reasoning found in modern Thomism. This is what Ramsey had in mind when he spoke of "what is usually meant by the doctrine of the just war" and it is what liberal Catholics are opposing when they repeat conciliar language on the need for "a completely fresh appraisal of war." Thomism carries conceptual residues of ancient Judaism and early Christianity, of classical and modern theories of natural law, of Stoicism, and of Aristotelian ethics, but it appeals to the authority of Aquinas with the same sort of conviction that Ramsey appeals to Augustine. Among its most distinguished advocates in recent years is the Cambridge philosopher, Elizabeth Anscombe. The essays on war reprinted in the third volume of her *Collected Philosophical Papers* can be used to demonstrate the respects in which Thomistic reasoning conforms to neither Ramsey's ethics of Christian love nor the American Catholic bishops' presumption against violence.[25]

The most intriguing of these essays was originally published as part of a pamphlet opposing Britain's resort to war against Germany in 1939. The essay argues entirely from the natural law, by which Anscombe means those principles that show how human beings must act in matters where their will is free, if their nature is to be fulfilled and their happiness achieved.[26] The natural law requires justice—"the proper working out of relations between man and man, and between societies, each having his due"—and its reflection can be discerned "in the ordered activity" of God's creation. What the natural law demands of us we "can discover by reason, checked and guaranteed by the divine revelation of Scripture."[27] The conditions of the just war derive directly from the natural law. They specify what justice requires of us in a particular area of human life.

In introducing this framework, Anscombe moved easily within a relatively settled moral tradition that had not yet arrived at Vatican II or experienced the subsequent debates over natural law and absolutism that have made Charles Curran a cause célèbre. She felt no need to elucidate the framework in any detail, for she knew that her Catholic readers would find it immediately recognizable. For detailed exposition, she referred them to the relevant passages from Aquinas or to "any textbook of moral theology."[28] Aquinas counted in this context as *the* moral theologian, just as Aristotle was, for Aquinas, *the* philosopher. His authority and proper interpretation, as codified in the textbooks, could simply be taken for granted. Anscombe was also able to cite standard texts on the conditions of the just war (Eppstein's *Catholic Tradition of the Law of Nations* and Regout's *La doctrine de la guerre juste*). She worked from a set list of criteria, and asked only how they should be applied to the case at hand.[29]

Given her opposition to British involvement in the war and the fact that she has more recently been dubbed a "nuclear pacifist," it may be worth emphasizing that she does not rule out resort to war in principle. Her skepticism about Britain's declaration of war and, more recently, about the possession and use of nuclear weapons does not derive from an absolute principle prohibiting killing as such or even all killing in war. Anscombe insists that there are some circumstances in which killing is not only permissible but obligatory. She makes no mention of a presumption against harm or violence. She does not introduce a general rule against killing, allowing for exceptions in certain special circumstances or for competing considerations that might override the rule. Nor, for that matter, does she speak of agape as the guiding principle of Christian ethics. Instead, she proceeds from a classical conception of justice, convinced that a just God would hide nothing of great moral significance from the natural light of human reason and that he demands nothing less than absolute justice from citizens of earthly communities.

Anscombe began another essay, this one originally published in 1961, with themes from Augustinian realism:

Since there are always thieves and frauds and men who commit violent attacks on their neighbors and murderers; and since without law backed by adequate force there are usually gangs of bandits; and since there are in most places laws administered by people who command violence to enforce the laws against law-breakers; the question arises: what is a just attitude to this exercise of violent coercive power on the part of rulers and their subordinate officers?[30]

The tone here resembles Ramsey's, but Anscombe exhibits none of his reluctance to invoke the concept of natural justice. Fallen or not, we are morally required to be just. If there are thieves and frauds and murderers to take account of at home, so too are there tyrants to take account of abroad. Tyrants do not deserve to have their way. Their victims deserve protection. We cannot determine how to protect the common good justly, either at home or abroad, without a clear view of possible and probable threats to that good. It cannot be prudent or just to act as if such threats did not exist. We had better take full measure of the threats and then ask how, when, and by whom they might be justly repelled, if at all.

The absolute pacifist goes wrong, according to Anscombe, in blurring the distinction between killing as such (or making war) and murder, the unjust taking of human life. Absolute pacifism, she holds, is not only false but evil in the effects it induces in those who do not fully subscribe to it. It is false in its assumption that all killing (or all killing in war) is murder. Its corrupting effect upon others lies in how it leads them to lose sight of the proper limits on killing. People who believe that some killing is morally necessary but who have been convinced by pacifists that all killing is murder will be tempted to say that in war murder is morally necessary. Start talking in this way, according to Anscombe, and you will soon find yourself willing to commit crimes of the worst conceivable sort. The pacifists will have corrupted you by undermining your sense of the difference between some killings and others—the moral difference between killing an innocent person as a means to some end, however good, and killing, say, an army of unjust aggressors as a means to an end of protecting justice. To put the point in Thomistic terms, such acts do not have the same object and thus should not be conflated. Anscombe, in short, holds precisely the attitude toward pacifism that the U.S. bishops were trying to put behind them and which their account of the tradition renders invisible.

The same conception of justice that requires us, on occasion, to use force in defense of the innocent also prohibits murder, either as an end in itself or as a means to some other end. Resort to war is sometimes, though not always, murderous. Not even the just end of righting some wrong or defending the innocent against attack can make a murderous war just. Murder is unjust killing. It is unjust because it denies its victims their due. It denies its victims their due in a particular way—by taking their life. It is therefore a species of injustice. Not every taking of a life, however, denies someone his or her due. For society to punish criminals by execution may well be a way of giving them their due, if the crime is so bad that the criminal "could not justly protest 'I have not deserved this' " (italics in original).[31] And it can be just for a state to wage war in defense of a common good by ordering "deliberate killing in order to protect its people or to put frightful injustices right."[32] Indeed, such killing can be *required* by justice. The state and its representatives are obliged to use whatever just and prudent means are required in defense of the common good, even if that entails waging war. Failure to do so, by Anscombe's reasoning, is itself an offense against justice.

To say that an act is an act of killing, according to Anscombe's ideas, is not yet to place it in its moral species. It is merely to describe an act in relation to one of its physical or natural effects. The notion of killing as such does not make even implicit reference to the central moral notion of justice. It is therefore not the sort of notion that figures into genuine moral principles. That is why she is prepared to speak of just war, even though waging war involves killing. Waging war, she holds, is sometimes required by justice. It is not an exception to a general moral principle against killing, for there is no such principle at work in her reasoning. She might be willing to grant that most acts of killing, statistically speaking, are unjust, but the principles she actually employs have the form: "Always act justly," and "Never act unjustly." They are absolutes in the sense that they admit no exceptions and cannot be overridden by other considerations. Anscombe's reasoning takes these absolutes for granted and asks which acts are just and which are not. Her name for this mode of reasoning is "the method of casuistry."[33] It does not begin with the idea that any act of killing is presumed wrongful until proven innocent. To know only that an act is an act of killing is, from her point of view, to know too little about it to classify it morally.

Anscombe condemns as sinful and decadent another mode of reasoning, which she terms "consequentialism." Consequentialists hold that our moral responsibility as human beings is essentially to maximize the balance of good over evil in the consequences of our acts. For a consequentialist, it might make sense to say that moral reasoning about war should begin from a presumption against bad consequences, like death, injury, and other kinds of harm. But from Anscombe's point of view, this mode of reasoning gives too much prominence to consequences. For the casuist, consequences matter, but they must not be allowed to dominate our ethical thinking. Bad consequences are always something to regret, even when they result from acts we cannot justly avoid. And we always have reason to avoid bad consequences that we can justly avoid. But why is this so? Because those who suffer from consequences of *that* kind necessarily deserve whatever protection we can justly extend to them. Consideration of bad consequences has its place within the method of casuistry, but it is neither the point at which moral reasoning begins nor the main concern.

The casuist maintains that we should try to make the world a better place—one in which peace reigns and justice obtains in the relations among persons and groups. This is called pursuing the common good. Just people pursue the common good. They do so justly. With just peace as their end, they will employ only just means, acting with or under proper authority when using force and waging war only with just cause. Justice defines the limits of their responsibility for results. If beneficial consequences cannot be obtained by just means, the just must be patient. If they have just cause but lack the authority to wage war, justice requires restraint. If they could maximize the balance of good over evil effects by waging war but they lack just cause, they must refrain nonetheless. They bear no responsibility for an unfortunate outcome they could have prevented only by violating the requirements of justice.

Exactly where do expected consequences enter into Anscombe's reasoning about resort to war? First, in the requirement that war be the means of last resort. This may be viewed as a gloss on the requirement of just cause (which she calls "just occasion"). It implies that we do not have just cause for war unless other, less drastic, means of just statecraft have been ruled out. It assumes that it would be unjust (as opposed to presumptively or prima facie wrong) to use violent means not actually necessary in the pursuit of one's just ends. The bad consequences of such means would fall, either through negligence or ill will, upon people who deserve protection from them. Justice remains the primary consideration.

There are two other criteria on Anscombe's list that relate to the avoidance or minimization of bad consequences. Both can be viewed as glosses on the requirement of right intention. One implies that waging war must be directed toward ends we can reasonably hope to achieve without violating the standards of justice. The other entails that foreseeable bad consequences must be proportionate to the benefits sought. If we cannot reasonably expect the achievement of just ends as a consequence of our fighting or if just ends can be achieved by fighting but only by making things worse, our resort to war is vitiated and responsibility even for the unintended damage we cause by waging it falls to us. Again, justice is the issue. It would be just to complain, on behalf of those who have suffered death, injury, or harm as a result of a hopeless or disproportionate war. Do they not deserve protection from this?

## RALPH POTTER ON THE MORAL LOGIC OF WAR

In a footnote to paragraph 84 of *The Challenge of Peace*, the American Catholic bishops cite two scholarly articles, both of which have helped promote the notion that traditional just war reasoning begins with the presumption against violence: Ralph Potter's "The Moral Logic of War" and James Childress's "Just-War Criteria."[34] I now want to ask whether these essays give me any reason to qualify the suspicions I have been expressing about the bishops' account of *jus ad bellum* reasoning.

Potter's essay sets itself the task of scrutinizing "the moral logic of war." "Logic" here does not designate the science of deductive implication but rather the structure of principles and the pattern of reasoning people use to justify or condemn a war. Which people? Apparently everybody, according to Potter, or at least all the reasonable people. For Potter is prepared to say, as a conclusion of his analysis, that the massacre at Song My in 1969 was wrong not because it violated "the distinctive moral norms of this or that sect" or offended "the values of one segment of the public," but because it constituted "a logical contradiction which violates the minimal standards of reasonableness which must be observed if thinking, speaking, and acting are to serve human purposes through time."[35] Potter does not clarify the sense in which an act of massacre can itself constitute a logical contradiction, so we may interpret him charitably as meaning simply that the act violates principles and patterns of reasoning all reasonable people share. But Potter does not show that all reasonable people reason along the lines he describes or accept the principles he formulates.

"All of us are aware," Potter writes, "that our life together in society depends upon our mutual respect for the principle that we must do no harm to our neighbor."[36] Yet it is by no means obvious that our life together in society depends upon our mutual respect for a principle. The right set of habits and dispositions distributed in the right way across the members of a society should suffice to make life together possible. Everybody's conscious assent to a principle might help, but it hardly seems necessary, and it seems in any event like too much to ask for. Nor is it obvious what Potter means by the principle prohibiting harm to neighbors. Does the principle rule out all actions with harmful consequences? all actions with foreseen harmful consequences? all actions involving willful or intended harm? all actions causing unjust injury? none of these actions? Potter gives no direct answer to such questions. Which reading of the principle we should attribute to him remains unclear.

A paragraph later, Potter shifts without explanation from talk of harm to talk of force and then to talk of killing, and he refers not to a principle but to a presumption against using force. If we focus simply on this presumption, however, some of our judgments about war become puzzling, as Potter himself seems to admit:

It is remarkable . . . that there is a way of thinking and talking that can transmute the act of killing into an act of heroism. By what logic can it happen that a young American gun-lover who kills fourteen strangers from the top of the tower on the University of Texas campus in Austin is summarily slain and denounced as a psychopath, while another young American who kills fourteen strangers in a village in Vietnam is decorated, welcomed at the White House, and acclaimed a model for the youth of the nation?[37]

Ignore for now the question of whether the young American in Vietnam was acting justly and thus perhaps deserved his honors. A moralist like Anscombe would want to ask why it should be remarkable that one use of lethal force be just and another not unless expressions like "using force" and "killing" place an act in a moral species (in Aquinas's sense). Clearly, for Anscombe they do not, any more than "removing property from the possession of another" does. Murder and theft, in contrast, are moral species. They make implicit reference to justice. One must therefore employ the concept of justice to determine whether a given act is an instance of murder or theft. What would be remarkable, from Anscombe's point of view, would be a way of thinking and talking that could transmute an act of murder or theft into an act of heroism. For a Thomist, our life together in society does not depend upon our mutual respect for the moral principle that we must do no harm to our neighbor, unless "harm" is taken to mean something like unjust injury. For Anscombe, there is no moral principle against causing injury as such. The same holds for killing and using force.

When Potter says that "the term 'war' can be used to excuse conduct that would, under other circumstances, be condemned as an inexcusable assault upon the life and property of fellow human beings,"[38] the conduct he has in mind remains defined in what a Thomist would call its natural, not its moral, species. You can determine that an act is an instance of causing injury, using force, or killing without considering its justice, so it should not be surprising to discover that such an act can be just or unjust depending on the circumstances. It is also true that an act of holding a gun or pulling a trigger can be just or unjust depending on the circumstances. Is this remarkable? From Anscombe's point of view, it is not. Her reason would be that such acts need further description before they can be said to fall under a moral principle. We do not say that there is a standing presumption against holding guns or pulling triggers. Someone who has simply held a gun or pulled a trigger does not need to be excused by mention of further circumstances (such as that the gun was unloaded). We do not say that anyone who has had sexual intercourse needs therefore to be excused by use of expressions like "marriage" and "mutual consent." No mysterious logic has transmuted an act in need of excuse into an excusable act.

Potter might respond at this point by saying that "causing injury," "using force," and "killing" are different from descriptions like "pulling a trigger" or "having sexual intercourse." Each of the former expressions makes implicit reference to bad consequences, whereas the latter two do not. Pulling a trigger or having sexual intercourse need not cause any bad consequences. If, however, you knowingly bring about harm, coerce someone, or cause death, you will have done something you should avoid if possible. If we know about a certain act only that it brought about bad consequences of some kind, it is a truism to say that, other things equal, it would have been better for the act not to have been done. In this very weak sense, there is a moral presumption against the act, even from Anscombe's point of view.

But to judge that it would have been better, other things being equal, for an act not to have been done is simply to make an assessment of consequences. It does not follow from such a judgment that the agent should not have performed the act, let alone that he or she should be blamed for its bad consequences or needs to offer excuses of some kind for behaving in that way. For a moralist like Anscombe, if I have brought about injury, used force, or caused death, I need no excuses, provided I was following the requirements of justice (including the requirement of due proportion). Willfully using lethal force, when demanded by justice and ordained by proper authority, requires no excuses and incurs no guilt.

From the vantage point of Anscombe's Thomism, there is no point in ignoring justice while concentrating abstractly on acts described solely in terms of their bad consequences. For Potter, however, the moral logic of war is "simple in its basic structure. First, there is a strong presumption against the use of force. . . . But secondly, it is conceded that certain exceptions must be made for the sake of the common good."[39] The just war criteria, for Potter, specify exceptions to a general principle against using force. Just wars, he says, are rule-governed exceptions. Yet once we acknowledge the challenges Anscombe would want to raise against Potter, it is not clear why "the moral logic of war" *need* begin with a presumption against the use of force and only then proceed to considerations of justice in order to specify exceptions. Indeed, it is not clear that it should.

If the principle stating the presumption does not place acts in a moral species by making implicit reference to justice, "exception-clauses" informed by a conception of justice need to be appended. With the exceptions built in, the principle can become an absolute of the form "Never use force, whatever the consequences, unless . . ." But the exception-clauses pull nearly all the conceptual weight. The presumption against using force adds little. Making it central to a reconstruction of just war thinking is apt to disguise or distort the priority of justice. Why treat just war criteria as exception-clauses appended to a principle of marginal moral significance without them?

If we treat the principle stating the presumption as already making implicit reference to justice, there will be no need to append exceptions to the rule. At one point, Potter does import considerations of justice into the rule itself. He says that the use of force "always involves an exception to the rule which forbids us to do harm to our neighbor without due cause."[40] Harming our neighbor without due cause would, of course, have more than marginal moral significance, but only because it constitutes a species of injustice. As such, it falls under the absolute prohibition, "Never act unjustly." For this reason, however, the rule thus stated does not need an exception clause to permit harming one's neighbor with due cause, as in a case of self-defense against unjust attack.[41]

If I am right, then, Potter's "moral logic" is at odds with at least one major strand of just war thinking in Christian ethics—the Thomistic one. It would be a mistake, however, to stop short of a stronger conclusion, for most of the objections I have been raising against Potter on Anscombe's behalf are not specific to Thomism or even to natural law theory. They would arise for anyone who ascribes central importance to a classical conception of justice in thinking about resort to war, including various secular philosophers (like myself) and Christian thinkers (like Edmund Burke) who rely heavily on Aristotelian and republican modes of reasoning. And that includes a list of just war thinkers far too long to dismiss as exceptions that prove the rule.

## JAMES CHILDRESS ON THE LOGIC OF PRIMA FACIE DUTIES

Like Potter, James Childress argues that just war thinking begins with a presumption against harming or killing others. Much of what I have said about Potter's position therefore applies, mutatis mutandis, to Childress's as well. But Childress does not speak of just wars as exceptions to a general rule against harming or killing. Rather, he proposes to map just war criteria onto "the logic of prima facie duties." Childress borrows the notion of prima facie duties from W. D. Ross and explicates it as follows:

To hold that an obligation or duty is prima facie is to claim that it always has a strong moral reason for its performance although this reason may not always be decisive or triumph over all other reasons. If an obligation is viewed as absolute, it cannot be overridden under any circumstances; it has priority over all other obligations with which it might come into conflict. If it is viewed as relative, the rule stating it is no more than a maxim or rule of thumb that illuminates but does not prescribe what we ought to do. If it is viewed as prima facie, it is intrinsically binding, but it does not necessarily determine one's actual obligation.[42]

Just wars, if there are any, according to Childress, are cases in which the prima facie duty of nonmaleficence is overridden by what is, under the circumstances, a more stringent prima facie duty. The just war criteria are best understood, he says, as attempts to specify conditions under which the prima facie duty of nonmaleficence can be overridden.

Childress says surprisingly little about the duties that might take precedence over the duty of nonmaleficence or why they might be considered more stringent. Presumably, this is where a substantive theory of justice would have to be brought in, and Childress wants to steer clear of such matters in his reconstruction of just war criteria. He wants his proposal "to be accessible to many different theories of justice,"[43] thus providing a "framework within which different substantive interpretations of justice and morality as applied to war can be debated."[44] This means, however, that his reconstruction of the criteria does not, by itself, explain their force or imply anything at all about how they should be applied to cases.[45] Indeed, Childress is careful to leave open the possibility that pacifists are right in denying that satisfaction of the standard criteria, properly understood, makes a war just. He is saying only that the criteria are best viewed as attempts to specify conditions under which the prima facie duty of nonmaleficence can be overridden. Whether they succeed is another question.

Yet another question is why anyone with a substantive conception of justice should desire access to his framework. Someone like Anscombe is in a position to explain, in terms of her own theory, why gratuitous violence is unjust. Gratuitous violence fails to give others their due. No prima facie duty of nonmaleficence, derived without help of a theory of justice, need be mentioned. If she wishes to engage theorists of other persuasions in debate, she can do so in the usual way by moving back and forth between the opposition's vocabulary and her own in the hope of displaying the respective strengths and weaknesses. She need not seek some third vocabulary as neutral ground for the debate. Nor would she be inclined (or well advised) to view Childress's vocabulary as neutral ground. As Childress himself says, his reconstruction of just war criteria is not purely formal: it includes commitment to at least one substantive moral principle. What it lacks is a theory of justice. And his view that we ought to recognize the prima facie duty of nonmaleficence as having force without help from a view of justice is every bit as controversial as any Thomist's theory of justice.

Childress might respond, however, by arguing that Anscombe and her pacifist opponents are already implicitly working within his framework:

Just-war theorists sometimes overlook the fact that they and the pacifists reason from a common starting point. Both begin with the contention that nonviolence has moral priority over violence, that violent acts always stand in need of justification because they violate the prima facie duty not to injure or kill others.[46]

"The pacifist," he writes, "finally cannot be satisfied" with just war criteria, "just as the just-war theorist finally cannot be satisfied with the weight pacifism gives to the duty not to injure or kill others."[47] But both, in Childress's view, take the presumption against violence as their point of departure.

I find no serious grounds for concluding that just war thinking generally begins with a prima facie duty of nonmaleficence. Anscombe does not suggest anywhere, to my knowledge, that violent acts (defined without reference to justice) always stand in need of justification because they violate the prima facie duty not to injure or kill others. Nor do I think Anscombe would (or should) be pleased to see her objections to pacifism redescribed as dissatisfaction with the weight pacifism gives to the duty not to injure or kill others. Her most famous essay, "Modern Moral Philosophy," explicitly includes W. D. Ross within the scope of its sweeping condemnation of "all the best-known writers on ethics in modern times."[48] Not only does Ross tolerate injustices, such as procuring the condemnation of the innocent under certain circumstances, he does so, she thinks, because he is prepared to *weigh* any intrinsic value or prima facie duty against any other. The logic of prima facie duties lacks the very element she considers essential to all genuinely moral reasoning: a classical conception of justice. As Anscombe sees it, Ross's ethical theory is therefore the moral equivalent of consequentialism. We can hardly expect her to look kindly on the proposal that his logic be made the framework of debate.

If we view pacifists and just war theorists as differing principally on the weight assigned to competing prima facie duties, we shall soon need to know how such weighting is done. Childress does not say. A substantive theory of justice would, of course, help us determine the weight various prima facie duties should carry in our reasoning, but if we had such a theory in place, a theory of prima facie duties would be redundant.

Someone approaching Childress's proposal from Anscombe's direction would, at the very least, want to ask the following questions: If there are many prima facie duties, why begin with one prescribing nonmaleficence? Would not a duty to give each their due serve just as well or better? What suggests that the duty to act justly requires the qualifying clause, "other things being equal," as Childress's duty of nonmaleficence so clearly does? If we shall eventually need a substantive theory of justice to complete an account of the ethics of war, why begin with principles apt to seem superfluous once a substantive theory of justice has been supplied? And if we do, for some reason, decide to begin with prima facie duties in abstraction from considerations of justice, how can we explain their force or determine what weight to assign them in particular situations?

## AQUINAS AND THE PRESUMPTION AGAINST VIOLENCE

Potter and Childress might object at this point that Aquinas himself begins his discussion of war in the *Summa Theologiae*[49] (2a2ae, Q. 40, A. 1) by acknowledging a presumption against resort to war. And if that is so, perhaps Anscombe's links to earlier stages of just war tradition are weaker than I have made them seem. David Hollenbach, for one, cites Aquinas's discussion as if it provided especially clear evidence of such a presumption at the core of the just war tradition:

The *quaestio* with which Thomas begins his reflection is this: "Is it *always* a sin to fight in war?" The just war tradition, therefore, is not the result of ignorance or rejection of the biblical and theological evidence of Jesus Christ's challenge to a peaceful and nonviolent way of life. Rather the just war tradition, again when it is properly understood, rests on the conviction that violent warfare should be presumed to be morally unacceptable and even sinful.[50]

But why should the question quoted by Hollenbach suggest that violent warfare, in Aquinas's view, should be presumed to be morally unacceptable and even sinful? In fact, Aquinas begins here, as he so often does elsewhere, with a question readers might be tempted to answer incorrectly. And, as usual, he is preparing us for a systematic dismantling of all considerations that might tempt us to give the wrong answer: "It would seem that . . ."; "On the contrary . . ."; "I answer that . . ."; and so on, until he has handled all the objections to his position that he deems worthy of response. Arguing in this way involves acknowledging a presumption against resort to war in something like the following limited sense: that some of his readers, for whatever reason, might already be presuming that resort to war (or any other kind of violence) is inherently a species of sin or injustice. That is not, however, the sort of moral presumption Potter and Childress seem to have in mind.

What might lead a reader to think that it is always sinful to wage war? The first two objections offer what Aquinas takes to be misunderstandings of biblical passages (Matt. 26:52, 5:39; Rom. 12:19). The third presupposes what for him is a misunderstanding of the aim of just warfare. The fourth (and last), he thinks, misunderstands the Church's prohibition of "warlike exercises in tournaments" (2a2ae, Q. 40, A. 1). So it is only misunderstandings of one sort of another that create a presumption against waging war as such in this passage, and Aquinas's aim is to help readers beyond overly simple presumptions like this and toward a comprehension of the conditions under which waging war can be just.

The body of his answer to the quaestio is his (eventually) influential statement of the criteria of proper authority, just cause, and right intention. He does not begin by citing a general principle and asking under what conditions exceptions to it might be allowed. He does not begin by listing prima facie obligations and asking which might outweigh another under conditions of armed conflict. He proceeds instead by employing a substantive conception of justice to define the moral species to which certain acts belong. He is at pains to show that resort to war, like resort to violence generally, is not, per se, a species of injustice. Whether engaging in a particular war is a just act or not depends upon such matters as the authority under which it is fought, the cause that provides its occasion, and the intentions of those who undertake it. He does not say that these are sufficient conditions of the just war. The Aristotelian ethical theory he gives elsewhere in the *Summa Theologiae* (in the first twenty-one questions of 1a2ae) implies that he would recognize other necessary conditions as well. The implication follows from his conviction that any act can be vitiated either by having an improper object or by virtue of a deficiency in any of its circumstances.[51] And in his treatment of war (though not his treatment of truth-telling or sexuality), it is his Aristotelian conception of justice that performs the crucial ethical work in distinguishing, according to their objects and circumstances, the vitiated acts from those that are not.[52]

Saying that Aquinas's quaestio itself proves his implicit allegiance to Potter's "moral logic" or Childress's framework would be more plausible if it could be integrated with a systematic reading of other passages in the *Summa Theologiae*. If the question "Is it always sinful to fight in war?" acknowledges a moral presumption against war as such, what shall we make of the question posed in the next article: "Whether it is lawful for clerics and bishops to fight?" Does this suggest a presumption in favor of allowing clerics and bishops to fight? Surely not, except in the limited sense already noted: that some *readers* might be making *mistaken* presumptions that Aquinas wishes to identify and to oppose. Take any other quaestio at random. When Aquinas asks in 1a, Q. 25, whether there is power in God, whether his power is infinite, and whether it is almighty, is he acknowledging a genuine presumption in favor of negative answers? Obviously not.

Richard B. Miller is another scholar who claims that a fairly strong presumption against violence is operative in Aquinas's reasoning, but the evidence he cites comes mainly from the discussion of killing in self-defense in 2a2ae, Q. 64, A. 7. Summarizing Aquinas's view, Miller writes:

When I am the victim of aggression, I may never directly kill the attacker either as a means or an end of self-defense. Preserving myself may be lawfully intended, but the injury of another must be "beside" the intention, as an accident of the act. This kind of logic, where legitimate self-defense may never include direct harm of another, can only make sense if there is an abiding presumption against the use of force.[53]

Miller's argument is similar to the one Ramsey once made in support of the idea that Christian love, not natural justice, is the controlling notion in Aquinas's passages on the ethics of violence.[54] Both men assume that Aquinas's conception of justice cannot, by itself, make sense of his refusal to permit someone actually to intend to kill another in self-defense, but both men neglect the reason Aquinas himself offers in the very next clause: "since the [intentional] taking of life is reserved to the public authorities acting for the common good."

At this point Aquinas alludes to articles 2 and 3 of the same question and then continues as follows:

Killing in self-defense in this sort of way [i.e., by intending the death of the attacker] is restricted to somebody who has the public authority to do so; such a man may indeed intend to kill a man in self-defense but he does so for the general good. This is exemplified by the soldier who fights against the enemy, and the official of the court who fights against robbers. And even such men sin if and to the extent that they are moved by some private passion. (2a2ae, Q. 40)

The theme of this passage is related to the first of Aquinas's stated conditions of just war—"the authority of the sovereign on whose command war is waged" (2a2ae, Q. 40, A. 1). His concern is a requirement of justice, namely, that certain acts be restricted to those who possess genuine public authority to perform them. The restriction is meant to dissociate such acts from private passion and to direct them properly to the common good. It is the sort of concern Cicero expresses when he says that someone who is not legally a soldier has no right to go into battle (*De Officiis*) or that Aquinas has in mind when he says that "a private person has no business declaring war" (2a2ae, Q. 40, A. 1). By the same token, a given individual, qua private person, has no business *intending* the death of an attacker outside the context of war. Intentional killing is reserved, under the rule of justice, for people to whose protection the commonweal has been committed. If you find yourself under attack, it matters greatly *who* you are. This will be a morally relevant circumstance of whatever response you make. If you are a private person, Aquinas would permit you to act in defense of your own life, but only if your intention were merely self-preservation and if the attacker's death, were it to result, would fall outside your intention. The point is to make retribution and civil defense public business—not a matter for private enterprise. Justice, he thinks, requires such a division of labor, with the monopoly on intentional killing awarded entirely to public authorities. Not love, not a presumption against violence per se, but justice.[55]

This reading is confirmed by what Aquinas says in articles 2 and 3. In article 2, he allows intentional killing of someone who "is dangerous to the community and is subverting it by some sin." The analogy he offers is with the surgeon's amputation of a diseased limb. In article 3, he restricts this sort of act to the appropriate public authorities:

As we have already noted, the killing of malefactors is legitimate in so far as it is ordered to the well-being of the whole community. And so this right belongs only to those who are charged with the care of the whole community, just as it is the doctor who has been entrusted with the health of the whole body who may amputate a gangrenous limb. But the care of the whole community has been entrusted to the rulers who exercise public authority, and so it is they, and not private persons, who may execute malefactors.

Acts involving harm to another need to be judicially decided by just authorities precisely because private persons are especially apt to commit such acts on the basis of private passions, like spiteful revenge and hatred. This aspect of Aquinas's thought is best seen as part of the long struggle of Christian civilization to subdue and displace local honor codes that equate justice with the private vengeance of an individual, family, or clan. Just war, like just punishment, could come, as he saw it, only from relatively disinterested parties charged with and practiced in the high duties of public service. Public officials may of course occasionally succumb to private passions, and that is one reason for including "right intention" among the conditions of the just war. But if rulers fail to intend the common good, they also destroy their authority to rule.

This Aquinas makes clear in the question on sedition (2a2ae, Q. 42, A. 2). Genuine public authority must be distinguished from the mere holding of political power. A tyrannical government obviously holds political power, but it is unjust, he says, echoing Aristotle, because it is directed toward the private good of the ruler. Such a ruler therefore lacks genuine authority.

Consequently, disturbing such a government has not the nature of sedition, unless perhaps the disturbance be so excessive that the people suffer more from it than from the tyrannical regime. Indeed it is the tyrant rather that is more guilty of sedition, since he fosters discord and dissension among his subjects in order to lord over them more securely. For this is tyranny, to govern for the ruler's personal advantage to the people's harm.

Notice how Aquinas's reasoning works here. Sedition (like murder) is declared a species of injustice and is therefore absolutely prohibited. Sedition is not, however, defined as forcible overthrow of a government. It is something of which a ruler, as well as his subjects, can be guilty. Aquinas does not say that forcible overthrow of a government is generally or prima facie wrong. He defines the moral species in relation to the virtue of justice and then asks which acts belong to it.

Aquinas does not mention proportionality in his brief discussion of war, but he does in his discussion of sedition—and in a way that helps us see how bad consequences enter into his reasoning. The disturbance caused by overthrowing a tyrant must not be disproportionate to the good of having him deposed. Concern for proportionality in the pursuit of justice does not swing free of the other requirements of justice, imposing a general responsibility for maximizing the balance of good over bad consequences. It operates within a theory of justice, and specifies a condition that must be met for a rebellion to qualify as just. It follows from the theory that the same condition would apply to war, which, "properly speaking, is against an external enemy" (2a2ae, Q. 42, A. 1). Aquinas's remark about disproportionate rebellion draws a line between just and gratuitous violence. Gratuitous violence is a species of injustice, a kind of harming out of line with the requirements of justice. As such, it is absolutely prohibited, for it unnecessarily lets loose harm upon people who deserve protection from it. From Aquinas's point of view, to say that there is a presumption against gratuitous violence would be to say too little; to say that there is a presumption against the kind of violence required of us in a just war or a just rebellion would be to say too much.

Aquinas would surely affirm each of the following four propositions: first, that to kill, injure, or harm people is to bring about bad consequences; second, that such consequences are bad because of the violence they entail to human life and well-being; third, that, other things being equal, knowingly bringing about violent consequences is illicit; and fourth, that if you know that an act will have such consequences, you had better determine that other things are not equal before committing it. This last proportion may sound equivalent to the bishops' presumption against violence. But to Aquinas the clause "other things being equal" in the third proposition would have to mean something like this: that neither the act's other circumstances (including its good consequences) nor its object, when fully and wisely considered, make it a just thing to do. Any such act, it should now be clear, will be an act of gratuitous violence. It will therefore be not presumptively or prima facie wrong but simply illicit or unjust.

As for what Ramsey calls the quasi-legal sense of the presumption, Aquinas does not generally treat acts of violence as gratuitous until proven just. He does not begin his systematic inquiries into particular types of actions by considering their bad consequences, citing an "other things being equal" judgment or prima facie obligation and then weighing other considerations. If you offered him a particular case, he would of course begin his casuistic reasoning with whatever information happened to be at hand concerning a given act, its object, and its circumstances, and he would then endeavor to fill in the other information needed to complete his appraisal. But in resort to war, as in any other kind of act, the "most important of all the circumstances is that which affects the act as to the end, namely the *why*." And "the moral act is most of all specified by the end" (1a2ae, Q. 7, A. 4). He explicitly downgrades consequences to secondary importance. So it is in keeping with his analysis of human action for Aquinas to stress just cause and right intention, as opposed to consequences, in his treatment of war. We have seen why the circumstance of who resorts to war strikes him as worthy of mention, while the reference to proportionality in his treatment of sedition shows one way that consequences do figure into his reasoning.

Another way that consequences figure in is through the concept of velleity, or subjective willing. In 1a2ae, Q. 8, A. 5, Aquinas distinguishes between complete and incomplete willing. Your willing of a means or an end is complete if you actually will it, and this can be done only when execution of the means or achievement of the end is possible. Incomplete or subjunctive willing involves what you *would* will if a change in circumstances were to make different means and ends possible. Velleity relates the will to counterfactual possibilities. It can be expressed in counterfactual conditionals of the form: If it were the case that P, I would will (or refrain from willing) D. Incomplete willing, like complete willing, is subject to moral evaluation. What you *would* will under circumstances somewhat different from yours can be a highly significant fact about you as a moral agent. Justice may require you to perform some acts that involve willing death, injury, or harm to someone in your attempt to uphold or protect the common good. But when you perform such acts, as a virtuous person, you have negative velleity with respect to the bad consequences you are willfully bringing about. That is to say, if it were possible to avoid willing death, injury, or harm to someone without doing an injustice, you would. This idea allows us to explicate a sense in which even just wars are regrettable for Aquinas, a sense distinct from the consequentialist notion that a just war is the lesser of two evils and one that does not commit him to Childress's notion that overridden prima facie obligations leave "traces or residual effects" in one's conscience.[56]

Potter claims that using force "always requires an explanation."[57] This seems a harmless platitude at first glance, yet would Aquinas accept it? He would grant, of course, that using force often requires an explanation. But there are many cases in which the justice of a particular use of force is too obvious to require explanation. The palace guards who use coercive force with all due restraint to subdue a would-be assassin in full view of the ruler and his court are not expected to explain themselves publicly, as if they shouldered the burden of proof. Were they to refrain from using force under such circumstances, they would need to explain themselves. Whether an explanation is needed in a given case depends, first, upon which persons, if any, are entitled to an explanation in that sort of case and, second, upon which of the circumstances of the act become clear to the relevant parties without benefit of explanation.

Aquinas does not say that going to war always requires formal explanation, but it does seem consistent with his ethics to hold that in all matters of such gravity, rulers owe their own subjects, their allies, their enemies, and other affected parties a truthful account of their reasons and ends. This can be viewed as a debt of justice, an explanation owed to someone, without being taken as a sign that going to war is inherently more difficult to justify than other available courses of action might be. If we are obligated by treaty to assist our allies in fending off unjust attacks, and an obviously unjust attack is now in progress, it may well be the pacifists among us who bear the burden of proof. If we fail to meet our treaty obligations, we will have some explaining to do. The explanation due when resorting to war belongs, likewise, to the just exercise of public authority by rulers. It is sometimes by hearing such an explanation, and testing it against behavioral evidence, that we are able to judge whether the conditions of just cause and right intention have been met and whether rulers have the authority over their subjects they claim to have. Rulers owe us such an explanation because we need it in deciding whether justice requires us to stand with them or against them.

One last passage ought to be noted before I conclude. In A. 2 of the quaestio on war, Aquinas argues that clerics and bishops have no business engaging in warfare. He offers two reasons. The first refers once more to the need for functional differentiation in service to the common good. Just as there is a distinction between the proper roles of public authorities and private individuals with respect to the use of force, there is also a distinctive role to be played by clerics and bishops. This latter role is incompatible with engaging in commerce as well as in war, indeed with any activity that interferes with a religious vocation by excessively entangling or upsetting the soul. "The second reason," Aquinas says, "is special." It has to do with being "ordained for the ministry of the altar in which the passion of Christ is represented sacramentally." For clerics or bishops to shed the blood of others, "even if they have done so without sin," is to become ritually irregular, given the spiritual meaning of blood in the eucharist (2a2ae, Q. 40, A. 2).

Here we have the last sense in which Aquinas might be said to recognize a presumption against violence, albeit one that applies only to one class of individuals. It is a very important matter to him, as a Christian and as a cleric. It is not, however, a matter that bears on whether there can be just wars, let alone the premise from which his just war thinking begins. He makes clear that ritual irregularity, not sin or injustice, is his concern in this passage. And he does not hesitate to add that clerics and bishops "may make their presence felt at war ... by spiritually helping those who fight on the side of justice, exhorting, absolving them, and giving other like spiritual assistance" (2a2ae, Q. 40, A. 3). Even those who are prohibited by their vocation from spilling of blood, then, have a contribution to make to the just war. They too must sometimes determine which side is just in order to do the work to which they have been called. They have a peaceable vocation but not a pacifist one.

## CONCLUSION

I do not deny that some Christian thinkers have begun their reasoning about resort to war from a presumption against violence. Potter, Childress, and the Catholic bishops seem to have done so. And while I question the wisdom of their normative proposals, I do not question their right to claim standing for them in just war tradition or to make conciliatory gestures toward the present-day followers of Erasmus and King. I am pleased to let each proposal take its place, alongside the Augustinian pattern of reasoning found in Ramsey and the more classical ones found in Aquinas and Anscombe, as evidence of one religious tradition's remarkable conceptual diversity. That diversity, which we have only begun to sample here, shows itself in the sometimes heated contest between just-war thinkers and Christian pacifists, in disputes among the former over how to formulate the *jus ad bellum* criteria, and also in the varied usages and arguments that have permitted seemingly identical criteria to acquire distinct interpretations and to support opposing conclusions about particular wars.

My pluralistic view of the tradition has its own normative biases, which I have not tried to conceal. It also has some advantages, but the least of which is the promising (though daunting) basis it affords for comparisons with other traditions, like Islam, in which a conception of justice inherited from classical philosophy also plays a major role. Only time will tell whether this promise is fulfilled. In the meantime, another advantage will have to suffice. It is a vision of Christian ethics as a cultural inheritance too variegated for either the Church or the theologians to control. There is a way of reading the past that allows it to answer back, to criticize the present, to enhance our freedom. By doing justice to the otherness of the past, we discover that familiar habits of thought are not universal, and if they are not universal, they are not necessary either. They are subject to change.[58]

## NOTES

1. I thank James Johnson and John Kelsay, both for offering me this assignment and for their helpful comments on the penultimate draft of this chapter.

2. National Conference of Catholic Bishops. Ad Hoc Committee on War and Peace, *The Challenge of Peace: God's Promise and Our Response* (Washington, DC: United States Catholic Conference, 1983), paragraph 70.

3. Ibid., paragraph 80.

4. In paragraph 82, the bishops do acknowledge in passing that just war reasoning "has taken several forms in the history of Catholic theology," but their use of definite articles and singular nouns repeatedly reinforces the impression that only one theory, which varies only slightly from one author to another, is involved.

5. The criteria as listed by the American Catholic bishops, briefly stated, are as follows: that the cause be just; that those declaring war have competent authority to do so; that the party waging war be, comparatively speaking, just; that the war be fought with right intention; that it be a last resort; that its success

be probable; and that its costs be proportionate to the end being pursued. See ibid., paragraphs 85–99.

6. Ibid., paragraph 74.

7. Ibid., paragraph 120.

8. This is the bishops' reason for overriding the presumption against violence in certain circumstances. In paragraph 82, they refer to it as an "Augustinian insight" that is the "central premise" of the "just-war argument." But as we shall see, not all Augustinian realists would be as friendly as the bishops are to pacifists who reject this insight.

9. See Gilbert Harman, "Relativistic Ethics: Morality as Politics," in P. French, T. Vehling, and H. Wettstein, eds., *Midwest Studies in Philosophy*, vol. 3, *Studies in Ethics*, (Minneapolis: University of Minnesota Press, 1980), pp. 109–21.

10. Stanley Hauerwas, *Against the Nations: War and Survival in a Liberal Society* (San Francisco: Winston Press, 1985), p. 194.

11. John Howard Yoder, *The Original Revolution* (Scottdale, PA: Herald Press, 1971), p. 58.

12. As translated in Arthur F. Holmes, ed., *War and Christian Ethics* (Grand Rapids, MI: Baker Book House, 1975), p. 186.

13. Paul Ramsey, *Speak Up for Just War or Pacifism* (University Park, PA, and London: Pennsylvania State University Press, 1988). This book focuses mainly on a pastoral letter published by the United Methodist bishops: *In Defense of Creation* (Nashville: Graded Press, 1986). But it also devotes considerable attention to *The Challenge of Peace*.

14. For Hauerwas's epilogue, see Ramsey, *Speak Up*, pp. 149–82. For his critique of *The Challenge of Peace*, see Hauerwas, *Against the Nations*, pp. 160–68.

15. As colleagues and friends for the last dozen years of his life, Ramsey and I worked out our overlapping objections to the bishops' account in conversation with one another. It would therefore be inappropriate for me to place too much weight on Ramsey's late writings as evidence for my conclusions, as if they provided independent corroboration of my own view of just war tradition. I first drafted much of this essay, and shared it with Ramsey, shortly after the American Catholic bishops' pastoral letter appeared in 1983. The section on Ralph Potter and some material on Aquinas became part of a paper I delivered at the annual meeting of the American Academy of Religion in 1985. Ramsey and I began talking regularly about such matters shortly after I joined the faculty at Princeton in 1975. Another colleague, Victor Preller, and various students were drawn into these conversations in the early 1980s. It is to Preller that I owe much of what I shall be saying about Aquinas in later sections of this paper. Matters of interpretation of Aquinas aside, it would be impossible for any of us to say precisely where one person's contribution began and another's left off.

16. Ramsey criticized David Hollenbach and Richard B. Miller along these lines in *Speak Up*, pp. 109–10. The quoted material, italics included, comes from p. 109.

17. Ramsey, *Speak Up*, p. 83; I have deleted Ramsey's italics.

18. Ramsey, *Speak Up*, p. 109.

19. Paul Ramsey, *Basic Christian Ethics* (New York: Charles Scribner's Sons, 1950).

20. Paul Ramsey, *War and the Christian Conscience: How Shall Modern War Be Conducted Justly?* (Durham, NC: Duke University Press, 1961), p. 14.

21. Ramsey, *War and the Christian Conscience*, p. 32.

22. Differences on this issue can be discerned well before Augustine—for example, in the contrast between the arguments Athenagoras and Lactantius offer for policies of nonviolence and forgiveness. The former jettisons justice as a standard too lax for Christians, who, he says, rightly refuse to retaliate against those who wrong them and are revolted even by just executions of wrongdoers. The latter makes justice central but holds that Christian mercy and kindness are themselves requirements of justice.

23. See Alasdair MacIntyre, "Epistemological Crises, Dramatic Narrative and the Philosophy of Science," *The Monist* 60, no. 4 (1977), pp. 453–72.

24. For a concise summary of Johnson's work, see his "Historical Roots and Sources of the Just War Tradition in Western Culture," in John Kelsay and James Turner Johnson, eds., *Just War and Jihad: Historical and Theoretical Perspectives on War and Peace in Western and Islamic Traditions* (Westport, CT: Greenwood Press, 1991). For the details, see his trilogy: *Ideology, Reason, and the Limitation of War: Religious and Secular Concepts, 1200–1740* (Princeton and London: Princeton University Press, 1975); *Just War Tradition and the Restraint of War: A Moral and Historical Inquiry* (Princeton and Guildford, Surrey: Princeton University Press, 1981); and *The Quest for Peace: Three Moral Traditions in Western Cultural History* (Princeton and Guildford, Surrey: Princeton University Press, 1987).

25. G.E.M. Anscombe, *Ethics, Religion, and Politics* (Minneapolis: University of Minnesota Press, 1981), chs. 6–8.

26. In contrast, *The Challenge of Peace* appeals to the absolute requirements of natural law only in passing. It never shows how such appeals are to be made consistent with a style of thought in which one begins with a nonabsolute presumption against war and then weighs it against other considerations to determine whether the presumption is overridden. The letter bears the marks of compromise between more than one kind of bishop.

27. Anscombe, *Ethics, Religion, and Politics*, pp. 72–73.

28. Ibid., pp. 73, 79.

29. See John Eppstein, *The Catholic Tradition of the Law of Nations* (Washington, DC: Catholic Association for International Peace, 1935) and Robert Regout, *La doctrine de la guerre juste de saint Augustin à nos jours d'après les théologiens et les canonistes catholiques* (Paris: A. Pedone, 1934). Interestingly, Anscombe's list makes no mention of what the bishops call "comparative justice." In her conception of justice, a party waging war is either just or not. Being comparatively just, relative to Hitler's Germany, was not for Anscombe a count in Britain's favor. Britain too was to be condemned as unjust. It could take no moral comfort in the greater sins of its enemy.

30. Anscombe, *Ethics, Religion, and Politics*, p. 51.

31. Ibid., p. 69.

32. Ibid., p. 90.

33. Anscombe claims that this pattern of reasoning is practiced by Aristotelians and believers in divine law like herself but not, generally, by modern moral philosophers. See her essay, "Modern Moral Philosophy," ibid., ch. 4, especially p. 36.

34. Ralph B. Potter, Jr., "The Moral Logic of War," *McCormick Quarterly* no. 23 (1970), pp. 203–33; James F. Childress, "Just-War Criteria," reprinted in James F. Childress, *Moral Responsibility in Conflicts: Essays on Nonviolence, War, and Conscience* (Baton Rouge and London: Louisiana State University Press, 1982). Ramsey discusses these essays and their possible influence on the American Catholic bishops' ghost writer, Father Bryan Hehir, in *Speak Up*, pp. 83–84, 108–10.

35. Potter, "The Moral Logic of War," pp. 223–24.

36. Ibid., p. 203.

37. Ibid., p. 203–4.

38. Ibid., p. 204.

39. Ibid., p. 205.

40. Ibid., p. 206.

41. See Ramsey, *Speak Up*, p. 84, especially the indented quotation from Childress.

42. Childress, *Moral Responsibility in Conflicts*, p. 68.

43. Ibid., p. 83.

44. Ibid., p. 90.

45. "It has been clear for some time, in any case, that Childress's uses of *prima facie* and *actual* duties in moral analysis are not *explanatory* of the just-war tradition but instead are *replacement* terms for its fine-tuning. Unfortunately, his proposal is widely used." Ramsey, *Speak Up*, p. 108, his italics.

46. Childress, *Moral Responsibility in Conflicts*, p. 93.

47. Ibid.

48. Anscombe, *Ethics, Religion, and Politics*, p. 33. The reference to Ross occurs in a footnote on the same page.

49. St. Thomas Aquinas, *Summa Theologiae*, trans. Blackfriars (New York: McGraw-Hill, 1972), 2a2ae, Q. 40, A. 1. All subsequent references to this work by Aquinas are from this translation.

50. David Hollenbach, *Nuclear Ethics: A Christian Moral Argument* (New York and Ramsey, NJ: Paulist Press, 1983), p. 14, Hollenbach's italics.

51. See in particular Q. 7, articles 3 and 4, and Q. 18. In Q. 7, A. 3, Aquinas lists the circumstances of the act as follows: who, what, where, by what means, why, how, when, and about what. The first seven circumstances are drawn from Cicero, the last from Aristotle. Aquinas discusses the consequences of an act in relation to *what* an agent does.

52. Aquinas's contribution to just war thought was to take criteria that had previously been formulated and to place them within the context of an Aristotelian ethical theory, thereby giving them fresh significance. The theory's analysis of human action offers a recipe for moving beyond rigid application of the received criteria, a recipe later thinkers used when formulating and defending new criteria as the circumstances of war changed. To accept the theory is to hold that any aspect of war-making might prove as important in a given case as the three aspects Aquinas explicitly singles out for attention.

53. Miller was the respondent to the version of this paper I read at the Annual Meeting of the American Academy of Religion in 1985. I am quoting from the typescript of his remarks, but I have deleted his underlining. I thank him both

for the care he put into those remarks and for his kindness in having them typed up and sent to me.

54. Ramsey, *War and the Christian Conscience*, ch. 3.

55. Hence Miller is wrong when he concludes: "If . . . we follow Stout's line of argument, the direct killing of another as a means of self-defense could be a legitimate exercise of justice."

56. Childress, *Moral Responsibility in Conflicts*, pp. 70–71.

57. Potter, "The Moral Logic of War," p. 206.

58. Comparative religious ethics can have a critical function relative to religious institutions and to theology, like the one David Bromwich has proposed for literary criticism relative to the state: "It cannot itself attain, or even supply others with tools for attaining, control of the present. But it can insert itself between those who control the present and their wish to control the past. It can, that is, weaken the state's inertia and qualify its authority, by affording a few of its citizens a backward glance which is not the same as the look sanctioned by the state. To the degree that it teaches the differentness of the past, criticism acts on behalf of a future." David Bromwich, *A Choice of Inheritance: Self and Community from Edmund Burke to Robert Frost* (Cambridge, MA: Harvard University Press, 1989), pp. 290–91.

# 2

## The Development of *Jihad* in Islamic Revelation and History

### Abdulaziz A. Sachedina

#### INTRODUCTION

I should like to begin with some indication of my approach to Islamic
materials. In this essay, I shall make use of certain categories that are
most at home in the field of comparative religious ethics, as that discipline is developed by Little and Twiss.[1] In particular, I shall make use
of the distinction between religion and morality in analyzing the various
justifications for war that are present in the Qur'an, the Prophetic traditions (Sunna), and the works of the great jurists. This approach has
made me cognizant of the fact that the religious and moral struggle of
the Muslim community from the time of Muhammad to the present is
part of the historical struggle of all humanity to make sense of its responsibility. Accordingly, my efforts are directed at interpreting the
Islamic sources and how they deal with the resort to war, in terms of
an awareness that every text must be read in connection with a context—
in particular (in this case) the historical development of the Muslim
community.

I have employed this approach in my earlier research on the apparent
discrepancy between the teachings of the Qur'an on freedom of religion
and justifications for *jihad* in the works of Islamic jurists. I am convinced
that the exegetical and juristic thought of Islamic scholars were inspired
by the socio-political circumstances of the Muslim community. Consequently, these scholars had to formulate terminological stratagems that
could reconcile the apparently tolerant tone of the Qur'an with the use
of *jihad* as a means of "calling" (*al-da'wa*) people to the divine path. The
frequent references by jurists and exegetes to the abrogation of certain

verses in the Qur'an that support the notion of tolerance, and thus to the primacy of those verses that sanction the use of defensive force in the face of persecution, provide an important example of such a stratagem. Through this exegetical device, such scholars were able to legitimize the *jihad* for purposes of "calling" persons to Islam—thus rendering the *jihad* a form of holy war.[2]

It is important to bear in mind that these exegetes and jurists were responding to questions about the *jihad* as individuals and that there was a lack of any definite organization or strict uniformity among them. Both the Sunni and Shi'i scholars were private individuals who, because of their piety and learning, were accorded reverence by the people and recognition as leaders by the Muslim community. Their writings reflect their individual and independent reasoning in an attempt to formulate an appropriate response to the socio-political realities of the Islamic public order.

The works of such scholars reflect several sorts of tensions. On the one hand, there is the problem of reconciling an apparent discrepancy between the Qur'anic treatment of the *jihad* as a means to make "God's cause succeed" (8:39)[3] and the manipulation of *jihad* by the de facto Muslim authorities to increase "the sphere of Islam" (*dar al-islam*) by engaging in territorial expansion. There is, further, the tension between religious and moral justifications for the *jihad*, which although not explicitly distinguished in Islamic jurisprudence are, at any rate, alluded to in the Qur'an. Undoubtedly, concrete political situations forced the scholars to be pragmatic and realistic in their formulation of the justifications for undertaking the *jihad*, especially if the de facto rulers were willing to uphold the supremacy of Islamic religious law in a Muslim public order. In the process of providing a religious legitimation for the territorial expansionism of the Muslim rulers, the jurists preferred on many occasions to overlook those passages of the Qur'an that point toward moral justifications for the *jihad*. Consequently, their rationalization of the *jihad* as the means by which the world might be converted to the "sphere of Islam" obscures the distinction between the Qur'anic concept of a "just war" fought to stop aggression and a "holy war" aimed at conversion to Islam.

The difficulty of keeping the moral (just war) and religious (holy war) justifications for engaging in *jihad* distinct in Islamic jurisprudence is inevitable because of the interdependence between religion and politics in the creation of an Islamic world order. The promise of the creation of a just and equitable public order that would embody the will of God was central to the Islamic revelation and also to the social, political, and economic activity of the Muslim community. The connection between the divine will and the creation of such an order was significant in the tendency of scholars to regard the *jihad* as an instrument in the fulfillment of the divine promise. Thus, in the highly politicized world of early Islam, it was not difficult to interpret the Qur'an in such a way that the relatively limited justification for *jihad* contained in the sacred text was broadened: the *jihad* came to be associated with the concepts of justice and divine guidance and with the desire to secure the well-being of all humanity.

At this point, I wish to note that one of the most important sources for my thinking in this paper has been *Kitab ikhtilaf al-fuqaha'* (Differences of opinion among the jurists [on the question of *jihad* and *jizya*]), by the famous jurist-exegete-historian Muhammad b. Jarir al-Tabari (d. 310 A.H./ 923 C.E.) While Tabari and others dealt with the subject of *jihad* as exegetes in the various works on *tafsir* (Qur'an commentaries), the more systematic treatments of *jihad* are in juridical works. In *Kitab ikhtilaf al-fuqaha'* Tabari compiled the opinions of all the major jurists individually and, to some extent, chronologically. He thus points to the differences between individual scholars (e.g., al-Shafi'i, al-Awza'i, Abu Hanifa and those who followed him, Malik, and so on), rather than to the so-called schools.[4] More significant, Tabari provides a kind of synopsis of the Qur'anic treatment of the *jihad* and discusses the issue of the "abrogated" verses in a way that reveals the discrepancy mentioned earlier.

## JIHAD IN ISLAMIC REVELATION

The Qur'an uses two distinct terms for military activity: *qital* and *jihad*. The former always connotes "fighting," whereas *jihad* means "struggle," or "striving," usually followed by the phrase "in the path of God." Those who have responded to the call of Islam to establish the divine order on earth, that is the believers, are exhorted to "strive" (*jahada*) with their possessions and their selves for the complete success of God's cause. In a sense, *jihad* is seen as a method of "bringing religion into practice."[5] In the Qur'anic usage, specifically military activity is consistently identified by terms other than *jihad* (e.g., *qital*), whereas *jihad* is reserved for the overall religious struggle, whether in the form of personal purification or the collective effort to establish an Islamic social order.

In the wake of the phenomenal conquests achieved by Muslims during the 1st/7th century, the scholars of Islam began to apply the term *jihad* to military action and to efforts to expand the "sphere of Islam" (*dar al-islam*) through the extension of the boundaries of the Islamic polity. The juridical works produced during the 2nd/8th century support the view that the treatment of the *jihad* in connection with the task of converting the "sphere of war" (*dar al-harb*) to the sphere of Islam was, in effect, an ex post facto legitimation of the early conquests.[6] In fact, the division of the world into the two spheres of "war" and "peace" (Islam) was based on the jurists' inference from the (implicit) Qur'anic division of the world into the spheres of "belief" (*iman*) and "disbelief" (*kufr*). By the time Tabari compiled his book on the "difference of opinions" in the 4th/10th century, the term *jihad* had acquired the characteristic meaning of military action undertaken to create a universal Islamic polity.

Tabari begins his discussion of *jihad* by affirming the divine promise made to the "righteous" servants of God, and by asserting the universal goals of the Islamic faith. He cites the following passage:

For We have written in the Psalms, after the Remembrance, "The earth shall be the inheritance of My righteous servants." Surely in this is a Message delivered unto a people who serve. We have not sent thee, [O Muhammad,] save as a mercy unto all beings. (21:105–7)

He then cites another passage that makes explicit the universal mission of the Prophet and indicates the primacy of Islam over all other religions:

We have sent thee not, except to mankind entire, good tidings to bear, and warning; but most men do not know it. (34:27)

According to Tabari, these passages from the Qur'an point toward a revealed justification for engaging in *jihad* for the purpose of making the entire world aware of the divine path, and of requiring humanity to obey the divine will manifested through the Prophet of Islam.[7] In other words, the call to faith (*al da'wa*) is closely linked to the *jihad*.

That there is a relationship between the call to faith and the undertaking of *jihad* is supported by the insistence of the Qur'an that it has been revealed as a guide for the establishment of an ethical order on earth that will reflect the divine revelation and the divinely established authority of the Prophet. But what are the means that the Prophet may use to create such an order? Does the Qur'an justify *jihad* in this connection?

If the aim of the Qur'anic revelation is to "command good and forbid evil" (3:104, 110; 9:71), then it would seem that any means—including military—would be obligatory. Failure to make use of such means would then involve disregarding a religious and moral obligation and would be blameworthy. Accordingly, the Qur'an gives the Prophet, in his capacity as the leader of the Muslim community, the right to control "discord on earth" by means of *jihad* (or actually, *qital*). This right points to the possibility—even obligation—for the Prophet to resort to *jihad* when, in his judgment, such action is necessary as a means to combat a breakdown of the public order. In particular, the Prophet may resort to the sword in response to a situation of general lawlessness that results from someone's "taking up arms against God and His messenger" (9:33–

34), that is, from a rebellion against the established Islamic order. The repeated injunction to eradicate "corruption on earth," taken together with the Qur'anic justification of a human institution that has the power to carry out the function of "enjoining the good and forbidding the evil," represents a religiously sanctioned basic moral requirement: one is required to establish and maintain a social order that will protect the well-being of a human community. A logical outcome of this requirement is the permission to use force.

In light of the need to eradicate "corruption on earth" and to "command good and forbid evil," it is plausible to speak of a sort of rationally derived moral basis for *jihad* in Islam. Indeed, the ordaining of *jihad* (*qital*) occurred, according to the commentators, during the Medina period of the Prophet's ministry (622 C.E.) when the Muslims were given permission to fight back against the "folk who broke their solemn pledges":

Will ye not fight [*tuqatiluna*] a folk who broke their solemn pledges, and purposed to drive out the Messenger and did attack you first? (9:13)

If they withdraw not from you, and offer you not peace, and refrain not their hand, take them, and slay [*uqtulu*] them wherever you come to them; against them We have given you a clear authority. (4:91–93)

It is not difficult to adduce a strictly moral justification for this permission given to the Muslims to use force. That is, the permission is to fight in retaliation for attacks upon the Muslims. The Qur'an thus justifies defensive *jihad*, allowing the Muslims to fight against and subdue hostile unbelievers who are dangerous and faithless, whose actions show them to be inimical to the success of God's cause.[8] However, the Qur'an does not stop at this duty of self-defense against hostile forces. It also requires Muslims to work toward establishing a just public order. At this point, the *jihad* becomes an offensive endeavor in connection with efforts to bring about the kind of world order that the Qur'an envisions.

The possibility of offensive *jihad* as a means in the creation of the Islamic world order raises questions about my remarks thus far. The Qur'anic passages revealed in the later part of the Prophet's career (in Medina) seem to contradict the characterization of the justification of *jihad* as a response to aggression, namely, a moral rather than a religious justification. Note, for example, 8:39, which requires the Muslims to fight (*qatilu*) against unbelievers "until there is no dissension [*fitna*] and the religion is entirely God's."[9]

The issue is not a simple one, especially since the verse in question (i.e., 8:39) also occurs at 2:193. On the one hand, if the verse is interpreted in the context provided by the general Qur'anic justification for engaging in *jihad* (response to aggression or moral wrong), it can be construed in terms of a moral requirement to fight "persecution" (*fitna*) which, according to 2:191 "is worse than slaughter." On the other hand, if the verse is interpreted in terms of the development of Muslim political power, then it may be said to provide a warrant for wars of expansion. Undoubtedly, the Sunni jurists regarded the conquests up to the end of the 2nd/8th century as the outcome of a legitimate *jihad*. However, these conquests were undertaken with the explicit aim of expanding Islamic hegemony, not with the goal, as stated in the Qur'an, of ensuring that "the religion is entirely God's." Moreover, offensive *jihad* against "those who do not believe in God and the Last Day and do not forbid what God and His messenger have forbidden and do not practice the religion of truth, from among those who have been given the Book [i.e., the Jews and the Christians], until they pay *jizya* [poll-tax]" (9:29) points more to the complex relationship and interdependence of religious and moral considerations in the treatment of the "People of the Book" than to their conversion to "God's religion," Islam.

## *JIHAD* IN ISLAMIC HISTORY

### Sunni and Shi'i Perspectives

Careful scrutiny of the historical circumstances that influenced the decisions of Muslim jurists demonstrates that the jurists thought of *jihad* in connection with Muslims engaging in wars to increase the "sphere of Islam," a territory in which Islamic norms would be enforced and where Islamic acts of devotion are publicly observed.[10] However, the Qur'anic legitimation of *jihad* in the sense of fighting "until there is no dissension and the religion is entirely God's" (2:193), according to Tabari (who takes "dissension" or *fitna* in the sense of "unbelief"), is concerned with the question of the eradication of unbelief that causes a breakdown in the Islamic public order.[11] Accordingly, the sphere in which this *jihad* was to be waged was designated the "sphere of unbelief" (*dar al-kufr*), with the essential aim of uprooting unbelief and preparing the way for the creation of an Islamic order on earth (*dar al-iman*, the "sphere of faith.") On the other hand, the *jihad* that the jurists discuss and legitimize is waged in the sphere designated as the "sphere of war" (*dar al-harb*) and is for the purpose of subduing the forces of unbelief rather than of uprooting unbelief through the conversion of individuals or groups to Islam. Such an explanation of *jihad* reflects a historical rationalization of Islamic hegemony. That is, the jurists' interpretation of *jihad* reflects the interest of the established Muslim authority in the expansion of the sphere of Islam, rather than the Qur'anic insistence on the creation of a just social order.

In the final analysis, the Sunni jurists identified the historical conquests as the result of an offensive *jihad* undertaken to establish an Islamic social and political order. However, the Islamic revelation clearly points toward the establishment of a universal creed based on the affirmation of "the oneness of God" (*tawhid*), the necessity of "divinely guided leadership" (*nubuwwa*), and "the ultimate day of judgment" (*qiyama*).

It is in connection with this last statement that Shi'i jurists, by contrast with the Sunni scholars, argued that the presence of a divinely appointed leader (the *Imam*) would be a necessary precondition of any offensive *jihad*. The Sunni jurists did not consider it a necessity that the leader of the Muslims be a divinely appointed *Imam*. Rather, they argued that any de facto Muslim authority ought to carry out the purposes of God in the *jihad*.[12] This difference of opinion points not only to the fundamental differences between the two schools of thought in the matter of right authority, it also demonstrates their understanding of the political history of Islam and of the connections of the Qur'anic *jihad* with that history. However, before we turn to these differences in the interpretation of Islamic history, it is important to understand the problem of unbelief in the Qur'an, in particular as the Qur'an implicitly justifies the use of force by a just authority against influences inimical to the establishment of a just social order. Attention to this issue will throw light on the thinking that lies behind the jurists' justifications for the resort to force by a qualified leader.

## The Problem of Unbelief and the Use of Force

According to the Qur'an, humanity has not, by and large, submitted to the divine call. God has favored human beings with those cognitive and volitional capacities necessary for the comprehension of the purpose of life, but human beings have failed to act on this "natural" guidance.[13] The Qur'an indicates that this failure is tied to the narrow-mindedness and stupidity (self-cultivated, not innate) of human beings who fail to reflect on the signs that come their way. Preoccupied with worldly affairs, such people do not see that their lives and all that they have is given by the beneficent and merciful Lord, and that they will have to render an account for their actions on the day of reckoning. They live for the pleasure of the moment, not considering that the pleasures of the next world (not to mention the punishments) will exceed their wildest imaginings.

On the other hand, the Qur'an also upholds the lordship of the almighty, sovereign God. God has the power to make unbelievers into believers, and that is what would happen if God so chose (6:107). In other places the Qur'an says that those who go astray have been led astray by God, whereas those who follow the "straight path" are able to do so because God helps them (2:6–7). These verses stand alongside others that indicate that human beings have been given the knowledge and freedom to move toward the telos for which they were created (91:7–8). There are, further, passages that evidently resolve the apparent tension between these "predestinarian" and "free will" positions, indicating that in the case of those whom God has misled, God's action is a response to their previous rejection of God (59:19).

The relation of these various Qur'anic perspectives on the problem of unbelief (i.e., the failure to respond to divine guidance) was the object of the intense discussion among Muslim theologians following the establishment of the Islamic empire (i.e., 2nd/8th–3rd/9th centuries). The focus of this discussion was on the question of "misguidance" (*idlal*). With respect to this question, it is important to note especially those Qur'anic verses that consider "misguidance" or "leading astray" as God's activity in response to unsatisfactory actions or attitudes on the part of individuals who have chosen to reject faith. As such, misguidance is earned: "How shall God guide a people who disbelieved after they believed? . . . God guides not the evildoing people" (3:86).

With respect to the issues of concern to this essay, it would not be helpful to go into more detail on this point. It suffices to say that the problem of human persistence in unbelief and ingratitude is a major concern, even a preoccupation, for the Qur'an. Why do human beings fail to respond to divine guidance? For the Qur'an and the Prophet, unbelief came to signify not only a denial of truth, but a threat to the community of the faithful. To put it another way, unbelief came to be identified not only as a religious wrong, to be punished on the day of judgment, but also a moral wrong, to be subdued in the here and now—by the use of force, if necessary. The picture that emerges in the successive revelations of the Qur'anic verses during the career of the Prophet points to a growing sense by the Muslim community that it would have to engage in armed resistance to the threat posed by those who did not share its faith and the socio-political implications of that faith.

I have already indicated that the need for fighting first became evident when the Muslims established the first Islamic order, in Medina. The permission to fight was a response to the problem of unbelief posed by the Meccan tribes. The Qur'an indicates that this unbelief was, on the one hand, beyond the jurisdiction of the Prophet and the Muslim community. This was so because unbelief is (according to the Qur'an) a religious problem, to be construed as one dimension of the work of God. At the same time, the Qur'an indicates that unbelief can be, and in the case of the Meccans was, malicious—a willful action on the part of human beings who seek to deceive God or to deprive God of God's rights.

As willful disobedience, the unbelief of the Meccan tribes became a problem with moral as well as religious dimensions. The Qur'an indicates that various kinds of action were appropriate for the Prophet and the Muslim community in dealing with this situation. The important point for this essay is that the more the Qur'an stresses the moral aspects of the problem of unbelief (e.g., in terms of Meccan persecution of the Muslims) the more the use of force is justified. When unbelief takes on an actively hostile dimension, the Qur'an justifies, even commands the use of force by the believers:

Fight [*qatilu*] in the way of God against those who fight against you, but begin not hostilities. Lo! God loveth not aggressors. And slay them wherever ye find them, and drive them out of the places whence they drove you out, for persecution [*fitna*] is worse than slaughter. (2:190–91)

To reiterate, the Qur'an justifies the use of force by believers as a response to actively hostile unbelief. It is not unbelievers as such who are the object of force, but unbelievers who demonstrate their hostility to Islam by, for example, persecution of the Muslims. Nonetheless, in the context of the historical development of Islam, the jurists regarded this principle of the Qur'an as abrogated. They maintained that fighting was obligatory for the Muslims, even when the unbelievers had not begun hostilities.[14] This accommodation with the historical practice of *jihad* is not uncommon in the works of the jurists.

When unbelief among Jews and Christians takes the form of disregard for the moral standards prescribed by the Islamic public order, the Qur'an justifies *jihad* (i.e., *qital*) until the hostile forces are subdued and forced to pay the poll-tax (9:29). Reluctance to fight, in 2:190–91, which may be understood in terms of the priority of the rule against killing, is overcome by the security needs of a persecuted and outnumbered community. Consequently, Muslims are commanded to fight against the aggressive hostility of unbelievers, whether this hostility is shown by engaging in an armed attack or by a refusal to comply with the norms of an Islamic polity.

The command is given in such a way that the Qur'an shows that the security needs of the Muslim community and the demands of justice (2:194) could override certain regulations of a religious nature that were recognized among the Arab tribes concerning the "Inviolable Place of Worship" (2:191) or the "forbidden months" (2:194). Thus, the community of believers—which is steadfast in its service to God, and, according to the Qur'an, receptive to God's guidance—may engage in *jihad* to defend itself and strive to establish justice, or perhaps to reestablish a violated justice in the face of aggressive unbelief.

If *jihad* is understood within the notion of human responsibility consistently maintained by the Qur'an—that is, that human beings are to strive for the success of God's cause (9:41)—then sanctioning the use of force against moral and political offenses cannot be regarded as contradicting the Qur'anic dictum of 2:256: "No compulsion is there in religion." The Qur'an justifies the use of force in the establishment of an order that protects the basic welfare of the Muslim community against "internal" and "external" enemies—that is, against "tyrants" (those who take up arms against God and God's messenger [9:33]) and against "unbelievers" (those who break their oaths [9:12] or who "do not forbid what God and His messenger have forbidden" [9:29]), thereby obstructing the struggle to make "God's cause succeed."

This being the case, the use of force by an Islamic authority requires a rigorous demonstration that its purpose is "enjoining the good and forbidding the evil"—that is, if the use of force is to be termed a *jihad*. In other words, Muslim authorities must shoulder the burden of proof and establish that a particular use of force has not been undertaken primarily for territorial expansion, but for the purpose of ushering in the type of world order envisioned by the Qur'an.

As already indicated, the Sunni jurists thought of the *jihad* as a war for the expansion of Islamic territory—i.e., the sphere where the norms prescribed by the Shari'a would be paramount. In so doing, they offered a religious rationale for the historic practice of Muslim rulers. This way of thinking was critically evaluated by Shi'i jurists in light of the statements of their *Imams*, statements that did not regard the wars of expansion as motivated by the Qur'an. The Shi'i scrutiny of the Sunni explications of *jihad* gave rise to questions concerning right authority—Who can declare the *jihad*?

While Sunni jurisprudence is oriented toward the historic practice of the community, working out its ideas about *jihad* with respect to the reality of wars of conquest in the name of Islam, Shi'i jurisprudence characteristically focused on the ideal. It could thus remain adamant concerning the questions of right authority and just cause. The Shi'i jurists, therefore, questioned the motives of the Sunni caliphs with respect to the practice of war.[15] The original purpose of *jihad*, according to the Shi'i jurists, was not preserved under the Sunni rulers. This evaluation of the early conquests leads to the question, Who can declare *jihad*, that is in the Qur'anic sense of a struggle in the path of God?

For the Shi'i, the offensive *jihad*—the *jihad* for the purpose of calling upon people to respond to God's guidance by accepting Islam—required the presence of the just *Imam*, not (as the Sunnis argued) just any leader; or, in the absence of the *Imam*, the person deputized by him could authorize such a struggle. The Shi'i jurists made an explicit distinction between this offensive *jihad* and the defensive *jihad*, which would protect the welfare of the Muslim community against hostile aggression. The requirement of just authority (in the case of offensive war) was supposed to guarantee that the *jihad* against unbelievers would be undertaken strictly for the cause of God. In fact, it is only the just *Imam* who, because of his infallible knowledge of Islamic revelation, could initiate the *jihad* against unbelievers; according to the Shi'i doctrine of the just leader, only the divinely appointed *Imam* has the grace necessary to avoid errors of judgment. In particular, only the just *Imam* can avoid unnecessary killing and ensure that the *jihad* is truly in accord with the goals of Islam. It is interesting that Tabari cites several Sunni jurists who, although in essential agreement that there should be an *Imam* to lead the offensive *jihad*, are in disagreement with the Shi'i in regard to the necessity of the *Imam*'s permission for the initiation of a *jihad* for the purposes of calling people to Islam.[16]

But when the *Imam* or his specifically designated deputy is absent, as is the case in Shi'ism from the tenth century on, the obligation to engage in offensive *jihad* lapses, and, according to the Shi'i jurists, it is not proper to engage in *jihad* at all. However, when the Muslims are unexpectedly attacked by enemies, and they fear for the safety of the boundaries and peoples of Islam, it becomes necessary for the Muslims to undertake defensive measures and defend themselves against those who threaten their security—so the Shi'i jurists argue. This type of fighting is a defensive form of *jihad*, which is sanctioned by Shi'ism, even in the absence of the just *Imam*. The question of obtaining the permission of the *Imam* does not arise, because defense is a moral requirement according to such Qur'anic passages as 2:190–91.

The presupposition upon which Sunni jurisprudence based it notions of *jihad* was the existence of an authority exercising power in the affairs of the Muslim community. Consequently, Sunni jurists did not feel the need to pursue the discussion concerning the various types of *jihad* or the diverse justifications for it. By contrast, the Shi'i jurists presupposed their own lack of power. Hence, their indulgence in the exercise of defining the goals, the preconditions, the various types of *jihad*, and so on. Moreover, Shi'i jurisprudence was not restrained in its theoretical deliberations about the *jihad* in Islamic revelation by the need to rationalize the actual historic practice of the Muslim community. Consequently, there is a substantial discussion in the works of Shi'i jurists concerning two types of *jihad*: what I have called offensive and defensive.

First, *jihad* is used in the sense of furthering the cause of God until it succeeds. This type of *jihad* would include fighting (*qital*) against hostile forces, even against dissenting groups within the Muslim community, who are engaged in spreading "discord on earth" and in undermining the creation of the just public order demanded by Islamic revelation. In an important tradition, this meaning of *jihad* is explained by the Shi'i *Imam*: two groups of people require the response of *jihad*: the unjust and those who reject faith with hostility.[17] It is in this sense that the Shi'i jurists characterized the *jihad* fought by Ali during his caliphate (36–40/ 656–61) against those who "broke their covenants" by disobeying the rightful caliph; those who "deviated from divine guidance" by taking up arms against a righteous government; and those who became "renegades by seceding" from the caliph's camp. These people were, according to the Shi'i jurists, the instigators of the first civil war (*fitna*, here in the sense of "sedition"), a war ignored by the Sunni jurists in their discussion of *jihad*. Indeed, according to the Shi'i historian-theologian Mufid, Ali's appeal to his followers to join in the struggle against those who broke covenant with him included this reminder of the significance of the *jihad*:

Verily, God has imposed the obligation of waging *jihad* and has glorified it and made [participation in it a sign of] support for Him. I solemnly declare that worldly and religious affairs will not be in order without [participating in] it.[18]

Clearly, the theological implication of this type of *jihad* (against the unjust and those who reject faith in hostility) is that participation in it is obligatory. To ignore the call of the just *Imam* in this regard is tantamount to disbelief in God's ultimate purpose for creation. In another tradition, one of the Shi'i *Imams* states that he does not know of any *jihad* in his days except performing devotional acts of piety like the *hajj*, the lesser *hajj* (i.e., *'umra*), and living in the vicinity of the holy precinct in Mecca and Medina (i.e., *jiwar*). This tradition further indicates the way the Shi'i *Imams* interpreted the historical *jihad* of the Sunni rulers as nonrepresentative of the true *jihad*, exemplified by Ali's struggle.

Second, the term *jihad* is applied to all types of defense undertaken to protect the lives and property of Muslims threatened by either external or internal forces hostile to the Muslims. The underlying presupposition of this type of *jihad* is the morally derived obligation of self-protection demanded by the Qur'anic injunction. Accordingly, the Shi'i jurists allowed Muslims to undertake this form of *jihad* even in the absence of the just *Imam*. In other words, when the community is in danger, there is a collective responsibility to defend Muslim families, children, and property.

### CONCLUSIONS

In the final analysis, the Qur'anic understanding of the question of *jihad* points to the twofold signification of the term, as the Shi'i jurists understood and as was reflected in their opinion concerning the authority necessary for resort to *jihad*: A *jihad* intended to call people to faith, needs a just *Imam*. A *jihad* intended as a response to hostile aggression, has no such restriction.

Furthermore, there is a close connection between *jihad* and justice, which makes it indispensable to explore the question of the purpose of Islamic revelation (namely, the establishment of a just public order) and the forces that obstruct the realization of the divine plan for humanity. Such an examination is critical for the elucidation of the theological-political concern of the Muslim jurists, who were, on the one hand, engaged in explaining the historical practice of war within the context of the Qur'anic teachings about the religious-moral purpose of *jihad* and, on the other, in formulating the preconditions for engaging in the *jihad*. It is not difficult to discern the religious and moral presuppositions of the Qur'an in the case of the discussion of defensive *jihad*. Indeed, for this form of *jihad* the Muslim community is made responsible to judge the situation and to act accordingly. However, when it came to waging the offensive *jihad* (and here I speak in the context of Shi'i jurisprudence) to deal with the problems of unbelief and the way it affects the establishment of the Islamic public order, importance was attached to the guidance of a divinely appointed leader who alone is entitled to make binding decisions in matters affecting the welfare of humanity. By virtue of his being an infallible leader and an authoritative interpreter of Islamic revelation, the *Imam* is the sole legitimate authority for the establishment of the Islamic state.

Sunni jurisprudence, written under the impact of historical circumstances, treated the *jihad* as a divinely approved political tool for furthering the "sphere of Islam" and keeping the "sphere of war" in check. Hence, the twofold signification of *jihad* was of little relevance. *Jihad* in Sunni jurisprudence carried the sense of military action with the object of universalizing the temporal power of Islam. The main concern of the Sunni jurists was to provide guidance to rulers so that war would retain a connection with justice and peace under the aegis of Islamic rule.

In principle, the twofold conception of *jihad* outlined in this chapter (and in Islamic jurisprudence) indicates both the idea of a holy war ("an armed struggle on behalf of the constellation of values associated with religion and the concept of the divine—or, more broadly, ideological war—armed struggle against threats to the highest values accepted in the culture and against the values represented by the enemy")[19] and the idea of a just war (a war consonant with "the possibility that armed conflict may be justified to protect and preserve values [and the denial of] the justifiability of unlimited means of war in the service of such values").[20] In connection with the Qur'anic presuppositions about the existence of universally objective moral values "ingrained in the human soul" (91:8), one might say that Islamic revelation foreshadows the just war concepts conceived as grounded in natural law of modern Western theorists.[21]

In closing, I should say that the task of distinguishing the Qur'anic justifications of *jihad* from the historical connections of that idea with the politically motivated experience of the Muslim rulers awaits full treatment. Any treatment of Muslim political history will have to include a careful discussion of *jihad* and its relationship to the exercise of legal and moral authority in Islam. Such a treatment would explain the apparent discrepancies between the ideal and the real in the Islamic tradition as pointed out, for example, in my discussion of Sunni and Shi'i approaches to *jihad*. Truly, Islamic jurisprudence is the mirror in which the religious and social history of the Muslims can be observed.[22]

If anything, this chapter demonstrates the necessity of approaching the topic of war in Islam from a variety of directions: religious texts, history, jurisprudence, and so on. Such an approach can lead us to discover universally applicable categories in the study of the struggle of humanity to make sense of its responsibility on earth and to uncover the means to fulfill that responsibility. Needless to say, in this age of "specialization" it is too much to expect any scholar to do the work of a Tabari or of an Aquinas. But I believe we can become sensitive to Tabari and Aquinas.

## NOTES

1. See David Little and Sumner B. Twiss, Jr., *Comparative Religious Ethics: A New Method* (San Francisco: Harper & Row, 1978).

2. It is inaccurate to render *jihad* as "holy war" without qualifying the term in the context provided by the Qur'an. As we shall see, Muslim jurists, at times in contradiction to the Qur'anic concept of *jihad*, have in many cases seen the goals of *jihad* as those of a holy war, at least as such a war is described by James Turner Johnson in "Historical Roots and Sources of the Just War Tradition in Western Culture," in *Just War and Jihad: Historical and Theoretical Perspectives on War and Peace in Western and Islamic Traditions*, ed. John Kelsay and James Turner Johnson (Westport, CT: Greenwood Press, 1991).

3. In this chapter I shall make use, with my own alterations, of the translation of the Qur'an by A. J. Arberry in *The Koran Interpreted* (New York: Macmillan, 1967).

4. Tabari, *Kitab ikhtilaf al-fuqaha'*, ed. Joseph Schacht (Leiden, Netherlands: E. J. Brill, 1933). Tabari's focus on individual jurists is important in that it reflects the truth of Joseph Schacht's judgment that Islamic law came into being and developed through the efforts of "pious specialists" against a varied political and administrative background. It is for this reason that Schacht characterizes Islamic law as a "jurists' law." The "schools" developed during the first decades of the 2nd/8th century, building on the work of private, individual jurists whose rulings reflect the socio-political realities of the various regions within the Islamic empire. See Joseph Schacht, "Islamic Religious Law," in *The Legacy of Islam*, 2d ed., ed. Joseph Schacht with C. E. Bosworth (Oxford: Oxford University Press, 1974).

5. Ignaz Goldziher, *Muslim Studies*, vol. 2, ed. S. M. Stern (London: George Allen & Unwin, 1971), p. 354, citing Tabari, *Ta'rikh*, 2/544.

6. Prior to Tabari's work, the *Muwatta* of Malik and *Kitab al-kharaj* by Abu Yusuf both set forth detailed rules for engaging in *jihad*.

7. Tabari, *Ikhtilaf*, pp. 1–3.

8. That the Qur'an justifies "defensive" *jihad* only has been challenged by some activist Muslim authors as a view "fairly common among Muslim apologists." See Mehdi Abedi and Gary Legenhausen, eds., *Jihad and Shahadat: Struggle and Martyrdom in Islam* (Houston: Institute for Research and Islamic Studies, 1986), p. 13. However, my categorization of the Qur'anic *jihad* as a "defensive" one is based on the complete absence of any reference in the Qur'an that would justify an "offensive" *jihad*, i.e., a *jihad* undertaken in order to "convert" all of humanity to Islam. As I shall demonstrate, the Muslim jurists, especially the Shi'ites, had great difficulty justifying the "offensive" *jihad* without some type of divine intervention (e.g., the designation of an infallible leader who could protect against the shedding of innocent blood, and so on).

9. Muslim exegetes disagree on the meaning of the term *fitna*. In addition to "dissension," it may signify "persecution," "temptation," and "sedition." See E. W. Lane, *Arabic-English Lexicon* (Beirut: Librairie du Liban, 1968) under FTN. Tabari interprets the term to mean "disbelief," which would provide religious justification for waging *jihad* "until religion is entirely God's" (*Tafsir* [Beirut: Dar al-Ma'arif, 1972], 1/129).

10. W. Montgomery Watt, "The Significance of the Theory of Jihad," in *Akten des VII. Kongresses fur Arabistik und Islam Wissenschaft* (Gottingen, West Germany: 1974), p. 393.

11. Tabari, *Tafsir*, 2/113 cites various opinions that are in agreement that *fitna* meant *shirk*, that is, a form of disbelief in which a person would ascribe divinity to things not worthy of such ascription. It is also translated as "associationism." Other exegetes agree with Tabari on this point. See, for instance, Zamakhshari, *Kashshaf* (Cairo: al-Halabi, 1966), 1/550; Baydawi, *Anwar* (Cairo, 1887), 41. For a modern interpretation, see Tabataba'i, *Mizan* (Beirut: al-A'lami, 1974), 3/89.

12. Tabari, *Ikhtilaf*, p. 12. He uses the word "Imam" in the general sense of the leader of the community.

13. For further details on the concept of guidance in the Qur'an see my chapter on "Freedom of Conscience and Religion in the Qur'an," in *Human Rights and the Conflict of Cultures*, co-authored with David Little and John Kelsay (Columbia: University of South Carolina Press, 1988), esp. pp. 58–62.

14. See the article "Djihad" in *Encyclopedia of Islam* (London: E. J. Brill, 1970), 2nd ed., 2/538.

15. That the Shi'i leaders did not regard the various *jihads* of the Sunni caliphs as motivated by the Qur'anic demand to make God's cause succeed is the point of a number of narratives related in Shi'i sources. See Majlisi, *Bihar* (Tehran: Islamiyya, 1957), 100/18.

16. Tabari, *Ikhtilaf*, pp. 11–13.

17. For the sources and their discussion see my work *The Just Ruler in Shi'ite Islam* (New York: Oxford University Press, 1980), pp. 105–17.

18. Mufid, *Irshad* (Tehran: Islamiyya, 1972), pp. 118–19.

19. Johnson, "Historical Roots . . ."

20. Ibid.
21. Ibid.
22. Joseph Schacht, "Law and Justice," in *The Cambridge History of Islam*, vol. 28, ed. P. M. Holt, A.K.S. Lambton, and B. Lewis (Cambridge: Cambridge University Press, 1970), pp. 539–68, has observed the significance of juridical works as the most important sources for the investigation of Islamic society.

# 3

## Approaches to Limits on War in Western Just War Discourse

### Stephen E. Lammers

## INTRODUCTION

### Limits on War or Limits on Fighting

One of the first things that one notices about the title of this chapter is the term "limits." In our era, the context for the use of the term has been the conflict between the United States and the Soviet Union. Given that both powers had (and have) enough weapons to inflict enormous damage upon the other and given that the damage in case of large-scale war would be unacceptable, some Western theorists spoke of "limited war" as a goal of United States policy. In thinking about war, these theorists were explicit in assuming, as one put it, "The existence of thermonuclear weapons and the lack of any mechanism for guaranteeing the absence of war makes it necessary to take seriously the problem of how war . . . can be kept limited."[1] In limited war, one theorist was thinking of "a military encounter in which the Soviet Union and the United States see each other on opposing sides and in which the effort of each falls short of the attempt to use all of its power to destroy the other."[2] In most cases, these conflicts would be waged through proxies. If war between the superpowers did occur, limited war meant that there would be some attempt to constrain the horrors of war by making some targets off-limits.

Discussion of limited war is common in the modern era, and this includes discussion of limitations upon what can be accomplished in war as well as discussion about limitations upon conduct in war. If one turns to the Western religious and secular traditions of discussion about war with this in mind, one tends to first focus upon the *jus in bello* criteria that are part of that tradition of just war discourse—that is, limitations upon the means of war. Major contemporary just war theorists, such as Paul Ramsey, have, by emphasizing *jus in bello* concerns in their writings, fed the tendency to identify the problem of limitation of war with this part of just war tradition: the principles of discrimination (or noncombatant immunity) and proportionality. Very little attention is paid to the other part of the tradition, the *jus ad bellum* criteria, though this formed the major focus, especially for Christian thinkers, in earlier periods. Further, though the classic just war theorists held that justice must be served in order for a war to be just, so that wars fought strictly for reasons of realpolitik would not, for them, be justified, in the modern era there is no publicly acceptable way of limiting war by talking about the demands of justice in going to war. Insofar as commentators within the just war tradition in the past insisted upon talking about justice, they are thought to be irrelevant to discussions about limited war.

Yet the bias in contemporary discussion hides the fact that as a whole, just war tradition imposes restraints on war through both the *jus ad bellum* (which sets limits on when it is justifiable to engage in war) and the *jus in bello* (the locus of limits on what it is justifiable to do while fighting a war). For a full treatment of the limitation of war in the just war context, it is necessary to look at both, not simply at the *in bello* limits.

Nonetheless, because of the contemporary focus, the stress in this essay will be devoted to the *jus in bello* criteria as exemplifying how thinkers in the West have tried to limit war, especially in the twentieth century. The *jus ad bellum*, though, will also be treated in an effort to show how the criteria that define it functioned in the past to limit war. This will not only provide a fuller, more representative analysis of the implications of just war tradition for the limitation of war; it will also help to show why, in the contemporary context, reliance on *jus ad bellum* criteria has waned and *jus in bello* concepts have received increased emphasis.

### Limiting War in the Christian Just War Tradition

As a backdrop to discussion of Christian theorizing about limiting war in the West, it must be admitted that some Christian apologists have historically seemed mainly concerned not to limit war but to justify and support the wars of their particular states or rulers, including raising money to finance these wars.[3] Even those Christian thinkers who took seriously the need for moral criteria to define the justification of a war often did not go on to insist that the means of war also had to be justified if Christians were to participate. The available means seem simply to have been taken for granted and factored into the larger calculus of whether or not the war was justified.

Given this backdrop, it is not surprising that a great deal of historical Christian writing on war has focused on the theological problem of justifying the ways of God to man: in particular, justifying the horrors of a certain war and either the justice or beneficence of God. In this theological context, war functions much like a natural disaster, and the first question that is asked is not "How may we work to limit war, either its occurrence or its extent?" but "How could God possibly have allowed the terrible devastation of this particular war?" or "What, if any, are the deity's purposes?" In such cases, the primary problem for Christian theology has been how one plausibly might claim that the horrors of war were not outside of the powers or purposes of the divinity. It was (and is) an especially crucial consideration to those who think of themselves as in some sense the heirs of the Hebrew Bible and who thus were ready to find God working in the context of warfare, even when that warfare led to the defeat of the armies of Israel or their successors.[4]

The question of limitation arose only after Christians had come to assume that they had to take some responsibility for what the political powers were doing, a development that began to take place gradually from the second century onward and was ratified when Christianity became the state religion of the Roman Empire in the fourth century. The earliest concentrated theological attention to issues of justification and limitation in war, that given in writings of Ambrose and Augustine, date to this latter period. That is, contrary to the way in which just war criteria are used by some twentieth-century pacifists, the developing discussions of just war assumed that Christians, for a variety of reasons, had to take responsibility for what was being done by the political order. Further, just war ideas arose in the context of people trying to understand how war might serve moral purposes despite its destructiveness, not simply trying to defend the possibility of war against pacifist criticism.[5] The very requirements of the gospel or of humanity were themselves given as reasons why one ought to go to war.

When the earliest Western Christian discussions of limitations of warfare took place, they took place in a context in which it was assumed that not only could official activities of the state and the church provide legitimation for wars, but that there were other societal practices and conditions that were helpful in limiting war. War was not total, in the sense that it involved the entire population of a belligerent power; rather, it was limited to soldiers, who made up only a fraction of the entire population. The means of war were principally those of face-to-face combat with hand weapons, not means of massive destruction capability. Difficulties of supply and adversity of weather imposed further limitations on the practice of war. In this historical context, which for

practical purposes has only dissolved in the modern era, the practice of
war was limited by the inherent conditions, and theorists instead focused
their energies on whether it was just to engage in war and how to prevent
going to war unjustly. The situation today is far different, as indicated
by the shift in theoretical discussion to limits on the means of fighting.

Yet historical Christian commentators on war did recognize that it was
possible to sin in war. In the words of Albertus Magnus, writing in the
thirteenth century, "According to customary usage warfare is only with
difficulty engaged in without sin."[6] But the problem was not conceived
in terms of wrong means or targets in war (issues central in contemporary
*jus in bello* discussions) but in terms of the possibility that a soldier might
act in war out of a wrong intention. Killing an enemy on the field of
combat as a public servant operating under the authority of those responsible for political order, justice, and the return of peace, and with
no intention but to serve these ends, was regarded by medieval theorists
as of a decisively different moral stripe from killing the enemy out of
hatred or rage directed at him. The possibility that, even in a just war,
individual soldiers might have been motivated by the latter sort of intention led to serious ecclesiastical efforts to deal with the resultant guilt
and allow soldiers to expiate their sin. This perspective determined how
church and society in the Middle Ages dealt with the returning warrior.
By contrast, modern discussions do not presume and cannot rely upon
systems that not only express this presupposition about sinfulness arising from war but also attempt to deal with the issues raised by that
presupposition for the returning soldier and the society into which he
had to be reintegrated. Let me mention two practices from this period
that have no resonance in our own day, one concerning soldiers and
one concerning political leaders.

First, in the medieval context there was a way of dealing with returning
warriors liturgically, not simply to forgive them their sins but also to
cleanse them from any ritual impurities. This was done regardless of
the justice of the war. That is to say, the discussions of limitations on
means and targets of fighting arose in just war tradition as part of a
broader cultural system addressing not only how war should be conceived but also how its ill effects should be dealt with for the individual.[7]

Second, the soldier was not alone in receiving special attention from
the society. Classic Christian just war discussion aimed its advice primarily at princes and rulers and assumed a consensus about what constituted good rule and the good ruler. If the person who leads the
political unit is important because it is that person who can limit the
extent and occasions of war, then a duty of moral theorists is to provide
that person with the kind of perspective necessary to accomplish that
task. The Christian tradition on just war developed as part of a larger
political tradition that sought to train political leaders to have character

traits such that they would not be subject to those evils that give rise to war and that war creates. As in the case of the possibility of sin on the part of individual soldiers, the core issue is a *right intention* on the part of the ruler with respect to war. Specifically, greed, lust, desire for domination, revenge, and the like—examples of wrong intention—are the evils that bring about wars or which wars encourage.[8] Political leaders must become the kind of people who will resist these evils, and in order to do that they need certain virtuous habits. Such Christian teaching about the virtuous ruler is presupposed by the Western just war tradition in its early development through the Middle Ages.

Again, the contemporary situation is strikingly different. Current discussions of limitation of war take place in a context where there is little attention to the situation of the soldier returning to the community and little attention to the personal virtues required of political leaders. Rather, contemporary discussion seems to assume that the problem of establishing moral restraints on war is chiefly a matter of establishing the right moral rules applying to war. The assumption seems to be that a person who knows and understands these rules is well placed, assuming goodwill, to enforce or follow them.[9] Contributors to the earlier Western just war tradition never saw the issue that simply.

To summarize, early Christian discussion of the limitation of warfare within the tradition of just war often took place in contexts that simply are not available today. Thus, how one extends that tradition to talk about limits in the contemporary context is itself a question that has to be considered. Discussion of the criteria for justifiable war must take place with attention to the contexts within which the criteria developed and how these criteria functioned within those contexts.[10] Even though the terminology remains the same, the actual functioning of the various just war criteria in the different historical contexts leads to different emphases and to different insights about when war is justified and how it ought to be limited. Further, the present focus upon criteria as the way to limit war masks the fact that in the past there were practices that also imposed limits—practices not available to us today.

In this chapter, I will try to be sensitive to these issues as I develop the discussion of the criteria of the just war. It is these criteria that will be the focus of this chapter. I will not be developing the history of the tradition; time does not permit and it has been done elsewhere.[11] I will examine how the criteria of the *jus ad bellum* were used to limit war in the past and how the current discussion of the *jus in bello* criteria serve contemporary theorists as a way of discussing limitation of war today.

## THE JUST WAR CRITERIA

I will begin with the *jus in bello* criteria, since those are the ones that have received the most attention in the modern period. After having identified the most commonly discussed criteria for the *jus in bello*, I will follow the same procedure for the *jus ad bellum*. After both sets of criteria have been identified, I will show how the makers of the tradition developed the criteria as a way of limiting war. Then I will explain how the *jus ad bellum* limits have diminished usefulness in today's context. At that point, I will return to the discussion of the *jus in bello* criteria, with special attention to the discussion of these criteria since the Second World War. It is in that period that many developments have taken place that shape the contemporary discussion of limitation.

Whatever the historical context, though, Christian discussion of the justification and limitation of war has proceeded because of certain aspects central to Christian religion itself, including belief in the overriding justice of God's plan for the world, a faith that linked moral behavior with salvation, and normative claims about the character and common humanity of the enemy. John Langan has listed these in more detail and in greater length.[12] The link they provide across the history of development of Christian thought establishes the commonality of contemporary Christian reflection on just war and its limits with that which earlier commentators produced. However these aspects might be translated into concrete normative claims about the normative limits they impose on war, no Christian could deny them at the level of faith and doctrine. This provides Christian just war thinking its own coherence within the larger Western tradition on the moral justification and limitation of war.

Despite its distinctiveness as a body of religious reflection on war, Christian just war thought has contributed to this larger tradition, principally through the idea of universal moral ideas found in natural law and more recently expressed in international law. The natural law discussion assumes that there are moral constraints that can be known by human reason unaided by any form of divine revelation: thus one does not have to be a believer in order to know them. These constraints are to be followed in any war that could be called just. In the past, one of the effects of claiming that these constraints were part of the natural law was that political authorities would be justified in punishing persons who did not follow the constraints, since it was assumed that these constraints could be known by anyone of goodwill. That is to say, the norms were universal and all peoples could be held accountable under them.

This universality also appears in modern international law, which is a major framework within which just war tradition operates today. However, whatever universality is claimed for the norms of international law today is that which arises from agreements between nations. The natural law, on the other hand, was conceived as applying to all persons whether or not they agreed in advance to adhere to its norms. Accordingly, just war tradition is manifested more narrowly in international law than in natural law or Christian theological reflection.

## The Jus in Bello Criteria

Recent discussion on the limitation of war within the framework of just war tradition has focused heavily on the two moral principles that define the idea of *jus in bello*: the principles of proportionality and discrimination. Application of these principles to the contemporary conditions of war had led many commentators to the judgment that all wars with nuclear weapons, and many other contemporary wars beside, are impermissible. Others maintain that it is possible to conceive and fight contemporary wars within these limits and that just wars remain a moral possibility in the present age.[13]

The first principle of limitation states that actions in war must be discriminate. This is often known as the principle of noncombatant immunity from directly intended attack. What it forbids, in general terms, is direct, intentional attack upon persons not involved in the war. Defenders of this principle have long recognized, as they do today, that there will be times in war when civilians will be killed or injured as a result of military operations. What is central, according to the principle of discrimination, is whether or not those deaths were intended, whether they were sought as part of the scope of a military operation or whether they were unwanted results of an otherwise justifiable military action.

Besides forbidding attacks upon noncombatants, this criterion also forbids attacks upon places and buildings dedicated to activities not related to war. Thus, hospitals and museums should be exempt from attack, for example. Finally, this principle implies that one may not be careless with one's use of military force. It is the moral responsibility of every military commander to take positive steps to prevent even unintended, indirect deaths of noncombatants.[14]

The second *jus in bello* principle requires that actions in war must be proportionate. While political leaders must also pose the question of proportionality to the overall issue of whether to engage in war, within the *jus in bello* context this principle applies mainly to the military commander. The military leader must consider the harm that will be caused by a particular action or campaign and judge whether the harm is worth the good that will be achieved. The harm must not be disproportionate to the good.[15] Again, the question is not simply one of physical value but one of moral value. An example chosen by Michael Walzer to illustrate this principle makes this clear.

During the Korean War, American commanders often responded to sniper attacks by having artillery barrages directed at the area from which sniper fire originated. This saved them from risking their troops in ferreting out the snipers. The cost, however, was that many Korean villages were subjected to artillery barrages and there was (it is estimated) a heavy loss of civilian life. The Americans clearly did not *aim* at the Korean villagers, that is, they did not intend to kill them. However, there was so much damage done by this practice that it has been judged disproportionate to any good that it achieved, in this case, the preservation of the lives of American soldiers.[16]

Note what the criterion of proportionality demands. The commander must make an evaluation about the harm done by the unwanted killing of noncombatant civilians and weight that against the equally unwanted (if not more so) deaths of his own troops. Note further that the troops and the civilians—combatants and noncombatants, respectively—do not count equally. Soldiers, as Walzer argues, must expect to endure more death and destruction than civilians.[17]

### The Jus ad Bellum Criteria

Proportionality and discrimination aim at limiting the destructiveness of war in process, that is, *how* a war should be fought once begun. The criteria of the just war *jus ad bellum,* typically ignored in contemporary discussions of limiting war, have to do with restraining the incidence of resort to war, that is *when* it is morally legitimate to begin war.[18] Further, *ad bellum* constraints were ones that traditionally applied primarily to political leaders while *in bello* considerations were ones that applied primarily to soldiers and their immediate commanders. Among the limitations on when war might be fought are the following:

In order to be fought justly,

1. War must be publicly declared.
2. War must be declared by a competent authority.
3. War must be fought with the right intention.
4. War must be fought for a just cause.
5. War must be fought for a proportionate reason.
6. War must be fought for a just peace.
7. War must be a last resort.[19]

*Just war must be declared.* Originally this criterion involved the idea that war was a public event, that it should not be prepared and initiated sub rosa.[20] Contemporary critics worry that this constraint is anachronistic and unrealistic in the present context, in which most armed conflicts are never formally and publicly declared. The limit may, however, still have relevance in that it can function as a way of keeping officials honest in their commitment of military forces. When taken seriously, it is a way of making clear that one is not permitted to engage in war without some kind of public announcement of the action.

*Just war must be declared by a competent authority.* This is a requirement that dates back at least to the medieval period. In its original context, that of a hierarchy of knights with the hereditary right to bear arms, it was an attempt to limit war by insisting that only certain persons, those who had no political superior, had the authority to declare war. In the medieval context, many petty princes and ordinary knights were thereby deprived of their authority to initiate war. The assumption of this requirement was that if there are fewer persons who may rightfully declare war, then it is more likely that there will be fewer wars. In modern democratic societies, this requirement is a constraint on the political leader if the leader does not have exclusive warmaking power. (For example, the debates during the Vietnam war on the role of Congress in committing troops could have been and sometimes were framed in terms of the competent authority to declare war.)

*Just war must be fought with the right intention.* This requirement, which was at the core of medieval moral teaching about war, is little attended to in the modern context.[21] In the context of medieval assumptions about morality, the presence or absence of right intention was closely connected to determining who was seeking peace, who was seeking simply to gain something for himself, who was fighting out of hatred or vengeance, or who intended simply to destroy the enemy, not to establish justice. In that context, subjective hatred of the enemy was evidence of wrong intention and was not morally permitted, nor was revenge. As previously mentioned, concern for the possible presence of wrong intention led to the establishment of ecclesiastical and social structures for the reintegration into church and society of soldiers returning from war. This manifested a pastoral concern diffused throughout society; it depended on the existence of common moral assumptions and close links between church and world, as well as a thematic connection between the virtuousness of rulers and their judgment in resorting (or not resorting) to war. In the present context, none of these conditions exists; as a result, in practice, the *jus ad bellum* criterion of right intention is substantially ignored.

Reflection on this criterion raises important differences between the classical discussions of justifiable war and the modern ones. The differences are at the level of moral psychology. For example, in the classical writings, hatred is seen as growing out of envy of a neighbor's flourishing. In that schema, "When I hate someone, I wish him injury, not to redress an injustice but as a consequence of my envy."[22] As a result, in a war undertaken out of hatred, it *may be* that I will redress a wrong, but my intention is to do injury for its own sake. Needless to say, in this view of the world, hatred is never justifiable. Contrast this with the following:

The difficulties concerning hatred can perhaps be resolved by distinguishing justifiable from unjustifiable hatred. Hatred of leaders who choose to wage unjust war is justifiable; hatred of their compatriots and coracialists is not, since hatred of human beings as such—apart from their voluntary acts—is not a morally acceptable emotion.[23]

Hatred, in the latter formulation, has become acceptable when it focuses on persons who perform unjustifiable actions. It is clear that this is a quite different sort of claim about the nature of right intention than a medieval writer could make.

*Just war must be fought for a just cause.* This is a conceptually difficult constraint today, not because people are opposed to the use of force in order to bring about some kind of justice, nor because we would want wars fought for anything less than a just cause, but because of disagreements about what justice is and about who can decide what is just in the case of a particular war. Who is to provide the definition of justice and judge the justice of the cause? Where there is no one authority who can plausibly claim to be neutral, this kind of a criterion seems inappropriate.

In the modern context the issue is resolved with the claim that only those wars that are fought in self-defense can be considered just, and then only if those wars are wars of self-defense in response to aggression.[24] This has meant a substantive change in the discussion of this criterion. In the classical formulation of just war theory, as found in Augustine, Aquinas, and other commentators, just cause existed if the war in question were to punish evildoers, to repulse an injury that was in the process of being committed, or to recover property that had been unjustly taken previously. In the writings of contemporary commentators and in positive international law this list is sharply restricted, so that self-defense is recognized as the only legitimate aim in justifiable war.[25] In practice, however, the idea of self-defense has been stretched beyond the medieval concept of a reaction against an injury in progress. Contemporary discussion treats retaliation and recovery of territory as forms of self-defense, even if the aggressive act is not ongoing.

*Just war must be fought for a proportionate reason.* This criterion asks the political leader to consider whether the harm that can be foreseen in the waging of war will outweigh what might be accomplished through war. It is a difficult criterion to apply, since most commentators insist that it requires not only the assessment of physical damage but also a judgment on the loss of value that will come about through either fighting or refusing to fight. Although difficult to apply, it would appear that its intent is clear with respect to limiting war. War should not be undertaken lightly. In the present era, when the means available for war have enormous destructive power, many commentators have concluded that there can be no just wars because any and all wars will prove disproportionate. Others argue that the destructive capabilities of modern weapons do not in themselves obviate the possibility of just wars; the moral issue for them is to employ available weapons so as not to violate proportionality.

*Just war must be fought for a just peace.* This criterion demands that the political leader consider what will be established in the relations among nations if the war is successful. This criterion poses a limitation not only on going to war but upon the manner of conducting and concluding a war. Obviously, the aims of a belligerent party can be important during a war since the other party can respond in different ways to surrender based on being at the whim of the victor or retaining some rights after surrender. The Allied demands for the unconditional surrender of Germany and Japan during the Second World War are sometimes argued to be the kind of demand that would violate this criterion.

*Just war must be fought as a last resort.* There is a great deal of recent discussion of this criterion. Fundamentally, this criterion would limit war by making sure that all steps short of war have been accomplished. Some modern commentators reason that the criterion assumes a condition that only existed in a past era, when armies took a long time to mobilize and patient diplomacy could be used to forestall war. In contexts where the weapons are more powerful, when attack can take place quickly, and where there is no place to recover from an initial attack, a nation can move from a state of peace to a state of war (and to defeat) rather rapidly. In such a setting, there is a question about what this requirement adds to the requirement of proportionality.

Yet other commentators have argued that the contemporary meaning of the criterion of last resort is that nations should always seek peaceful solutions to their disputes—not only by patient diplomacy but also by availing themselves, if necessary, of international arbitration—and that they should seek to establish and perpetuate a world order such that resort to force among nations will be progressively made less likely. Coupled with the redefinition of just cause as allowing only self-defense, this means that any first use of force to settle a dispute could never be the last resort.

### Development of the Jus *ad* Bellum Criteria

The criteria of the *jus ad bellum* developed over a long period of time. A brief description of some of the important changes in the development of the criteria will help to show how the contributors to the tradition tried to establish and maintain them as means of limitation.

The concepts of right authority and just cause went through similar critical changes. Medieval commentators made a correlation between the authority and the cause. If the authority were secular, so should the cause be secular. If the authority were religious, so the cause could be for some religious purpose.[26] Only gradually did religious authorities— and religious causes—disappear from the concepts accepted by just war commentators.

In this historical context, as already noted, much attention was given to the intention of the actor. Thomas Aquinas, for example, joined Augustine in rejecting "the desire to inflict harm, . . . vengeance, . . . the fever of rebelling, . . . and the lust to dominate" on the part of the person who would enter into a war.[27]

Right authority, just cause, and right intention formed the core of the medieval *jus ad bellum*. The content of these ideas underwent evolutionary change as the modern era dawned. In the sixteenth century Franciscus de Victoria argued explicitly that there could be no just cause for war for difference of religion. His authority was not sufficient to prevent the century of bloodshed following the Protestant Reformation, but by the end of that era the rejection of religion as cause for war was a settled piece of the developing just war tradition. Also, by the time of Victoria, it was clear that secular rulers were too self-interested to be good judges of the justice of their own causes. Thus Victoria recommended that more people become involved in the process of deciding whether or not to go to war, perhaps with the expectation that the more people involved in the process, the more likely it is that the decision will be against going to war.[28] Even then, he recognized that both sides may think, because of invincible ignorance, that they have just cause for war. He argued that in such cases belligerents should observe moderation in their actions toward each other.[29] This was the historical beginning of the shift in emphasis in just war tradition away from the *jus ad bellum* and toward the *jus in bello*.

I have already noted that one of the ways the thinkers in this tradition tried to limit the occasions of war was by limiting the justifiable cause of war to self-defense. Once the objective reasons for justifying the use of war are limited, the question remains of how certain the person deciding to go to war must be of the existence of these reasons. Must one be absolutely certain that one's cause is just? Must the justice of the cause be apparent not only to the ruler but to the subjects as well? These and similar questions were raised during the early modern development of just war discussion. What appeared over time, reflected in the restriction of just cause to self-defense, is a trend to arguing for a higher and higher standard of objective certainty on the part of the decision maker and a broader consensus on the part of the ruler's advisors and subjects.[30] These changes foreshadowed the changed political structures of modern liberal democratic states, in which the decision to resort to war is a shared one. It is not clear, however, that this necessarily leads to limiting the probability of making war.

In the medieval context, only the ruler had the right to make war, and in almost all cases, actions against the ruler would have been considered sedition, a special sin.[31] This limitation on the power to declare war, however, can be in direct conflict with the desire to see justice done. Thus later theorists, beginning with Victoria, argued for an expansion of the right of war to lesser magistrates. The eventual democratization of the right to declare war is one place in which the tradition has been somewhat at odds with itself. One cannot expand the power to declare war and hope thereby to limit war.[32]

## Modern Reservations about the Jus ad Bellum

For a number of reasons the criteria of the *jus ad bellum* have lost favor in efforts to limit war, no matter what the intention of their creators at an earlier period. The reasons are various.

First, as already has been noted, there is no dominant conception of justice in our pluralistic world. Without the ability to agree on what is meant by justice, it is impossible to have a discussion of the justice of the cause.[33] Such a discussion might proceed within particular communities that have their own agreed upon conceptions of justice, but they cannot proceed between communities with radically different conceptions of justice. Reduction of the idea of just cause to self-defense against aggression adds an element of objectivity to the judgment, but exactly what constitutes aggression and what self-defense remains controverted. It is conceivable, moreover, that first use of force would, in some instances, serve justice. Finally, as already noted, the concept of self-defense has become stretched so as to include other forms of use of force than response to an armed attack in progress.

Second, the criteria of the *jus ad bellum* always assumed that there was someone who could act as a judge of the justice of the action of war. But the disinterestedness presumed by this, already questionable by the time of Victoria, is simply not believable in our world.

A plausible, if limited, contemporary use of the *jus ad bellum* criteria is suggested by Bruce Russett. Russett argues that these criteria were never intended to be applied formally by objective observers, but rather were created in order to provide a basis for some kind of restraint upon action by political leaders.[34]

Seeking more objective ways to limit war, contemporary commentators within this tradition have turned elsewhere and looked to the *jus in bello* criteria for attempts to restrain immoral conducts of war. By focusing upon conduct, they hope that the modern world can come to some agreement about how to limit the destructiveness of war, even when there is no agreement about the moral principles to be observed in limiting the occasions of war.

## *JUS IN BELLO* IN HISTORY AND IN RECENT DISCUSSION

One of the striking things about discussion of the *jus in bello* in the history of Western religious reflection upon war is how little attention is paid to limitation within war, especially by the specifically religious writers, before the modern period. This does not mean that limitation within war is not discussed; it is not, however, the center of attention. In what follows, I will offer some examples of the kinds of discussions that took place in the past and then contrast them with the lively discussion of the *jus in bello* criteria in our own era.

### Historical Discussions of the *Jus in Bello*

Thomas Aquinas, an authoritative source for much Christian just war thought, provides a useful first example. Aquinas is surprising in that he did not pay much attention to two principal ways in which the medieval church attempted to limit the conduct of war: the Peace of God and the Truce of God. The Truce of God required that warfare be forsworn on certain days of the week and on certain feast days; Aquinas did not support this limitation if it threatened the public good in any way. Otherwise he accepted it.[35]

He was also strangely silent on the Peace of God, which stated that certain persons, clerics among them, were not to be attacked in war. Aquinas did limit the participation of clerics in war to the spiritual support of just war; he said clerics should not fight in war.[36] The canon law of his time paired this with a restriction on attacking clerics, pilgrims, and others on church business, as well as certain classes of other persons: women, children, the aged, the infirm. Aquinas made no mention of this. Limitation on the times of war or the targets of war does not appear to have been among his primary concerns.

At the same time, Thomas was willing to set drastic limits on what one could intend to do to the enemy during war, and this limitation turned out to be the basis of much later discussion. Aquinas claimed that one could not harm one's enemy more than was necessary in order to prevent the evil the enemy was trying to do. In his discussion of self-defense, he said that one could not have the killing of the enemy as part of one's intention. Some later commentators claim that this assertion is the first statement of the principle of double effect, which is important for later discussions of limitation of the means of war.[37]

By the sixteenth century, matters were much different. Franciscus de Victoria spent much more time than Aquinas discussing limits upon the means of war. First, he put restrictions on what might be done assuming one wins the war: the victor could only take what was stolen and monies to cover the expense of the war. In his thinking war was still regarded as a punishment process carried out by a judge, but he made clear that the judge did not have unlimited discretion about what might be done to the guilty party.

Second, Victoria was concerned with protecting the innocent, though he defined the innocent differently in two different contexts. In the first context, he saw the innocent as people who ought not to be attacked directly because of their status. This included women, children, ambassadors, clerics, etc.: those persons who were protected in the canon law of his time and would today be considered noncombatants. The second definition of the innocent was made in the context of the punishment due to people after the war. Victoria here defined as innocent the soldiers of the conquered enemy ruler. This second class of innocents can be killed in war but should not be punished once the war is over. After the war they are noncombatants. Enemy leaders, obviously enough, are not among the innocent. Thus Victoria limited both who could be attacked during a war and who could be punished later. However, Victoria was willing to have the financial punishments of war extended to all of the people of the enemy side.

Victoria did permit the killing of the noncombatant innocent in one significant case: such killing was permitted during a war known to be just if the killing was unavoidable, that is, if it was necessary for victory. Thus people who are in a besieged fortress and who are noncombatants are not killed wrongly if the capture of the fortress is necessary and the noncombatants are killed as a result of the siege process and not as a result of killing after the siege. Further, the siege commander is under no obligation to allow civilians to leave a besieged area once the siege has begun. In this case, in Victoria's reasoning, the justice of the war and the necessity of taking the city to bring victory are the overriding considerations, suggesting that in his thought the *jus ad bellum* has priority over the *jus in bello*. This contrasts sharply with the contemporary emphasis on the *jus in bello* criteria.

One further point should be made. Even though Victoria was unwilling to concede that difference of religion might provide just cause for war, he distinguished between those wars fought on both sides by Christians and those wars in which only one side had Christian participants. Women and children could not be enslaved, he held, if the war was between Christians. Such was not the case, he felt, when the women and children were not Christian, whether or not they participated in the war at all.[38] His restrictions on the conduct of war thus apply unequally to persons outside the Christian faith. The notion of limits that are universal in scope and application had yet to be realized.

In the next century Hugo Grotius took up this same discussion in more detail and with more clarity as to the issues at stake. The key was his distinction between the natural law and the laws of nations. Because of his interest in the laws of nations as he understood them, Grotius recognized two levels of argumentation with respect to conduct in warfare. First, there is the level of the natural law, which is quite strict about conduct in warfare. On a second level is the practice of nations, which permits far more than the natural law. Grotius expresses the distinction between these levels when he speaks of the "permissions" of the laws of nations and the "moderations" of the law of nature. For example, he writes that although it is "permitted" to kill all of those who are subjects of the enemy ruler, the natural law requires that the victor not only spare women and children but also those who were participating in the war only as subjects of the enemy ruler.[39] The discussion of limitation here works on two levels. First, who is actually participating in the war? Second, what is the responsibility of those participating for the war itself? Here Grotius follows Victoria in his conclusions, though not in the reasoning that leads to those conclusions.

At this point, Grotius introduces a new element into the discussion of limits. Contrary to others who were arguing that one did not have to keep faith with one's enemy if they were of a different religion, Grotius argues for the centrality of promise keeping with all persons, whether they are tyrants, pirates, or persons of different faiths. He spends more time making clear that the limits upon the means of warfare apply to all equally, according to the moderations of the natural law. In his thought, natural law thus moves to center focus as the source of limits to war.

This natural law can be known solely through reason. Grotius completes what other theorists of just war had begun earlier, establishing just war thought squarely on a natural law basis, thus making possible the development of the secular discipline of international law.[40] The positive consequence of this was that a body of thought emerged, later codified into positive laws regulating the conduct of nations, which extended to all persons regardless of religious belief, cultural difference, or historical context. An unfortunate result, as Leroy Walters has noted, is that the theological discussion in the West and the international legal discussion have subsequently gone on with barely a reference by each to the other. That has begun to change only recently.[41]

## Jus in Bello in Recent Discussion

The impetus for a renewed discussion of the *jus in bello* criteria by moral philosophers, theologians, and others was the Second World War. Over the last generation, thinkers from widely different academic fields and intellectual traditions have reflected upon limitation within warfare, using elements of the just war tradition. For the first time in this century, the theological and international legal discussions have returned to a conversation with one another.

After the war it gradually became clear that nuclear deterrence presented just war thinkers with a new set of problems. To understand the historical background to those problems, it was necessary to reevaluate some actions taken during the Second World War, particularly the policy of bombing cities in order to affect civilian morale as well as to destroy places of production. Scholars reflecting upon the Second World War in terms of the just war tradition had an opportunity to discuss the morality of the means of warfare without the complications of relating those means to a war of doubtful or uncertain justice. Virtually no one among them thought that this war was unjust in terms of its cause. The only question concerned the means of warfare and how the means used in that war—including area bombing and the use of nuclear weapons—led to the possibility that there would be a new, even more terrible form of warfare in the future.

The possibility of that more terrible type of war was the catalyst for a number of religious thinkers to take up the question of limitation within war. In particular, development of the strategy of nuclear deterrence provided the occasion for much discussion and debate, since deterrence, by its dependence on counter-city targeting of nuclear weapons, seemed to involve the intention to do direct harm to noncombatants, a violation of the principle of discrimination/non-combatant immunity.

Finally, renewed theological reflection on war also was spurred by the fact that deterrence made the world "safe" for other kinds of war, especially guerrilla war, which raises many special problems when analyzed from a just war perspective. In the United States the war in Vietnam occasioned much debate on whether the war in fact was just and whether the means used in the war were discriminate and proportionate.

Among the major figures in the contemporary development of just war analysis directed at both nuclear deterrence and the Vietnam war are Paul Ramsey, a theologian, and Michael Walzer, a political philosopher. In the remainder of this section I briefly examine their views as prominent examples drawn from a larger context of discussion and debate.[42]

## Paul Ramsey on Conduct in War

Ramsey, in *War and the Christian Conscience*, published in 1961, and
*The Just War*, a collection of essays published in 1968, is to be credited
more than any other one person with reestablishing just war thinking
as a source for moral analysis directed at war. His position is marked
by two features important for the present discussion. First, rather than
arguing from a basis in natural law, he established just war thinking as
a concern for Christian theological ethics by insisting that the *jus in bello*
principle of discrimination is rooted centrally in the implications of Christian love. Second, on the basis of this argument, he focused his analysis
entirely upon *jus in bello* issues, leaving aside the *jus ad bellum* of just
war tradition. In both these respects Ramsey has had great influence on
subsequent Christian just war analysis.

Ramsey's discussion of limiting war includes a sharp critique of what
he regards as the typically American assumption about war, namely,
that war itself is the fundamental moral problem. As the result of this
assumption, he argues, most Americans think that they should avoid
war at all costs. However, once these same Americans go to war, they
place no value upon restraint in waging war; since war is immoral any-
way, the point is to finish the war as quickly as possible. Americans are
thus pacifists when they are not in war and crusaders once in war.[43]

For Ramsey, this characteristically American view of war is encouraged
by thinking about war as a way of accomplishing utopian, unlimited
goals. Rather, he counters, war should be conceived as limited in its
aims, and then it can be limited in means. Observing the rise of nuclear
weapons capable of mass destruction, he argues that it will be impossible
for Americans to limit the means of war so long as we continue to think
in terms of unlimited goals for war. Our approach to the means of war,
resulting in weapons of mass destructive power, grows out of our unlimited goals.

Despite these *jus ad bellum* considerations, the great bulk of Ramsey's
analysis is concentrated on *jus in bello* concerns: whether it would be
possible to fight a contemporary war in a way that did not violate the
twin limiting principles of discrimination (directly implied by love for
neighbor) and proportion (an implication of natural reason). Applying
these concerns to the case of nuclear deterrence and the possibility of
nuclear war, he focused principally on the key concept (for Christian
ethics) of discrimination—the principle establishing the immunity of
noncombatants from direct, intentional attack. Counter-population targeting as a means of deterrence violates this principle and so is morally
disallowed.

For Ramsey, the argument that in a modern war all are combatants
is invalid. Rather, in modern wars as in wars of earlier times combatancy

and noncombatancy are defined not by political views or citizenship in a belligerent nation but by the functional closeness of each individual to the activities of war. It does not matter in any case, he argues, how many of the inhabitants of a targeted city are noncombatants, because discrimination forbids the direct, intentional killing of even one.[44] In this way, he radically limits the number and types of targets one is morally permitted to define for purposes of deterrence or attack in war. This does not mean that Ramsey finds that all civilian death in war is morally impermissible: only those noncombatant deaths that were (wrongly) directly and intentionally caused fall into this category. It remains possible, in his analysis, for legitimate military targets to be defined and attacked, despite the indirect, unintentional deaths of noncombatants in the vicinity. In such cases the limiting principle is proportionality, not discrimination.

Before leaving the question of combatancy, one other point should be made. Ramsey argues that noncombatant immunity from directly intended attack has implications not only for how to conduct a war already begun, but also for thinking about war during times of peace. For example, he finds it reprehensible that legitimate military targets of great importance are placed in highly populated areas. The moral burden for the civilian deaths that would occur if war should come, he argues, would rest upon those persons who placed the targets there.

It is no surprise that Ramsey, working from an ethical position that gives the principle of discrimination such prominence, is concerned about policies of deterrence that threaten to destroy other societies through the use of massive retaliation. Central to his early work is the view that these doctrines have to be thought through from a new basis. Nuclear deterrence may be retained as a moral option, but to be so it must be limited to counter-force targeting; it cannot rely on massive retaliation or indeed on counter-value targeting at any level. Yet even counter-force targeting must be subjected to judgment in terms of the principle of proportionality. Ramsey points out that the cumulative effect of thermonuclear strikes on even legitimate military targets would likely cause so much destruction, including unintended, indirect death of noncombatants, that such strikes would violate proportionality. Thus together these two principles of the *jus in bello* impose strict moral limits on the possibility that nuclear war could be conducted justly.[45]

In the debate over the war in Vietnam, Ramsey applied this same perspective to the question of whether it is possible to justly wage an insurgency or a counterinsurgency war. As in the case of nuclear war, when Ramsey turns to insurgency-counterinsurgency warfare he does not discuss the justice of the cause but rather examines the ways in which the war is to be fought. Given this outlook, it is not surprising that he generally condemns insurgency war as morally illegitimate, because it deliberately aims at the killing of civilians. The question then becomes whether counterinsurgency can be conducted in a morally responsible way.

Ramsey thinks that it is possible to do so, but that in practice the principle of noncombatant immunity will not be the most important limiting principle most of the time. He believes this because of the typical use by insurgents of individuals who are combatants by night and who carry on some civilian occupation by day, as well as the practice of quartering combatant insurgents among noncombatants. Following the same reasoning he applied to nuclear targeting, Ramsey reasoned that these combatants are legitimate targets in war. Of course, the military commander should make every effort to separate the combatant from the noncombatant. But where this is impossible, the important question then becomes whether what is being done is disproportionate or not.

Ramsey's purpose was not to make concrete judgments of fact about the conduct of insurgency-counterinsurgency war but to provide a framework within which political authorities could think about war. He left to them complex judgments of fact about what they and their opponents were doing. One point that he stressed again and again is that political authorities must be willing to confront the possibility that engaging in counterinsurgency war might cause more loss than gain and that negotiations always should be considered.[46]

Ramsey's effort to impose moral limits on war held to a consistent theme, whether the discussion was thermonuclear war or counterinsurgency war. The primary principle of limitation implied by Christian ethics is that of discrimination: war should be fought so as to avoid the direct, intentional killing of noncombatants. The secondary principle of limitation is proportionality, implied by natural reason: war should be fought in such a way that the harm done, even by otherwise legitimate military actions, not exceed the good results. While Ramsey sketched some general implications of these two principles for two major types of contemporary war, he left the detailed working out of the meaning of these principles to the political and military leaders. Thus his purpose was to provide moral counsel to such leaders. For Ramsey, the leader who kept noncombatant immunity from directly intended attack and proportionality in mind had some chance of keeping the horror of war limited. His view was that modern war, without attention to these two principles, would lead us to grave moral evil.

## Michael Walzer on Modern Warfare

The thrust of Walzer's *Just and Unjust Wars* is to reestablish just war thinking, not on a theological basis as with Ramsey, but on a basis in historical cases and philosophical reflection. His is a version of natural law argument, as he uses a diversified selection of historical incidents to introduce just war concepts, thus implying their universality in human experience. This is coupled in his method to philosophical analysis that is a form of utilitarianism. While Ramsey aimed at uncovering what the Christian conscience could allow in modern war, Walzer aims at a more universal context of discourse.

Also unlike Ramsey, Walzer pays attention to the question of *jus ad bellum*, though his treatment of it in "The Theory of Aggression" in *Just and Unjust Wars* is skewed by the modern focus on self-defense against aggression as the only just cause for making war. To allow direct comparison with Ramsey, however, I will highlight Walzer on *jus in bello*, specifically, what he says about the morality of guerrilla warfare and nuclear deterrence.

At the core of Walzer's analysis is a conception of individual rights. All human beings have rights, and these individual rights ultimately are the basis for claiming that states have rights vis-à-vis other states. For Walzer, these rights imply limitations upon conduct toward others. Thus all forms of utilitarianism that simply calculate the "best" way to reach an objective are ruled out, since these forms of utilitarianism cannot account for rights as limits upon action. Ordinarily, these rights are thought of as something that civilians possess. Walzer regards rights as something all of us possess, but which some of us may give up. For example, in war a soldier gives up the right not to be killed.

Walzer understands the moral problem of guerrilla warfare in our age as follows. Resistance to occupying armies is legitimate, and punishment of those who resist the occupation is also legitimate. He argues for this conclusion because he thinks that it recognizes that people have a right to resist armies of occupation but at the same time members of those armies have a right to defend themselves.

But matters rarely remain at such equipoise. What guerrillas try to do is enroll the entire civilian population in their struggle, either directly through intimidation or indirectly by affronting the occupiers so that the army of occupation attacks the civilian population in order to defeat the guerrillas. The fact that guerrillas fight among civilians introduces, for Walzer, the moral problem. Walzer argues that where guerrillas have the civilian population's support, the guerrillas acquire whatever war rights the people possess. This claim, however, only shifts the moral question. The question then becomes, what rights do those civilians who support the guerrillas have?

Walzer responds by arguing that these civilians may be interrogated, detained, etc. but that they still have rights that protect them from being tortured or killed. Walzer comments at length on the American Rules of Engagement in Vietnam in this context. He finds that they allowed a disproportionate amount of social upheaval, in that in order to work, the Americans would have had to forcibly resettle most of the rural population of Vietnam. Second, the rules created two classes of non-combatants, those who were friendly to the South Vietnamese government and those friendly to the Vietcong. The latter could be attacked with impunity. Such a form of classification is not a way to limit war but to expand it. Walzer thinks that if you are forced to make war on people who simply disagree with you but who are not soldiers, you should cease making war because at that point you are making an unjust war.[47]

For Walzer, then, the moral problem of limitation in guerrilla war seems principally to imply restrictions on the conduct of the army fighting the guerrillas; he simply accepts the intentional intermixture of guerrillas and noncombatant population that, in Ramsey's perspective, raises some of the most serious moral problems, those having to do with discrimination.

The same rights of civilians, according to Walzer, are threatened by the policy of nuclear deterrence. Walzer understands deterrence as a way of trying to keep war from happening and thus limiting the occurrence of war. This is a laudable goal, but achieving it by a nuclear threat against noncombatant civilians sacrifices an important moral principle. While he is not pleased with this situation, he is willing to accept it.[48] Deterrence, Walzer observes, is an easy strategy, easy in the sense that those persons being used for hostages are not physically constrained. Walzer rejects the arguments of Ramsey about the nature of deterrence as well as the conclusions of those arguments. Walzer's concern has to do with preventing nuclear war, while Ramsey is concerned with limiting certain kinds of nuclear war. Another significant difference is that Walzer imagines the situation of deterrence to be one of "supreme emergency" in which the ordinary rules for right conduct are put to their severest test. Both the degree of danger and the imminence of that danger lead to situations where the lives of innocents may not only be threatened, but in some circumstances, Walzer believes, taken. In the case of deterrence, the moral evil of the threat is so much smaller than the moral evils that would come with nuclear war that deterrence can be tolerated. This does not mean that one can rest with deterrence as a strategy forever. All examples of supreme emergency are unstable political situations, and ways to overcome them should be sought so that the world can return to situations in which the rules of war apply.[49]

It should be clear that by using the criteria of the *jus in bello*, modern commentators have been able to show the relevance of this tradition of discussion to the kinds of war fought in our times. This fact makes credible the claims of those who argue that the questions raised by this tradition are the ones that must be discussed if war is to remain a barely tolerable human enterprise.

## CONCLUSION

The purpose of this chapter has been to examine the two senses in which just war tradition seeks to limit war: by establishing restraints on the decision to wage war through the requirements of the *jus ad bellum* and by defining restraints on the conduct of war through the requirements of the *jus in bello*. I have argued that for most of the history of this tradition, the major focus of attention for Christian theorists contributing to its development was the *jus ad bellum*, the criteria for going to war, which sought to prevent the occurrence of unjust wars. This stands in contrast to the fact that recent commentators, Christian theologians as well as other contemporary writers, focus on the *jus in bello*, whose criteria define limits to be observed in the course of fighting a war.

During the medieval development of the *jus ad bellum*, its purpose seems to have been to guide the conscience of rulers, those in whose power lay the decision to make or not make war. Just war tradition, from this perspective, was related to the tradition of moral guidance for princes that had its beginnings in the classical era and flourished in the Middle Ages. A key element in the *jus ad bellum* was thus the criterion of right intention, first defined by Augustine, which implied that only just rulers—those with correct intention—could wage just wars. This moral requirement was also imposed on the individual warrior, who was expected to fight for justice and as an agent of a duly authorized prince—not out of hatred, desire for vengeance, or some other wrong intention and not for his own purposes but those of the political unit. So important was it to maintain the correct intentionality that the medieval church developed ritual means for cleansing soldiers after battle— lest they had sinned by having wrong intentions toward their enemies— so as to reintegrate them into society. Absent the medieval context, with its assumptions about the relation of church and society and the nature of the moral life, this concept of right intentionality has been stripped of much of its meaning, and it plays no important part in contemporary discussions of just war—even among Christian commentators.

The *jus ad bellum* criterion of just cause has also suffered from erosion of its content. For medieval Christian theorists, it would be just to fight only when necessary to regain something wrongly taken, to punish evil, or to defend against an injustice in progress. Recent commentary follows the lead of international law, which reduces just causes for war to one:

self-defense. This has fundamentally altered the understanding of this idea and its functioning in regard to the prevention of war.

While similar changes in meaning, minor or major, can be found in all the *jus ad bellum* criteria in their transition from the medieval era to the present, what is most striking about recent discussion of just war is the lack of attention given to this part of just war tradition. The full weight of moral limitation of war has shifted to the criteria of the *jus in bello*: discrimination (or noncombatant immunity) and proportionality. I have shown how this shift in emphasis began to develop in the early modern period, with writers such as Victoria and Grotius, and reached a climax in the works of such contemporary writers as Paul Ramsey and Michael Walzer. Ramsey, with his stress on discrimination as a require- ment of Christian love and as the primary principle of limitation in war, has defined a contemporary version of Christian just war theory, while setting it in the context of secular society. Walzer, by arguing from a concept of human rights and by coupling his moral argument to historical illustrations, attempts to establish his own contemporary version of just war theory as representing a moral consensus not limited by creed or society, but universal in human moral consciousness. At the same time, he undermines the *jus in bello* limits on war by introducing the concept of "supreme emergency," which allows the overriding of those limits in extreme situations.

In both its *jus ad bellum* and its *jus in bello*, just war tradition embodies serious attempts to establish limits on war. While contemporary reflec- tion on the meaning and implications of the *jus in bello* restraints is laudable, there is need for more attention to the *jus ad bellum* as a possible source for moral discussion of the prevention of war.

In addition, Christian moralists today might well give more attention to the implications of the *jus ad bellum* idea of right intention for defining the nature of good political leadership and for considering the obligation of society for reintegrating returning soldiers into civilian life. Both these concepts, central to the medieval just war tradition, require serious at- tention in the contemporary context.

## NOTES

1. Morton H. Halperin, *Limited War in the Nuclear Age* (New York: John Wiley & Sons, 1963), p. 2.

2. Ibid.

3. For an example of this, see A. K. McHardy, "The English Clergy and the Hundred Years War," in *The Church and War,* ed. W. J. Sheils (Oxford: Basil Blackwell, 1983), pp. 171–78.

4. John P. Langan, "The Western Moral Tradition on War: Christian The- ology and Warfare," in *Just War and Jihad: Historical and Theoretical Perspectives*

on *War and Peace in Western and Islamic Traditions*, ed. John Kelsay and James Turner Johnson (Westport, CT: Greenwood Press, 1991), pp. 19–28.

5. R. A. Markus makes this point in the context of assessing Augustine of Hippo's discussion of warfare. Markus is concerned that those who see Augustine as simply criticizing pacifists do not understand that in Augustine's context pacifism was not a lively issue. His more general methodological point is that the best way to understand the tradition of just war discussion is to first understand the antecedent conditions in the particular society. Once one knows the context, be it one of pacifism or bellicosity, then one can assess what impact the just war discussion of limitations might have had on the particular society. R. A. Markus, "Saint Augustine's Views on the 'Just War,' " in *The Church and War*, ed. W. J. Sheils (Oxford: Basil Blackwell, 1983), pp. 1–13.

6. This quote is found in Thomas R. Heath, "Appendix 2," in *Summa Theologiae*, vol. 35, St. Thomas Aquinas (London: Blackfriars, 1972), p. 197.

7. For one recent account of the treatment of returning soldiers in medieval times, see Bernard J. Verkamp, "Moral Treatment of Returning Warriors in the Early Middle Ages," *Journal of Religious Ethics* 16, no. 2 (Fall 1988), pp. 223–49. Verkamp argues that in the period mentioned, returning warriors were asked to undergo rites of passage back into the community after the war. Verkamp suggests that one of the reasons this was done was so that the soldiers might be aware of and subsequently deal with a sense of shame. Contrast this with the treatment of Vietnam war veterans by this society. It is only with some difficulty that American society realized that they should be helped and reintegrated into the society, if not religiously, at least psychologically. Note that this was not necessary for World War II veterans. As a society, we seem to hold to the view that reintegration is necessary for those persons who fought in a war of doubtful justice (Vietnam) but not in a war whose cause was just (World War II). The earlier processes of reintegration were not simply available but often mandatory for warriors, no matter what the justice of the war.

8. St. Augustine, "Reply to Faustus the Manichean," XXII, 74, in *A Select Library of the Nicene and Post-Nicene Fathers*, ed. Philip Schaff (Grand Rapids, MI: Wm. B. Eerdmans, 1956).

9. A friendly critic has suggested that this discussion of virtue might be taking place in the military establishment today. I simply do not know the literature of the modern tradition on the training of military officers and thus cannot comment on it in detail here. It does seem clear that there is renewed attention to the question of the ethics of warfare in the military academies but whether this also means that there is attention to the habits and discipline needed so that one is not overtaken by the vicissitudes of war is still unclear to me. For representative works, see Malham M. Wakin, Kenneth H. Wenker, and James Kempf, *Military Ethics* (Washington, DC: National Defense University Press, 1987); Joint Services Conference on Professional Ethics, *Moral Obligation and the Military* (Washington, DC: National Defense University Press, 1988).

10. This opens up the question of what it means to speak about a tradition at all. I will not address that question in this chapter, but will simply assume that there is such a thing as the tradition of just war discussion. That does not mean that I do not think that this is not an important question. Indeed, that may be the question facing those people who wish to continue to claim this

tradition as a good place to begin the discussion of what may and may not be done in and through war.

11. James Turner Johnson, *Just War Tradition and the Restraint of War*, (Princeton and Guildford, Surrey: Princeton University Press, 1981).

12. Langan, "Western Moral Tradition on War," pp. 10–12.

13. Some authors discuss a third limitation on the means of warfare. This is known as military necessity. I will not take up this form of limitation here, since military necessity has often been seen to permit actions in war that would otherwise have been forbidden. I would like to note here that this is not the only way it needs to be understood. The discussion of military necessity has not been as important in theological discussions as it has been in international law discussions. Compare Douglas P. Lackey, *The Ethics of War and Peace* (Englewood Cliffs, NJ: Prentice Hall, 1988), p. 59, with David Hollenbach, *Nuclear Ethics: A Christian Moral Argument* (New York and Ramsey, NJ: Paulist Press, 1983), pp. 37–46. Hollenbach, the theologian, is silent on the claim of military necessity. For a good discussion of military necessity in the context of just war, consult William V. O'Brien, *The Conduct of Just and Limited War*, (New York: Praeger, 1981).

14. See Hollenbach, *Nuclear Ethics: A Christian Moral Argument*, pp. 37–46, for his discussion of the criteria.

15. Lackey, *The Ethics of War and Peace*, p. 59.

16. The example is given by Michael Walzer, *Just and Unjust Wars* (New York: Basic Books, 1977), pp. 154–55.

17. Obviously, who counts as a civilian and a soldier is an important matter, especially in contexts where one may be a civilian one day and a conscript the next, even against one's will.

18. Lackey, *The Ethics of War and Peace*, p. 29.

19. One of the interesting features of the just war tradition is the fact that the list of the requirements for when war may be justly fought varies slightly from author to author. The particular list here is a compilation drawn from Lackey, *The Ethics of War and Peace*, pp. 28–97, and Hollenbach, *Nuclear Ethics: A Christian Moral Argument*, pp. 37–46.

20. Not all modern commentators mention this criterion. Hollenbach, *Nuclear Ethics: A Christian Moral Argument*, pp. 39–40, attempts to relate it to democratic government.

21. For one modern commentator who wants to hold on to right intention, despite the difficulties of doing so, see Lackey, *The Ethics of War and Peace*, pp. 31–33.

22. G. Scott Davis, "Warcraft and the Fragility of Virtue," *Soundings* 70, no. 4 (Winter 1987), p. 486.

23. Lackey, *The Ethics of War and Peace*, p. 33.

24. For an example of this, see Bruce Russett, *The Prisoners of Insecurity* (San Francisco: Freeman, 1983), p. 139.

25. Even the meaning of "self-defense" is, not surprisingly, disputed. Under one reading, one must wait to repulse an injury that is being committed; under another construction, one can engage in anticipatory self-defense when about to be attacked. For the implications of these meanings in a particular context, see the contrasting discussions of the Six-Day War by Walzer, *Just and Unjust*

*Wars*, pp. 80–85; and Lackey, *The Ethics of War and Peace*, pp. 35–37, 42, and 44–45.

26. LeRoy Brandt Walters, Jr., "Five Classic Just-War Theories: A Study in the Thought of Thomas Aquinas, Victoria, Suarez, Gentili, and Grotius" (Ph.D. dissertation, Yale University, 1971), pp. 81–87.

27. St. Thomas Aquinas, *Summa Theologiae*, 2a2ae q. 40, a. 1, in *Summa Theologiae*, vol. 35, ed. Thomas R. Heath (London: Blackfriars, 1972).

28. Franciscus de Victoria, *De Jure Belli*, 439, in James Brown Scott, *The Spanish Origin of International Law: Francisco de Vitoria and His Law of Nations*, (Oxford: At the Clarendon Press, 1934).

29. Franciscus de Victoria, *De Indis Noviter Inventis*, sections I and II, in Scott, *The Spanish Origin of International Law*.

30. Hugo Grotius, *De Jure Belli ac Pacis, Libri Tres*, II, XXII, III, 1, Trans. Francis W. Kelsey, (Oxford: Clarendon Press, 1925). See also Franciscus de Victoria, *De Bello*, I, 8, in Scott, *The Spanish Origin of International Law*.

31. Aquinas, *Summa Theologiae*, 2a2ae q. 42, a. 1.

32. Michael Walzer, *The Revolution of the Saints* (Cambridge: Harvard University Press, 1965), pp. 268–99.

33. Alasdair MacIntrye points to this in his *After Virtue* (Notre Dame, IN: University of Notre Dame Press, 1981).

34. Russett, *The Prisoners of Insecurity*, p. 141.

35. Aquinas, *Summa Theologiae*, 2a2ae, q. 40, a. 4.

36. Aquinas, *Summa Theologiae*, 2a2ae, q. 40, a. 2.

37. Aquinas, *Summa Theologiae*, 2a2ae, q. 41, a. 2.

38. Victoria, *De Jure Belli*, p. 454.

39. For example, see Grotius, *De Jure Belli ac Pacis*, III, VII, and VIII, where he discusses the rights victors have over the property and the lives of the vanquished in war. He makes clear distinctions between what is required by the law of nature and what is permitted under the laws of nations.

40. On this point, see James T. Johnson, *Just War Tradition and the Restraint of War: A Moral and Historical Inquiry* (Princeton and Guildford, Surrey: Princeton University Press, 1981), pp. 179–180.

41. Walters, *Five Classic Just-War Theories*, p. 275.

42. In doing this, I am leaving aside a number of important materials, including the letter of the American Catholic bishops: National Conference of Catholic Bishops, *The Challenge of Peace: God's Promise and Our Response* (Washington, DC: United States Catholic Conference, 1983).

43. Ramsey relies heavily upon Robert Tucker, *The Just War* (Baltimore: The Johns Hopkins Press, 1960), for his analysis of the American understanding of war.

44. Paul Ramsey, *War and the Christian Conscience: How Shall Modern War Be Conducted Justly?* (Durham, NC: Duke University Press, 1961) pp. 134–70.

45. James Turner Johnson, "Morality and Force in Statecraft: Paul Ramsey and the Just War Tradition," in *Love and Society: Essays in the Ethics of Paul Ramsey*, ed. James Johnson and David Smith (Missoula, MT: Scholars Press, 1974), pp. 93–114.

46. Ramsey's arguments on counterinsurgency war are found in *The Just War:*

*Force and Political Responsibility*, (New York: Charles Scribner's Sons, 1968), pp. 427–512.

47. Walzer, *Just and Unjust Wars*, pp. 176–96.

48. Walzer, *Just and Unjust Wars*, pp. 269–74.

49. Walzer, *Just and Unjust Wars*, pp. 269–83. For a critique of one of his applications of the idea of supreme emergency, see Stephen E. Lammers, "Area Bombing in World War II: The Argument of Michael Walzer," *The Journal of Religious Ethics* 11, no. 1 (Spring 1983), pp. 96–113.

# 4

## Al-Fârâbî's Statecraft: War and the Well-Ordered Regime

*Charles E. Butterworth*

In the Islamic tradition, especially the medieval Islamic tradition, those who engage in philosophy are ever mindful of the horizon revelation places upon expression. Among the political philosophers distinguished for their writings within this tradition, al-Fârâbî is preeminent. Though he does not address in the same way as later Christian thinkers the topics of what justifies just war or of what limitations are to be placed upon it once it has begun, he does address issues that clarify the first of these topics. His approach is to place his thoughts within the broader context of what makes political rule good, even excellent. In exploring al-Fârâbî's reflections on the character of just war and its place in a well-ordered regime, this chapter is attentive to the wider context within which medieval Islamic political philosophers wrote. It focuses on one philosopher, rather than many, so as to show how these arguments are to be explicated and thus how one might better appreciate the richness of that tradition. Because al-Fârâbî and his fellow political philosophers think first of the political regime and its demands, we can learn from them only by following them in their reflections on statecraft.

### INTRODUCTION

This chapter investigates the subject of warfare, in particular its justification, from the perspective of medieval Islamic political philosophy. The restriction of the subject is significant. Political philosophers within the medieval Islamic tradition are intent, above all, upon exploring the characteristics of the best political regime and, within that context, the question of what justifies resort to warfare. Consequently, they almost never address the issue of limitations on warfare. Or, to say the same thing positively and in the language of Western theologians and those schooled in the seventeenth- and eighteenth-century theorists of international law, the political philosophers of medieval Islam discuss what makes it right to wage war (jus ad bellum) rather than what it is right to do when waging war (jus in bello).[1]

To illustrate my point as sharply as possible, I propose to focus here on what the most prominent of the Muslim philosophers, Abû Nasr al-Fârâbî (257A.H./870 C.E.–339 A.H./950 C.E.), has to say concerning justified warfare. As distinct from the two other Muslim philosophers who come readily to mind when one reflects upon political questions—Abû Alî al-Husayn Ibn Sînâ (370/980–428/1037) and Abû al-Walîd Muhammad Ibn Ahmad Ibn Rushd (520/1126–595/1198), Avicenna and Averroes respectively—al-Fârâbî discussed just war and questions directly related to it in several of his writings. Avicenna and Averroes, on the other hand, discussed just war only indirectly and even then in no more than one or two of their writings.[2]

Addressing the subject that holds our common attention in this manner also has the merit of presenting the views of one who speaks primarily as a defender of reason rather than of revelation within the Islamic tradition and thus serves as a counterbalance to Abdulaziz Sachedina's presentation of views from the opposite perspective. In making this observation, I by no means wish to suggest that there is an irreconcilable difference between the political philosophers and the jurists or theologians. My goal, rather, is to emphasize the need to include the political philosophers in attempts to explain the dominant opinions within the medieval Islamic tradition. As will be seen in what follows, they add depth to what the theologians and jurists have to say about politics and statecraft. Indeed, the care taken by the political philosophers of medieval Islam to distinguish between jihad and "war" (harb) generally, not to mention their efforts to distinguish between jihad and just war, indicates how necessary it is to consider their arguments as part of any account of what the Islamic cultural tradition has to say about war, peace, and statecraft.

## AL-FÂRÂBÎ'S POLITICAL WRITINGS

At first appearance, nothing seems easier to follow or more accessible than al-Fârâbî's writings. Set forth in utterly clear prose, his explanations strike the reader as unobjectionable. Their subtlety and multiple layers of meaning come to light only as one becomes aware of the slight changes he introduces as he develops his various arguments. It is necessary, therefore, to preface this exposition of al-Fârâbî's teaching about politics in general and just warfare in particular with an account of how he views political inquiry. To this end, it may be helpful to follow up on a suggestion made by Muhsin Mahdi with respect to the discussion of political science in al-Fârâbî's *Enumeration of the Sciences*.[3]

Mahdi understands al-Fârâbî to have set forth two accounts of political science in this treatise. Both presuppose the validity of the traditional separation between the practical and the theoretical sciences, but neither is adequate for the radically new situation created by the appearance of revealed religion. The first account puts forth a political science that is simply practical.[4] The second goes beyond the practical limits of the first without becoming fully theoretical; it includes the "theoretical and practical sciences," but is not presented as able to handle the theoretical opinions set forth in religion.[5] More precisely, throughout the whole second account of political science in the *Enumeration of the Sciences*, such exclusive attention is paid to what political science has to say about actions that nothing is said about how it handles opinions.

Consequently, neither the first nor the second account of political science in the *Enumeration of the Sciences* can lead to an understanding of the kind of rulership or royal craft needed for the new phenomenon of revealed religion. According to Mahdi, such rulership or royal craft can come only from a political science that does more than explain the need for combining theoretical and practical sciences along with prudence. The political science that is a part of philosophy presented in al-Fârâbî's *Book of Religion* provides what is needed insofar as it shows how theoretical sciences, practical sciences, and prudence are combined and then how they are ordered in the soul of the ruler. Such a political science is more theoretical than the one first set forth in the *Enumeration of the Sciences*. Moreover, it goes beyond the understanding of the sciences presupposed in the second one, an understanding itself grounded in the exposition offered in the first four chapters of the *Enumeration of the Sciences*.[6]

According to this line of reasoning, political science as presented in the *Enumeration of the Sciences* falls short insofar as it is unable to explain everything alluded to in that treatise, especially the concerns of jurisprudence and theology. Even though the exposition of these two arts comes after that of political science, neither the first nor the second account of political science addresses the religious themes central to them. By closing the *Enumeration of the Sciences* with a discussion of jurisprudence and theology, al-Fârâbî alludes to what still needs to be taken into consideration. Insofar as the *Book of Religion* opens with a discussion of religion centered in political community, then moves to political science and even to a political science that is part of philosophy, it seems to represent his attempt to meet this need.

Religion or, more precisely, virtuous religion is rooted in concern for the adherents of the religion. The goal of the virtuous ruler in virtuous

religion is "only to obtain, for himself and for everyone under his rulership, the ultimate happiness that is truly happiness." To this end, the
ruler prescribes opinions about theoretical and voluntary matters in language that will lead the citizens to accept and abide by them. He also
sets down actions they are to follow and things they are to say. Belief
in these opinions and conduct congruent with these actions and
speeches will help the citizens attain ultimate happiness.[7] Virtuous religion, in other words, teaches nothing that does not have an immediate
relationship to the attainment of happiness. It does not pursue learning
for the sake of learning nor tolerate such a pursuit in the disciplines
subordinate to it, jurisprudence and theology.

Political science, as presented in the *Book of Religion*, differs from virtuous religion in that, though focused on practice, it is primarily an art
of inquiry. It investigates what happiness is and explains what constitutes happiness as well as what conduces to happiness. Not having the
direct concern with the citizens that is so characteristic of virtuous religion, it remains somewhat distant in order to explain how political life
functions without actually becoming involved in the day-to-day activities
of the regime. Whereas virtuous religion is concerned with what the
citizens need to believe and do in order to obtain ultimate happiness,
political science is concerned with investigating and then explaining
what the virtuous ruler needs to think and do in order to help the citizens
attain ultimate happiness.[8] Political science that is a part of philosophy
is even more distant, primarily because it investigates matters from a
universal perspective and has little or no concern with particulars.[9]

It is worth dwelling on these distinctions between virtuous religion,
political science, and political science that is a part of philosophy because
they are reflected in al-Fârâbî's other writings. He addresses similar
issues in different treatises in quite distinct ways, much as in the *Book
of Religion* each of these pursuits is said to approach ultimate happiness
in different manners. That is to say, al-Fârâbî speaks at times as someone
setting forth opinions and actions for a virtuous religion and at times
as a political scientist. With one possible exception, he never speaks as
though he were setting forth a political science that is part of philosophy.[10] Additionally, if we consider that he does nothing more than
explain what such a political science would look like were its actual
existence ever possible, it becomes clear that his whole body of writing
does not represent such a perspective.

The *Fusûl Muntaza'ah* (Selected aphorisms), or as it is more widely
known the *Fusûl al-Madanî* (Aphorisms of the statesman), the first treatise we will consider, presupposes a basic familiarity with ethics, politics,
and natural science on the part of the reader. It also enters into rather
detailed discussions about the divergent opinions different schools of
thought hold about good and evil, death, the first cause, and the way

God cares for his creation,[11] all of which suggests—given the parameters just set forth—that it is like political science. It is, in other words, some-what removed from the minute concerns and the detailed attention to opinions so characteristic of virtuous religion, but is not as universalistic in its pronouncements as a theoretical treatise would be.[12] The *Mabâdi Arâ Ahl al-Madînah al-Fâdilah* (Principles of the opinions of the people of the virtuous city) presupposes far less on the part of the reader than the *Aphorisms* and dwells much more upon fundamentals. It comes closer to a presentation of the opinions a virtuous ruler of a virtuous religion would seek for his citizens, and its various explanations should be read in that light.[13]

## AL-FÂRÂBÎ'S APHORISMS

Fauzi Najjar and D. M. Dunlop assign the *Aphorisms* different titles because of the various manuscript traditions in which the treatise has come down to us. According to the manuscripts on which Najjar bases his edition, the treatise has no distinct title. It opens with the following explanation:

Selected aphorisms that comprise the roots of many of the sayings of the ancients about that by which cities ought to be governed and made prosperous, the lives of the people of them improved, and they be led towards happiness.

One of the manuscripts on which Dunlop based his translation and edition, on the other hand, prefaces this statement with what purports to be a title, *"The Book of Aphorisms of the Statesman* by Abû Nasr al-Fârâbî," then, as a way of leading into the phrase quoted above, adds "these are selected aphorisms" and continues with the rest of that phrase.[14]

At the end of the section about the virtuous city, al-Fârâbî enumerates the various kinds of war (*harb*) that occur, as well as the ends they are waged for, then declares that some are unjust.[15] In other words, by the way he orders the text he intimates that an awareness of what political association is for and how it may best be ordered is necessarily prelim-inary to a fruitful discussion of the justice and injustice of warfare. All political associations wage war and all seek to justify recourse to it. By placing his discussion of just warfare within the context of wars waged by the virtuous city, al-Fârâbî suggests that regardless of what might be claimed on behalf of other regimes the virtuous city alone can engage in just warfare. It should be noted, nonetheless, that even the virtuous city is not impervious to unjust war.

The first five instances of warfare cited—namely, that waged for de-fense, acquiring a good the city deserves, reforming others, subjecting those suited for it, and taking back what is rightfully the city's—seem to be clearly justifiable. Of these, only the third,

carrying and forcing a certain people to what is best and most fortunate for them, as distinct from others, when they have not known it on their own and have not submitted to someone who does know it and calls them to it by speech,

comes close to what *jihad* is usually taken to signify. It should be noted, however, that neither *jihad* nor any of its derivatives occurs in this whole discussion. Nor, for that matter, does al-Fârâbî say explicitly that these kinds of warfare are just or even justified. Instead, he explains that these and two additional kinds of warfare all fulfill one or both of two conditions, acquiring some good for the city and bringing others to justice or making matters equitable, then juxtaposes these seven to four kinds of war he labels unjust (*harb jûr*). Thus, although it is reasonable to conclude that he does mean for these wars that are not explicitly termed unjust to be understood as just, he makes no clear statement of his intention. Moreover, none of these first five kinds of warfare, not even "warring against those who do not submit to slavery and servitude, but for whom it is best and most fortunate that their rank in the world be to serve and be slaves," is elaborated on by al-Fârâbî. Apparently, he deems it sufficient to mention them and to affirm that each fulfills one or both of the aforementioned conditions.[16]

Only with the two additional kinds of warfare does al-Fârâbî make an effort to defend their legitimacy. These two he mentions after declaring the two conditions served by the first five kinds of warfare, then strives to show how they serve the same purposes. The first,

warring against them in order to punish them for a crime they perpetrated, lest they revert to something like it and lest others venture against the city, coveting them,

has the merit

of acquiring a certain good for the people of the city and bringing that other people back to their own shares and to what is most proper for them and of repulsing an enemy by force.

Though not necessarily defensive warfare, such punitive attacks upon criminals could serve both a rehabilitative and a deterrent purpose. The second of these additional types of warfare raises more serious questions, for it involves

warring against them to destroy them in their entirety and to extirpate them thoroughly because their survival is a harm for the people of the city.

Throughout this whole enumeration, al-Fârâbî speaks so as to intimate that all of these justifiable wars are initiated and conducted by the city or its citizens rather than merely by the ruler. Although this presupposes that the citizens of the city engaging in these kinds of warranted warfare are more just than those warred upon, the condition is met insofar as the topic arises within the context of al-Fârâbî's account of the virtuous city. Still, this last kind of warfare, with its barely veiled suggestion that it is to be limited in no manner whatsoever, seems to need more justification than the hollow statement proffered by al-Fârâbî, namely, "that, too, is an acquisition of good for the people of the city."

On reflection, however, his silence may be instructive. Such warfare can be defended only if one is willing to argue that the happiness and the well-being of the virtuous are more important than the existence of the wicked, that is, of those who threaten the virtuous. Human beings, never reluctant to identify themselves as virtuous and their enemies as wicked, conduct themselves daily as though this principle were sound and pause only when it is taken—as here—to its ultimate conclusion. If the extreme case suggests its tenuousness, perhaps its fallaciousness, it would surely not be amiss to question whether it is sound even when leading to less dire results.

Unwarranted warfare, what al-Fârâbî terms unjust war here, consists in the pursuit of base goods by military means. Each instance enumerated is one of war waged by the ruler against the people of his city or against others. None of the four can be considered the obverse of those already enumerated, except insofar as each fails to fulfill either one of the conditions used as standards for assessing their merit. These unjust wars consist of bellicose actions undertaken for the sake of the ruler's increased honor or self-aggrandizement, pure conquest, venting of rage or achieving some other pleasure through victory, and over-reaction to an injustice committed by others. Here, just as in the discussion about just or justifiable warfare, our author is completely silent about the way the subject relates to the conditions for *jihad*.[17]

Warfare, justified or not, is dangerous to those who wage it, and part of what al-Fârâbî considers in the following section of the *Aphorisms* is the proper attitude of the virtuous man with respect to its dangers.[18] The virtuous man can no more shy away from these dangers, for that would be cowardly, than go to the other extreme and rashly charge into the midst of battle. He might, however, reasonably hold back lest his death cause the city a grave loss. The virtuous man, after all, is not a solitary, but a member of a city, perhaps even its ruler. He must, then, be ever conscious of what the loss of his life means to the city and be ready to acknowledge that occasion when he will benefit the city more by dying than by continuing to live.[19] Consequently, the virtuous man must have a proper appreciation of death and what it means. Aware of the ignorant or corrupt man's fears that death means the loss of worldly pleasure and convinced that the happiness he seeks is not diminished by a noble death, the virtuous man persists in asking what is to be gained by his continuing to live or risking death in battle.[20]

Al-Fârâbî makes the issue turn on the virtuous man's civic concern because he wants to emphasize the reason individuals pursue virtue. Speaking of the virtuous warrior, and here he uses the term derived from *jihad*, namely, *al-mujâhid al-fâdil*, al-Fârâbî says:

When he risks himself, he does not do so while holding within himself that he will not die through that action of his, for that is stupid; nor does he not care whether he dies or lives, for that is rashness; rather, he thinks that he will perhaps not die and will perhaps escape; but he is not frightened by death, nor does he become anxious when it comes upon him; he does not risk himself while knowing or presuming that he will obtain what he seeks without risk; rather, he risks himself when he knows that he will lose and not obtain what he seeks if he does not take the risk; and he thinks that he will perhaps obtain it if he takes the risk, or he thinks that the people of the city will without doubt obtain it through that action of his whether he dies or lives; and he thinks that if he survives, he will share [it] with them, and that if he dies, they will obtain [it] and he will achieve happiness because of his previous virtue and because he has now sacrificed himself.[21]

The point is that courage allows the virtuous warrior to aspire to victory over an enemy and thus to something good for himself as well as for the city. Moreover, just as courage differs from the other moral virtues in that its pursuit involves the risk of life, so does it differ in that it directly benefits the city. Moderation allows one to enjoy some pleasures without harming the mind or body by the excessive pursuit of pleasure, but provides only indirect benefit to the city. Even liberality, the correct use of personal wealth, does not vie with courage as a virtue. It becomes beneficial to fellow citizens and, more importantly, to the city only when it is exercised by a wealthy individual. Courage, on the other hand, benefits the city regardless of who exercises it.

This whole discussion is based on al-Fârâbî's earlier distinction between the necessary and the virtuous city and his decision to speak primarily about the latter. Only when people go beyond the satisfaction of immediate wants—the goal of the necessary city—does the question of happiness arise. There are many views of what constitutes happiness, but they all seem to fall within two categories: those corresponding to the popular view and those put forth by philosophers like Socrates, Plato, and Aristotle, all of whom al-Fârâbî names.[22] Popular views about happiness center on the pursuit of pleasure, wealth, or a combination of these, whereas philosophers begin to speak about happiness by drawing attention to the two sorts of life humans lead and claiming that there is a perfection and a happiness appropriate to each. Though only the second culminates in ultimate happiness, this being limited to the life hereafter, al-Fârâbî concentrates on the first kind of perfection and happiness. Its acquisition is crucial for striving toward the second, and it consists not only in being virtuous, but also in performing the actions of all the virtues—moral as well as intellectual.

Just as important as al-Fârâbî's turning away from the inquiry into ultimate happiness is his insistence upon its being a concern of pagan philosophers and his taking them as his guides for explaining what the virtuous city is, how it is constituted, and why its people alone strive to attain the perfection leading to ultimate happiness. The clear implication is that it is no more a topic arising solely in an Islamic context than one to be pursued only by reference to Islamic teachings. Similarly, what these pagan philosophers have to say about ultimate happiness and about the virtuous city or even about the first kind of happiness and politics in general is not to be prejudged as conflicting in any way with what Islam has to say about such topics. One sign of the harmony between their teachings and those of Islam is that a term usually reserved for a very specific kind of warfare sanctioned by the revealed law of Islam can be used to describe someone who engages in warfare that goes beyond the precise limits of Islamic warfare without going beyond the intention of Islamic warfare.

This becomes especially clear in al-Fârâbî's discussion of the qualities those who deserve to rule must have, a discussion that opens the section on the virtuous city, just as his discussion of the kinds of justifiable warfare closes it.[23] He begins by listing the different groups of human beings who administer the affairs of this city, tend to its various needs, and procure its sustenance. Called "parts" (ajzâ') of the city, they consist of the virtuous, the "possessors of tongues" (dhû al-alsinah), the assessors, the warriors, and the financiers. The warriors, ranked fourth, are called by a term derived from jihad, that is, mujâhidûn, and are further described as "fighters" or "combatants" (muqâtilah) and "guardians" (hafazah). Nameless others—"those who act in the same way as they do and are counted among them"—also make up the warrior part. Of significance here, however, is that the warriors are designated as those who wage defensive as well as offensive war. That is, a mujâhid engages not only in aggression or, to recall momentarily the echo of jihad mentioned above with respect to paragraph 67/63, not only in "carrying and forcing a certain people to what is best and most fortunate for them," but also in "repulsing an enemy who comes against the city from the exterior."

The virtuous mentioned here are "the wise and the prudent," "those who have opinions about major matters." That they are termed both "the wise" (al-hukamâ') and also "the prudent" (al-muta'aqqilûn) is suggestive of that combination of theory and practice said to constitute the virtuous royal craft in the *Book of Religion* and also in the second account of political science set forth in the *Enumeration of the Sciences*.[24] As will be seen, it remains central in al-Fârâbî's subsequent explanations here of the qualities the ruler or rulers of the virtuous city must have. The second part of the virtuous city, those called "possessors of tongues," he associates with the "transmitters of the creed" (*hamalat al-dîn*), then explains that the former are the rhetoricians, the eloquent, the poets, the musicians, the scribes, and "those who act in the same way as they do and are among their number."

By adding on to his fuller identification of each of the parts of the city other than the first—that is, the virtuous—that it also includes "those who act in the same way as they do," al-Fârâbî subtly indicates that each one is of lesser importance than the virtuous. The second and fourth parts, the possessors of tongues and the warriors, are nonetheless set apart from the assessors and the financiers by the additional qualification that "those who act in the same way as they do" are also either "among their number" or "counted among them." A minor point, to be sure, but one suggesting that these two groups are somewhat more selective.

Having thus identified the official parts of the virtuous city, al-Fârâbî now turns to a consideration of the qualities its rulers and governors ought to have.[25] Admitting from the outset that "the rulers of this city and its governors are of four sorts," he nevertheless insists on the primacy of the one who is "king in truth, that is, the first ruler." Such a ruler possesses the following six qualities: wisdom, complete prudence, excellent persuasion, excellent imitation,[26] bodily capability for *jihad*, and having nothing in his body that prevents him from carrying out things pertaining to *jihad*.

From the previous enumeration of the parts of the city, the list carries over qualities characteristic of the virtuous, the possessors of tongues, and the warriors. It makes explicit that those who transmit the creed and speak in public have persuasion as their goal, that they want to move the citizens to pursue or shun particular things, and how important it is for them to be skilled in creating images so as to achieve that goal. Whereas the functions peculiar to the assessors and the financiers are omitted from this list, those peculiar to the warrior group find twofold expression.[27] Capability for war is evidently far more important to the well-being of the city than anything offered by "accountants, engineers, doctors, astrologers, and those who act in the same way,"[28] or even "those who acquire riches in the city like farmers, herdsmen, merchants, and those who act in the same way." Above all, however, it emphasizes that such rulership depends on the theoretical and practical sciences along with practical wisdom being found in one human being.[29] Indeed, one in whom all of these qualities come together is the model, someone to be copied in his ways of life and his actions, someone whose declarations and recommendations are to be accepted, and one who may govern as he thinks and wishes.[30]

Usual human frailty is taken into greater account with the other three sorts of rulership. Recognizing that it may not be possible to find one human being who possesses all six qualities of rulership, al-Fârâbî speaks first of a group of four individuals, each of whom possesses one or more of the six qualities except for the last. Wisdom, complete prudence, and bodily capability for *jihad* are individual qualities each of which is to be found in one particular member of the group, while a fourth member is said to possess both excellent persuasion and excellent imitation. However, either because it is truly redundant or because it is too much to expect that a ruler should have nothing in his body that prevents him from carrying out things pertaining to *jihad,* no one in this group or in any of the other sorts of lesser rulers embodies this last quality.

In the two other sorts of rulership, wisdom and complete prudence are eliminated. They are replaced, either for a single ruler who is called a "traditional king" (*malik al-sunnah*) and whose rulership is called "traditional kingship" (*mulk sunnî*) or for a group who are called "traditional rulers" (*ruʿasâʿ al-sunnah*), by qualities more suited to those who follow "Laws" (*sharâʿ iʾ*) and "Traditions" (*sunan*)[31] set down by a previous ruler. These include: (a) being knowledgeable about the Laws and Traditions set down by the preceding leaders for governing the city, (b) being good at discerning the places and circumstances in which these Traditions ought to be employed in keeping with the intention of the earlier rulers, (c) being able to infer from what has not been declared in the Traditions that have been preserved and written down what is in keeping with them and with what has been inferred previously, and, finally, (d) being good at thinking about and prudently deliberating over new and unexpected events in order to preserve the city's well-being. Despite the absence of wisdom and complete prudence in these last two sorts of rule, neither seems particularly inadequate. Indeed, when it is recalled that the qualities of excellent persuasion, excellent imitation, and bodily capability for *jihad* are still said to be present in these rulers, it is difficult to fault them.

## AL-FÂRÂBÎ'S VIRTUOUS CITY

As already noted, the *Virtuous City* is a more popular work than the *Aphorisms*. It is not less extensive; in fact, if anything, several subjects are discussed in far greater detail in the *Virtuous City* than in the *Aphor-*

*isms.* The difference consists, rather, in that subjects treated in the *Virtuous City* are approached from the perspective of common opinion and that the discussion remains at that general level. In the *Aphorisms*, on the other hand, subjects are approached from the perspective of what is known in books and treatises, and, as we have seen, the discussion frequently leads to a new way of thinking about what at first seemed to be established doctrine. This basic difference between the two works is not immediately evident, for the language of the *Virtuous City* is much more laden with philosophic jargon. Distinctions are made between matter and form; the active, passive, and acquired intellects are spoken about at some length; and the parts of the soul as well as the organs of the body are explained in great detail. Upon examination, however, the speciousness of these distinctions becomes manifest.

The *Virtuous City* is divided into six major sections, apparently in keeping with al-Fârâbî's own understanding of the work.[32] The sections of concern to us here are the last two, those in which al-Fârâbî (a) enumerates the things man acquires through his will and because of which he needs to associate with other humans and then (b) discusses the erroneous opinions that lead to what he terms ignorant and errant cities as opposed to the virtuous city.

In section 5, chapter 15, al-Fârâbî explains that human beings need to associate because they do not naturally have all they need to reach their highest perfections. Though they need several kinds of associations, some of which are perfect and others not, only the association known as the virtuous city interests us. It is "the city in which association aims at mutual assistance in the things by which true happiness is obtained."[33] The ruler of the virtuous city, called indiscriminately "ruler" (*ra'îs*) and "king" (*malik*) at first,[34] is a most exceptional human being and appears to resemble the prophet described in section 5, chapter 14.[35] This ruler, declares al-Fârâbî, "is a man whom no other man can rule at all; indeed, that man is a man who has already become perfected and become an intellect in actuality."[36]

As a means of giving a fuller explanation of why this ruler is such a perfect human being, al-Fârâbî provides a more complex analysis of the human soul and the different levels of the intellect than he has offered heretofore:

The first rank by which man is man is for him to attain the receptive natural trait that is ready to become intellect in actuality. This is common to all. Between it and the active intellect are two ranks, attaining the passive intellect in actuality and attaining the acquired intellect. And between this man who has reached this much of the first human rank and the active intellect are two ranks. When the perfect active intellect and the natural trait are attained as a single thing, in the way the combination of matter and form is one thing, and the form of this man's humanity is taken as the passive intellect attained in actuality, there is between him and the active intellect only one rank. When the natural trait is set down as matter for the passive intellect that has become intellect in actuality, the passive [intellect] as matter for the acquired [intellect], and the acquired [intellect] as matter for the active intellect, and the sum of that is taken as a single thing, this man is the man upon whom the active intellect has alighted.[37]

To grasp fully the significance of this passage, one must be familiar with the account of the soul and of the ranks of being that have been explained either in what has preceded or in the first part of the *Political Regime*. For our purposes, it is perhaps sufficient to note that al-Fârâbî is describing here a man who has ascended to the very heights of a complex hierarchy of intellectual achievement. The significance of such an accomplishment is set forth in the following passage:

When that is attained in both parts of his rational faculty, namely, the theoretical and the practical, and then in his imitative faculty, this is the man who receives revelation, for God, mighty and exalted, reveals to him by means of the active intellect. Thus what emanates from God, blessed and sublime, to the active intellect then emanates from the active intellect to his passive intellect by means of the acquired intellect, and then to the imitative faculty. Thus by what emanates to his passive intellect, he is a wise man, a philosopher, and a man able to intellect things completely by a divine faculty within him; and by what emanates to the imitative faculty, a prophet, one who warns about what will be, and one who tells about the particular things that exist now.[38]

After such an elaborate explanation of what such a man can do, it should come as no surprise that al-Fârâbî would summarize his accomplishments by claiming immediately afterwards: "This man is in the most perfect of the ranks of humanity and in the highest level of happiness, and his soul is as though it were united with the active intellect in the way we have said."[39]

All this says nothing, however, about the qualities that make this man fit to rule. The detailed description of the way his soul is constituted and of his intellectual accomplishments provides no insight into what kind of a practical ruler he will make, unless we are to assume that practice follows so closely upon theory that a well-tuned soul is all one needs. At first, that seems to be the direction al-Fârâbî wants to take here. The qualities he demands of the ruler are both less numerous and less stringent than those he sets forth in the *Aphorisms*, and his summary praise of the ruler even a little stinting.

Al-Fârâbî begins by listing four conditions the ruler should meet, only two of which resemble those listed in the *Aphorisms*.[40] First, he must seize upon every action by which it is possible to attain happiness. Second, corresponding roughly to the third and fourth conditions mentioned in the *Aphorisms*, he must have the ability through his tongue to provide an excellent imitation in speech of all that he knows. Third, he must have the ability for excellent guidance to happiness and to the practices by which happiness is reached. Finally, he must have excellent endurance in his body for carrying out the operations of war. Here, too, there is something of a correspondence with the fifth and sixth conditions mentioned in the *Aphorisms*. But there is also a major difference in terminology here. That is, in this passage of the *Virtuous City*, al-Fârâbî speaks merely of "war" (*harb*) and not of *jihad* as he does in the *Aphorisms*.

Missing from this account is any explicit mention of wisdom or prudence. The first is, of course, more than represented in what was said of the ruler's soul in the two long passages already cited. Indeed, at one point, it is claimed that he is nothing less than "a wise man, a philosopher, and a man able to intellect things completely by a divine faculty within him." The second, prudence, is surely fundamental to the ruler's being able to grasp what leads to happiness and guide others to do what allows them to reach it. Moreover, revelation may take the place of prudence, especially since this ruler is also said to be a prophet by dint of his intellectual accomplishments. In calling him a prophet, however, al-Fârâbî speaks only of his warning others about what may befall them and of his having knowledge of the possible particular events that may occur. He says nothing about prophecy enabling such a man to rule others, that is, to be able to lead them to do what conduces to their ultimate happiness.

Perhaps this is why al-Fârâbî neither calls him a model nor claims that he can do whatever he wishes. It may explain why he emphasizes only the ruling titles by which this ruler may be identified and the vast extent to which his rule may reach: "This is the ruler whom no other man can rule at all; he is the imam; he is the first ruler of the virtuous city; he is the ruler of the virtuous nation and the ruler of all of the inhabited world."[41] Then, as though the description of the ruler were not yet complete, al-Fârâbî explains that no one can reach this state unless twelve additional properties or characteristics come together in him by nature.[42] Five of them have to do with learning or the intellectual virtues, five with the improvement of character or the moral virtues, one with eloquence, and one with justice. Though two of the five connected with the moral virtues relate to courage, there is no further mention of warfare with respect to this ruler.

Immediately thereafter, acknowledging that it is rare for such qualities to come together in one man, al-Fârâbî allows for a lesser sort of rule. In speaking of a ruler who has some of the qualities of the first ruler or who will follow the Laws and Traditions[43] made by the first ruler or the previous rulers, he raises the matter of warfare again. This second type of ruler must, under any circumstances, embody six conditions that are very similar to the ones required of the traditional king or traditional rulers in the *Aphorisms*. The first part of the sixth condition is precisely like the one required of the first ruler, namely, that he have excellent endurance in his body for carrying out the operations of war. To it, however, is added the clarification: "that is, he must have the serving and the ruling warring art." Here, too, the terminology is derived from *harb*, the broader term for war, rather than from *jihad*.[44]

Al-Fârâbî turns one last time to a discussion of topics relating to warfare when he considers how the opinions of people living in the ignorant city lead them to fight with one another. In section VI, chapter 18, much of the discussion focuses on the issue of conquest and whether people associate merely to avoid being conquered.[45] That line of thought leads eventually to the question of whether it is just for human beings to attack other human beings. Though the legitimacy of exploiting non-human beings—that is, of hunting some animals for food or clothing and domesticating others—is generally acknowledged, that of exploiting human beings is not. Nonetheless, because no group or nation can be secure as long as there is a threat that another group or nation will attack, provision must be made for defense.[46] Throughout this whole discussion, al-Fârâbî speaks of conquest, attack, defense, and aggression, but not once of war (*harb*) or *jihad*.[47]

## CONCLUSION

From this investigation of what al-Fârâbî has to say about warfare, it is evident that he is extremely reluctant to declare it ever just to wage war upon others and that he does not rigidly distinguish between the term for war (*harb*) generally and the term for the war usually considered to be in defense of Islam, *jihad*. His willingness to identify wars as clearly unjust because they are only in the service of the ruler and to castigate aggression or conquest carried out for its own sake allows him to identify several kinds of war that can be defended as warranted, justifiable, even legitimate or just. But it is important to note that he never explicitly claims these latter wars are in any way warranted, justifiable, legitimate, or just. If anything, they are necessary for the defense and the well-being of the virtuous city, a political association without which all but the most exceptional of human beings cannot attain ultimate happiness. Moreover, his reticence about total warfare, accepted only because it is in the service of the virtuous city, gives pause.

Al-Fârâbî recognizes that political life often begins, and more frequently abuts, in warfare. Thus he makes ability to carry out war one of the qualities of those whom he deems fit to rule the virtuous city in its various forms. In the *Aphorisms*, by referring to the ruler's or rulers' warring capability in terms derived from the word *jihad*, he underlines that the only kind of warfare such a ruler or rulers may reasonably resort to is warfare that serves the virtuous city. In the *Virtuous City*, however, where the exceptional moral qualities of the ruler or rulers are more clearly stated, he eschews such usage.

An explanation that views the works considered here as setting forth al-Fârâbî's personal prescriptions for the simply best city and that seeks, consequently, to read some kind of pious significance into his use of religious terminology is inadequate. In all of these works, al-Fârâbî is much more intent on explaining what political inquiry does and learns. He seeks to show what would make a political science or a political philosophy viable given the claims either of these investigations must meet from those who think revelation has solved all human problems. His speech, images, and general explanations of the universe as well as of the human soul all point to the great similarity of purpose, even of general understanding, that exists between the revelation accorded Muhammad and the inquiries of the pagan philosophers. By pointing to this similarity, directly as well as indirectly, al-Fârâbî preserves the possibility of philosophical inquiry. As one who pursues philosophical understanding and thereby tacitly acknowledges that the sciences are not yet complete, he must strive to preserve that possibility. What we see here of his reflections on warfare, justifiable and not justifiable, exemplifies that preserving activity. Its success is indicated in part by the fact that almost five hundred years later, as we have seen, Ibn Khaldûn deems it important to carry on that same enterprise.

## NOTES

1. Joel L. Kraemer makes a similar judgment in his thoughtful and thoroughly researched article, "The *Jihâd* of the *Falâsifa*," *Jerusalem Studies in Arabic and Islam*, 10 (1987), p. 312, n. 74.

2. Corroborating evidence for this claim may be found in the same passage of the article cited in the preceding note, where Kraemer describes al-Fârâbî's "discussion of just war" as "the most extended known to me by a Muslin philosopher."

3. See Muhsin Mahdi, "Science, Philosophy, and Religion in Alfarabi's *Enumeration of the Sciences*," in J. E. Murdoch and E. D. Sylla, eds., *The Cultural Context of Medieval Learning* (Dordrecht, Netherlands: D. Reidel, 1975), pp. 144–45.

4. This first account occurs at the beginning of Chapter 5, a chapter entitled "On Political Science, the Science of Jurisprudence, and the Science of Dialectical Theology" (*Fî al-ʿIlm al-Madanî wa ʿIlm al-Fiqh wa ʿIlm al-Kalâm*). The Arabic text of al-Fârâbî's *Enumeration of the Sciences* has been edited by ʿUthmân Amîn; see *Ihsâ al-ʿUlûm li-al-Fârâbî*, (Cairo: Dâr al-Fikr al-ʾArabî, 1949). Fauzi Najjar's English translation of the *Enumeration of the Sciences*, Chapter 5, with the Amîn page numbers in brackets, appears in *Medieval Political Philosophy: A Sourcebook*,

ed. Ralph Lerner and Muhsin Mahdi (New York: Free Press of Glencoe, 1963), pp. 24–30.

For the passage referred to here, see *Enumeration* 102:4–104:9; it corresponds to paragraph 1 of Chapter 5 in al-Fârâbî, *Kitâb al-Millah wa Nusûs Ukhrâ*, ed. Muhsin Mahdi (Beirut: Dar el-Machreq, 1968), pp. 67–76.

Mahdi maintains that *Enumeration* 104:10–15, that is, paragraph 2 of his edition, also belongs to the first account of political science; see Mahdi, "Science, Philosophy, and Religion in Alfarabi's *Enumeration of the Sciences*," pp. 132–33, 134–35, and 136. However, the great similarity between this passage and the *Book of Religion*, paragraph 15, leads me to differ with Mahdi and to urge that the passage from the *Enumeration* fits more properly with the second account of political science.

The Arabic text of the *Book of Religion* is to be found in *Kitâb al-Millah wa Nusûs Ukhrâ*, pp. 41–66, and an English translation by Charles Butterworth is in preparation.

5. This account, called by Mahdi the second one, is set forth in *Enumeration* 104:16–107:4, that is, in paragraph 3 of his own edition.

6. See Mahdi, "Science, Philosophy, and Religion in Alfarabi's *Enumeration of the Sciences*," p. 137 and *Book of Religion*, paragraph 10.

7. See *Book of Religion*, paragraphs 1 and 2–3.

8. See ibid., paragraphs 11–13; also paragraphs 14a–d.

9. Ibid., paragraph 15. See my n. 4 for an explanation of my differences with Mahdi on this issue.

10. I am thinking here of his treatise entitled *Nawâmîs Aflâtûn* (Plato's laws), because he is so willing in it to explain the tricks Plato used in order to conceal his writing from others.

11. See Abû Nasr al-Fârâbî, *Fusûl Muntaza'ah* (Selected aphorisms), ed. Fauzi M. Najjar (Beirut: Dar el-Machreq, 1971), paragraphs 74–75, 81, and 86–87.

Najjar's edition is based upon manuscripts that were not available to D. M. Dunlop and offers a more complete as well as a more reliable text than Dunlop's edition and translation, *The Fusûl al-Madanî, Aphorisms of the Statesman, of al-Fârâbî*, (Cambridge: Cambridge University Press, 1961). The corresponding sections in Dunlop are paragraphs 69–70, 76, and 81–82.

Henceforth references will be to both editions in the following manner: paragraphs 74/69–75/70, 81/76, and 86/81–87/82.

12. Though the *Tahsîl al-Sa'âdah* (Attainment of happiness) seems at first to be more theoretical, closer inspection shows that it is quite like the *Aphorisms* in what it presupposes of the reader and in the way it shies away from far-reaching theoretical investigation or sweeping generalizations. As noted earlier, not even the *Nawâmîs Aflâtûn* (Plato's laws), a commentary that speaks quite frankly about the different levels of Platonic discourse, qualifies as a theoretical book, though it does come the closest of those we will consider.

13. The same is to be said of the *Kitâb al-Siyâsah* (The political regime), especially given its many parallels with the *Virtuous City*, but it will not be possible here to investigate the teaching of this fascinating book.

14. Though neither of the critical editions proposes a formal account of the way this treatise might be structured, it seems to be divided into seven major sections:

A. How Reflection on Analogies between the Soul and the Body Leads to an Understanding of Political Activities (1/1–5/4)

B. The Human Soul, Its Virtues and Vices (6/5–21/19)

C. Politics and the Pursuit of Happiness (22/20–32/29)

D. The Intellectual Virtues (33/30–56/52)

E. The Virtuous City (57/53–67/63)

F. The Principles of Being and the Status of Happiness: Sound vs. Erroneous Opinions (68/64–87/82)

G. The Virtuous Regime (88/83–96/91)

Dunlop does, however, offer a paragraph by paragraph summary of the treatise's contents on pp. 23–24 of this edition. Following the manuscripts on which he bases his edition and translation, he divides the *Aphorisms* into two parts, paragraphs 1/1–65/61 and 66/62–96/91. One manuscript simply ends at paragraph 65/61. The other contains a formal conclusion denoting the aphorisms to this point as "the first selected aphorisms" and a new title, with formal invocation, denoting the aphorisms to follow as "the second selected aphorisms"; see Dunlop p. 145, nn. to lines 7–8, and pp. 20–21.

Najjar notes these variants at p. 75, n. 18 and p. 76, n. 1 of his edition. As my division of the text suggests, I follow Najjar in thinking that no major break in the argument occurs at paragraphs 65/61–66/62.

15. See *Aphorisms,* paragraph 67/63. The section on the virtuous city, the fifth of the major sections outlined in the preceding note, comprises paragraphs 57/53–67/63.

16. For a fuller explanation of the ranks of human beings and the idea that some are to serve others, just as some animals serve others, see *Book of Religion,* paragraphs 19–20 and 24–27.

17. In this respect, n. 74 of Joel Kraemer's "The *Jihâd* of the *Falâsifa,*" warrants a closer look. Observing that al-Fârâbî's discussion of just war "is not based upon Islamic legal principles or political theory," Kraemer urges that "[h]is criteria for just war (*jus ad bellum*) may be compared with those posited for both *jus ad bellum* and *jus in bello* by Richard Purtill." Yet neither here nor elsewhere in the article does Kraemer seek to explain how al-Fârâbî distinguishes between the general term for war, *harb,* and that usually termed "holy war," *jihad.* That failure is especially important given the point he insists upon at the beginning of this particular note:

The issue of just war is amply treated by Western theologians, political philosophers and theorists of international law, but it is not a relevant topic for Islamic political doctrine, for which the concept of just (or justified) war is comprehended by *jihâd.*

As evidence, he refers the reader to the opening pages of his earlier article, "Apostates, Rebels and Brigands," *Israel Oriental Studies* 10 (1980), pp. 34–73, where he lists the four kinds of warfare enumerated by Ibn Khaldûn in the *Muqaddimah.*

In that enumeration, Ibn Khaldûn (732/1332–808/1406) claims that war is natural among human beings and originates in a desire for vengeance prompted by four causes: (a) "jealousy and envy," (b) "hostility," (c) "zeal in behalf of

God and His religion," or (d) "zeal in behalf of royal authority and the effort to found a kingdom." The first cause gives rise to wars among "neighboring tribes and competing families" and the second to wars among "savage nations living in the desert," these termed "wars of outrage and sedition" (*hurûb baghî wa fitnah*). The third cause leads to "the one called *jihad* in the Divine Law" and the fourth to "dynastic wars against seceders and those who refuse obedience"; these he identifies as "wars of *jihad* and justice" (*hurûb jihad wa ʿadl*).

Contrary to Kraemer's assertion, then, Ibn Khaldûn distinguishes just war from *jihad* and allows neither to encompass the other. See *The Muqaddimah: An Introduction to History*, vol. 2, trans. F. Rosenthal, (New York: Pantheon Books, 1958), pp. 73–74; in three instances, I have made Rosenthal's translation more literal.

Subsequently (vol. 2, p. 107), Ibn Khaldûn identifies the preservation of religion as one of five things necessary for combatting *zulm* ("iniquity," "tyranny," or even "wickedness," but not "injustice" as per Rosenthal) and suggests thereby that, if anything, *jihad* is comprehended by just war rather than the converse (see also vol. 2, pp. 103–11 and vol. 1, pp. 79–83).

By citing Ibn Khaldûn as distinct from al-Fârâbî, whose "discussion of just war" is "not based upon Islamic legal principles or political theory," Kraemer implies that Ibn Khaldûn's discussion is rooted in one or the other. However, just war is no more comprehended by *jihad* in his account than in al-Fârâbî's.

18. See *Aphorisms*, paragraphs 68/64–87/82.

19. Ibid., paragraph 78/73.

20. Ibid., paragraph 77/72.

21. See ibid., paragraph 79/74. This translation, like those that have preceded, is my own; they differ considerably from Dunlop's.

22. Ibid., paragraph 28/25.

23. See ibid., paragraphs 57/63–61/57, esp. 57/63. As was suggested in my n. 14, the section on the virtuous city (paragraphs 57/53–67/63) is the fifth of the major sections in the *Aphorisms*.

24. See *Book of Religion*, paragraphs 14b–d, with paragraphs 18 and 27 and also my n. 5.

25. See *Aphorisms*, paragraph 58/54.

26. The term is *takhyîl* and is used by the philosophers to capture the sense of the Greek *mimêsis*. It might also be translated as "imitative representation" or even "imaginative representation," for *takhyîl* is used to create an image of something not easily grasped. The root *kh\*y\*l* preserves the notion that the imaginative faculty is involved in such representations. For a fuller discussion, see *Averroes' Middle Commentary on Aristotle's Poetics*, trans. Charles E. Butterworth (Princeton: Princeton University Press, 1986), p. 63, n. 18.

27. That Farabi speaks here of *jihad* and of *mujâhidûn* should, it seems to me, be taken as evidence of nothing more than a desire on his part to signal that the warfare called for in these circumstances has none of the characteristics of unjust war.

28. The reference is to *Aphorisms* 57/53, and the words translated as "accountants" and "engineers" are *hussâb* and *muhandisûn* respectively. Though they also mean "arithmeticians" and "geometricians" (see Kraemer, "The *Jihâd* of the *Falâsifa*," p. 298), the explicit political context and consequent need to think of

the political or civic functions such individuals perform seems to call for the translation suggested here.

29. For a fuller discussion of this theme, see *Aphorisms*, paragraphs 33/30–56/ 52, esp. 52/48–53/49. Toward the end of 53/49, Farabi declares: "It is wisdom, then, that seizes upon true happiness, and it is prudence that seizes upon what ought to be done in order to attain happiness."

30. Ibid., paragraph 58/54.

31. In other contexts, al-Fârâbî is not at all reluctant to use different terms for "law" and "laws," e.g., *qanûn* (pl. *qawânîn*) and *nâmûs* (pl. *nawâmîs*), which have a distinct resonance with "canon" and "nomos" respectively. It thus seems significant that he refers here to the plural of *sharî'ah* (*sharâ'i'*) and of *sunnah* (*sunan*), that is, to what I term "Laws" and "Traditions" here in order to indicate their special meaning.

My understanding of this problem is greatly influenced by what al-Fârâbî says in the passages cited in n. 29, above, and by his argument in paragraph 94/89, the only paragraph in the *Aphorisms* that has its own title: "On the Uses of the Theoretical Part of Philosophy and That It Is Necessary in Some Respects for the Practical Part." In the rest of that paragraph or aphorism, he makes it clear that the whole preceding account of the book was, indeed, a theoretical account of practical philosophy.

Theoretical philosophy starts from the most basic kinds of reflection about the principles of existence and eventually arrives at an insight into divine existence. The one engaged in theoretical philosophy then continues, according to al-Fârâbî

always investigating the purpose for the sake of which man was brought into being, which is the perfection man must reach, and all the things by which man reaches that perfection; then he is able to move over to the practical part and can begin to put into practice what he ought to put into practice.

From this perspective, revelation is understood as merely another way of coming to the same end: "He who is given the practical part of revelation is guided by it to a determination of each thing that ought to be preferred or avoided; and that is another way."

To make more sense of this, al-Fârâbî likens the one who receives revelation to a diviner and the person who has theoretical knowledge to a natural scientist:

They are both called knowers, for the name of knowledge is shared by both of them, just as it is shared by the possessor of natural science [i.e., *'ilm* knowledge or science] and by the diviner who relates what comes to be with respect to possible things.

In the next part of the argument, however, it becomes evident that this comparison does not really hold, for the diviner does not have knowledge of the *nature* of things that are possible as the natural scientist has knowledge of the *nature* of things that are. The diviner merely has knowledge of the possible. And even his knowledge of the possible is limited: possible things being without limit, he knows only about those possible things that happen to occur to him or to be brought to his attention.

At this point, al-Fârâbî should explain that the person receiving revelation is similarly limited. Instead, he introduces a new division of those who receive revelation: those who receive it and are perfected in theoretical knowledge as opposed to those who receive it and are not perfected in theoretical knowledge. These two share only the name of receiving revelation. What remains, then, is to explore the similarities and differences with respect to the person who has theoretical knowledge gained through investigation and the person who receives revelation and is also perfected in theoretical knowledge.

According to the context, these two are in the same relation to one another as the person who has natural knowledge is to the diviner. But al-Fârâbî does not state that explicitly. It seems, rather, that the person who has theoretical knowledge gained through investigation differs from the person who has both revelation and theoretical perfection only in that the former must still figure out how to apply what theoretical understanding teaches, whereas revelation works that all out for the latter.

By keeping the tension between divine Laws and man-made law or between tradition and custom always present to the mind of his reader, al-Fârâbî prepares for this fuller statement of the issue near the end of the *Aphorisms*. Were one to be persuaded by Kraemer's argument ("The *Jihâd* of the *Falâsifa*, pp. 293–297, nn. 9–14) that these terms are all synonymous, the far-reaching consequences of this last aphorism would be missed.

32. A small treatise entitled *Fusûl Mabâdi Arâ Ahl al-Madînah al-Fâdilah* by Ibn Abî Usaibi'ah, yet written by al-Fârâbî, explains the content of each section. The treatise is prefaced by the following explanation, clearly not from al-Fârâbî's pen, but found in the unique manuscript that preserves the treatise itself:

Abû Naṣr al-Fârâbî, may God have mercy upon him, had begun composing this book in Baghdad and he carried it to Syria at the end of 330 A.H. [942 C.E.]. He completed it in Damascus in 331 A.H. [943 C.E.]. He revised it, then, looking at the text after having done so, divided it into chapters. After that, some people asked him to place sections in the book so as to denote the division of his meanings. So he made these sections in Egypt in 337 A.H. [948 C.E.], placing them as an appendix to the book. There are six sections.

The translation, my own, is based on Muhsin Mahdi's critical edition of the Arabic text in *Kitab al-Millah wa Nusus Ukhra*, pp. 77–86.

33. See *Al-Farabi on the Perfect State, Abû Naṣr al-Fârâbî's Mabâdi Arâ Ahl al-Madîna al-Fâḍila*, ed. and trans. Richard Walzer (Oxford: Clarendon Press, 1985), p. 230 and see also p. 228. All the translation from this work, referred to here by the short title, *Virtuous City*, are my own.

34. *Virtuous City*, pp. 236 and 238.

35. Ibid., pp. 238–42, with pp. 218–24.

36. Ibid., p. 240.

37. Ibid., pp. 242–44.

38. Ibid., p. 244.

39. See ibid., p. 244; the reference at the end of the passage is to section 5, chapter 14, pp. 222–24.

40. See *Aphorisms*, paragraph 58/54. The qualities the ruler should possess are six:

wisdom

complete prudence

excellent persuasion

excellent imitation

bodily capability for *jihad*

having nothing in his body that prevents him from carrying out things pertaining to *jihad*.

The passage referred to at the end of the paragraph is found in the *Virtuous City*, p. 246.

41. *Virtuous City*, p. 246. Some words in this passage have a distinct resonance in Islam. Imam can simply mean "leader," to be sure, but its religious significance cannot be forgotten, especially since al-Fârâbî has already explained that this ruler receives revelation through the functioning of his active intellect (see p. 244 and the passage translated above). Though "nation" (*ummah*) is used frequently by al-Fârâbî as a way of denoting a political association larger than a city, the numerous Qur'anic references to the Muslim *Ummah* are not unknown to him.

42. See ibid., pp. 246–48.

43. See my n. 31.

44. The Arabic text of the passage in question reads: *"wa al-sâdisah an yakûn lah jawdah thibât bi-badnih fî mubâshirah a'mâl al-ḥarb wa dhalika an yakun ma'ah al-ṣinâ'ah al-ḥarbiyyah al-khâdimah wa al-ra'îsah"*; see *Virtuous City*, p. 252.

45. See ibid., pp. 292–98 and 308–12.

46. See ibid., pp. 312–14.

47. In the *Kitâb al-Siyâsah* (Political regime), when discussing the timocratic and despotic cities, al-Fârâbî speaks of these issues much more extensively. They are two of the sorts of cities he classes as ignorant, the others being called necessary, vile, base, and democratic cities; see *Kitâb al-Siyâsah al-Madaniyyah*, ed. Fauzi M. Najjar (Beirut: Imprimerie Catholique, 1964), pp. 58–73, esp. pp. 59–69. To the best of my knowledge, however, not once in the treatise does the term war (*harb*), *jihad*, or any term derived from either of them occur. When speaking of the fighting, raiding, resort to arms, and conquest prized and engaged in by the citizens of timocratic and despotic cities, al-Fârâbî uses other terms that are more limited in meaning.

# II

## Irregular Warfare and Terrorism

# 5

## Moral Responsibility and Irregular War

### Courtney S. Campbell

In an influential document on the laws of war, developed for the conduct of Union armies during the American Civil War, Francis Lieber observed; "Men who take up arms against one another in public war do not cease on that account to be moral beings, responsible to one another and to God."[1] This claim was conditioned by Lieber's particular interpretation of the civilizing influence of the nation-state system. In contrast to the "barbarous outrages" in "remote times," Lieber maintained that the "coexistence of modern nations" had both altered the conception of war into an instrument to obtain political ends and permitted the incorporation of moral and legal constraints on conduct. Thus, a key element in Lieber's notion of moral responsibility is that of "public war," which he defined as "a state of armed hostility between sovereign nations or governments."[2]

A question that immediately emerges is the scope of moral responsibility, for the most common form of contemporary conflicts falls outside "public war," or war between sovereign states. As Paul Ramsey suggested, the balance of terror that is nuclear deterrence "has made the world safe for wars of insurgency. . . . Therefore the type of warfare that deserves to be called truly 'modern' is 'insurgency' warfare, 'subversive' war, 'sub-limited' or 'sub-conventional' war, 'revolutionary war' or 'wars of national liberation,' 'guerrilla' war or the 'war of the flea'—or whatever you want to call it." Ramsey's nominalism may blur important distinctions among particular kinds of armed conflicts, but his general thesis that we are now dealing with various forms of "irregular warfare" rather than exclusively or even regularly with Lieber's "public war" seems valid.[3]

My concern in this chapter is to examine the significance of the norms of just war tradition for this context of modern and irregular war. The kind of moral responsibility expressed in the just war tradition, through its requirements of accountability, justification, and limitation of violence, may appear to have limited applicability to irregular war and a commonly associated method, terrorism, a feature perhaps best initially suggested by two distinctions implicit in the language of "public warfare." Insurgents, revolutionaries and guerrillas may lack the public authorization stipulated in the criterion of right or legitimate authority; the targets of terrorist activity, meanwhile, are most frequently "private" members of a society, civilians morally protected by the principle of discrimination.

The practices of irregular war are but one of several serious challenges to the credibility of the just war tradition in the contemporary world. Indeed, most recent discussion has focused on the ways the tradition might be accommodated to problems presented by nuclear war and deterrence strategy. Yet, given the fortunate fact that nuclear war remains a feared hypothetical situation, while insurgencies, national liberation movements, guerrilla war, and revolutions are an *actual* and pervasive phenomenon, the concerns of this chapter seem no less pressing or urgent.

## "FAIR RULES OF ACTION" IN GUERRILLA WAR

Some contemporary commentators have claimed that the just war tradition establishes a "presumption" against irregular war,[4] and the reasons for this presumption are anticipated remarkably well in a short essay by Francis Lieber, prepared at the request of Henry Halleck, general-in-chief of the Union forces, prior to the compilation of the *General Orders*. Halleck noted in correspondence that the line between combatant and civilian had been blurred by the guerrilla tactics of the Confederacy:

The rebel authorities claim the right to send men, in the garb of peaceful citizens, to waylay and attack our troops, to burn bridges and houses and to destroy property and persons within our lines. They demand that such persons be treated as ordinary belligerents, and that when captured they have extended to them the same rights as other prisoners or war; they also threaten that if such persons be punished as marauders and spies they will retaliate by executing our prisoners of war in their possession.[5]

What is the status of those who claim to be "ordinary belligerents" but wage war dressed as "peaceful citizens"? Lieber responded that this "is substantially a new question in the law of war," and set his legally trained mind to formulating definitions and "fair rules of action" in guerrilla war. Lieber did not, in some respects, directly answer Halleck's inquiry, but attempted to distance his interpretation of the laws and fair rules toward guerrilla parties from the question of whether or not they were applicable in the conflict with the southern states. Even so, he perceived the stakes in the basic question to be quite high and did not refrain from generalizing in his conclusion that any society that allowed assassination, robbery, and devastation by various kinds of irregulars to go unpunished would undoubtedly suffer "the deepest injury to itself and disastrous consequences which might change the very issue of the war itself."[6]

This conclusion depended in part on Lieber's conception of a guerrilla party, as contrasted with "ordinary belligerents," and he provided what he considered to be an understanding of "guerrilla" consistent with current usage: "[I]t is universally understood in this country at the present time that a guerrilla party means an irregular band of armed men, not being able, according to their character as a guerrilla party, to carry on what the law terms a regular war." He then specified three aspects of the "irregularity of the guerrilla party": (1) its *origin*, "for it is either self-constituted or constituted by the call of a single individual"; (2) its *lack of relation to a regular army*, particularly as regards "pay, provision and movements"; (3) its *lack of permanency*, for the guerrilla band "may be dismissed and called again together at any time," and "take up arms and lay them down at intervals."[7] A particularly crucial presupposition throughout Lieber's whole discussion is that a guerrilla movement is "self-constituting," for not only does this distinguish the guerrilla from others such as "partisans," who do have belligerent status, but one obvious implication is that a guerrilla party has no "public" authorization for fighting. In just war terminology, guerrilla war contravenes the condition of legitimate authority.

The authorization question is more complicated than a simple denial of legal protections to self-constituted parties, however, for Lieber perceived some overlap between guerrilla war and "the rising en masse, or the 'arming of the peasants.' "[8] He related a consensus in international law "that the rising of the people to repel invasion entitles them to the full benefit of the law of war," including respecting an obligation to "treat captured citizens in arms as prisoners of war." Lieber then immediately went on to claim, "Their acting in separate bodies [that is, as a guerrilla party] does not necessarily give them a different character."[9]

This seems like a fairly substantial concession to irregular war and away from a requirement for public war, which is reinforced by Lieber's subsequent contention that at times it is difficult to distinguish between guerrilla parties and "regular partisans, distinctly authorized by their own government." Lieber noted that the conduct of "humane belligerents" as well as scholarship on the laws of war toward guerrillas emphasized *jus in bello* considerations, thus "leaving the question of self-constitution unexamined." This position therefore gave captured "guerrillamen" treatment identical to that of the regular partisan, unless the guerrillas were known to be responsible for "special crimes," such as murder or the killing of prisoners.[10]

Yet the burden of Lieber's account is that guerrilla conflict almost unavoidably involves such crimes. Thus, while considering two ways in which guerrilla war might be transformed into a form of acceptable public (the rising en masse) or regular (the partisan) war, Lieber also addresses additional connotations of "guerrilla" suggested by other scholars that are, Lieber editorializes, confirmed by history. The evaluative content of these associated ideas permits Lieber to distinguish between those who "unite the fourfold character of the spy, the brigand, the assassin, and the rebel" from "a fair enemy,"[11] based principally on the common methods of guerrilla conduct: pillage; intentional, gratuitous destruction; necessitated murder, especially the execution of prisoners; minimal discipline that results in heinous criminality, robbery, and lust; and, perhaps invoking Halleck's own language, "the danger with which the spy surrounds us, because that to-day passes you in the garb and mien of a peaceful citizen, may to-morrow, as a guerrillaman, fire your house or murder you from behind the hedge."[12] Hence, guerrilla parties may be culpable for precipitating rapid moral degeneracy in compliance with the laws on combatant conduct, quickly undoing a long historical endeavor to set limits on killing in war: "It requires the power of the Almighty and a whole century to grow an oak tree; but only a pair of arms, an ax, and an hour or two to cut it down."[13]

Lieber did not conclude that guerrilla war necessarily introduces a "system of barbarity," but even "clean" conduct by guerrillas did not completely absolve them of moral and legal responsibility. For, as his frequent invocation of the "spy" imagery suggests, the moral problem of irregular war is, in addition to questions about authorization and appropriate conduct, significantly conditioned by *unrecognizability*. The aspect of "invisibility" is implicit in Lieber's second and third characterizations of the guerrilla party. Since guerrillas are typically not an integrated part of a regular army, but instead exhibit "the occasional assumption of the semblance of peaceful pursuits, divesting themselves of the character or appearance of soldiers,"[14] regulars are deprived of clearly knowing if the "peaceful citizen" is a lethal threat. The evasiveness of the guerrilla thus presents difficult questions about how to maintain fairness and trust in such a context, how the regular army can fight without itself violating *jus in bello* limits, and how citizens can be protected when the regular army has good reasons for assuming the enemy will frequently "appear" as civilians.[15]

The just war value particularly imperiled by this practice is that of right intention, which is constituted in part by an understanding that the end of war is peace. According to Lieber, "The ultimate object of all modern war is a renewed state of peace," and the use of "deception" could be justified and necessary to obtain this end.[16] But the practice of concealing or changing identity in irregular conflict is not mere deception; rather, when the "absence of the uniform is used for the purpose of concealment or disguise, in order to get by stealth within the lines of the invader, for destruction of life or property, or pillage," what is involved is perfidy and treachery.[17] Acts of this nature could never be justified, even by Lieber's rather expansive notion of "military necessity," because they constitute an "act of hostility that makes the return to peace unnecessarily difficult."[18]

The reasoning for this prohibition and its absolute scope is clear and sound: the practice of unrecognizability takes advantage of an enemy's adherence to the laws of war and its specific provisions for protecting "private," or "inoffensive," individuals and "unarmed citizens" to advance the objectives of irregulars. In so doing, the significance of these protections and *any* grounds for maintaining a modicum of trust between the opposing combatants is eroded. If combatants cannot trust that at least some persons do not pose lethal threats, the consequences of unrecognizability are likely to be just the kinds of retaliatory actions that concerned Halleck and, in Lieber's view, a return to the internecine brutality and barbarism that characterized the conflicts of remote eras. Thus, perfidy and treachery "essentially interfere with the mitigation of the severity of war, which it is one of the noblest objects of the modern law of war to obtain."[19]

One important way the laws of war have tried to transform irregulars into "fair enemies" is to require the open display of arms or the wearing of distinctive identifying clothing or badges. Lieber follows this convention fairly rigorously, but he does not consider it an absolute requirement or even conclusive evidence of one entitled to protected status. Lieber is willing to make a concession on this point for the same reason he made an allowance on the issue of authorization: "It does not seem that, in the case of a rising en masse, the absence of a uniform can constitute a difference."[20] What does make the difference is the purpose behind not wearing some identifying characteristic: It is one thing, Lieber seems to say, if it is a practical "impossibility" for combatants to be in uniform dress, as "in a levy en masse," and quite another if the uniform is discarded for reasons of stealth and concealment, which violate the prohibition of perfidy.

It might be argued that Lieber can take such a tolerant view toward certain practices he otherwise views as impermissible because the rising en masse doesn't blur the combatant-civilian distinction. In this type of conflict, civilian garb is the identifying characteristic. This reasoning has its own difficulties that merit further examination later, but I shall briefly identify two here. One problem, of course, is that typically the whole people is not in armed revolt; the real practical dilemma of distinguishing combatants in civilian clothes opens up a much broader issue about how the relation between "the people" who are fighting and those who are not should be understood morally. If, on the other hand, the rising en masse is a reality, the authorization of the regular army to fight seems seriously open to question.

We can extract from Lieber's delineation of "fair rules" toward guerrilla parties four general challenges to the moral tradition of justification and limitation of violence presented by irregular war. The authorization of a guerrilla conflict is at best problematic, if not nonexistent; the kind of deception involved in guerrilla war is such as to violate right intention and hence jeopardizes attaining even the minimal or negative peace of cessation of hostilities; a concession implicit in perfidy and treachery is that conformity to the conventional rules cannot reasonably be expected to result in success for irregulars; and the realization that the odds are stacked against them if they play by the rules makes indiscriminate violence an attractive, if not indispensable, temptation to irregulars.

These four considerations explicate the rationale for the presumption against irregular war found in the just war tradition. Yet, there seems to be support at various levels for considering the possibility of overriding this presumption. For instance, recent changes in the language of international conventions from using the term "war" to using that of "armed conflict" were prompted by a need to expand the scope of international law to account for the reality of and the conduct in "subinternational" warfare. Moreover, theories of "just revolution" have drawn heavily in structure and content on the just war tradition. I shall contend in the following sections that the principal way the presumption against irregular war is overridden within the just war tradition is by expanding or reinterpreting the meaning of the conceptions of authorization, cause, intention, success, proportionality, end, and discriminate conduct. Such a strategy can allow the tradition to incorporate the experience of irregular war in its empirically informed framework for moral reflection, but doing so can also carry certain risks to the credibility of the tradition.

## AUTHORIZATION

I want to outline two interpretations of irregular war that illustrate the perplexities it raises for *jus ad bellum* reasoning. One model, certainly more prominent in but not limited to previous centuries, affirms an absolute prohibition against war carried on by "self-constituted" combatants. The critical moral issue in the resort to violence in this perspective is that of authorization, which is vested only in the sovereign state and its public officials, who claim a monopoly over its legitimate use, no matter how oppressive their rule or how valid the grievances of a people. Typically, this reasoning also portrays the consequence of crossing the line from publicly validated to self-constituted warfare as social and moral anarchy; hence, there are also consequentialist reasons for holding that the line should never be crossed.[21]

A second model is reflected in the granting by many contemporary scholars of "ordinary belligerent" status, as well as all the protections accorded to exbelligerents, to at least certain irregulars. For example, Fotion and Elfstrom contend that the fact that "guerrillas do not always wear uniforms is no reason for the establishment armies not to treat them the way they treat uniformed personnel. But guerrillas even more so should not be mistreated when captured because they are fighting in the only way they can." In this model, the moral focus is on limiting the violence, on controlling the potential for anarchy, particularly since "the guerrillas are in a special position to fight a morally clean war."[22] What is absent in this model is considered attention to preliminary questions: whether the guerrillas *ought* to be fighting in the first place, and *who* authorized *them*. That is, in many contemporary discussions of irregular war, the logical priority and moral significance of the *jus ad bellum* seem to have been lost entirely.

Against this model, I want to maintain that moral responsibility requires us to consider authorizations for violence and the validity of a cause for irregular war. In contrast to the first model, I want to indicate that affirmative answers on both issues can be formulated out of sources within the tradition of just war.

The acceptance of the "rising en masse" by Lieber and many others is indicative of one important attempt at interpreting the concept of legitimate authority in a way that may bear directly on irregular war. As Michael Walzer has observed, "guerrilla war is 'people's war,' a special form of the levee en masse, authorized from below."[23] The notion that war might be authorized "from below," by "lesser magistrates" or even "the people" is compatible with some prominent perspectives in Western political ethics that have had revolutionary ramifications. In this influential tradition, mere possession of political power and military might is not a sufficient condition of legitimate authority to govern, let alone grounds for claiming a monopoly over the use of violence. Instead, legitimate authorities must conform to certain moral requirements, such as active seeking of the common good, right reason, or protection of the "inalienable rights" of the governed, which are typically grounded in a version of natural law.

A corollary of this point is that it is entirely conceivable that a de facto government that fails to conform to these standards no longer possesses (or never had) authorization to govern. Richard Overton summarized this line of reasoning in the context of the Puritan Revolution with morally significant imagery: "For tyranny is no magistracy. Therefore the resistance of tyranny is no resistance of magistrates, except it be of such [as are] so nominally, but really and essentially [are] monsters and pests of humanity." Thus, as "all just human powers are but betrusted, conferred and conveyed by joint and common consent," when "the betrusted betray and forfeit their trust . . . *their authority ceaseth* . . ." and "returneth from whence it came, even to the hands of the trusters."[24]

It is often claimed that recognizing the authority of the people as ultimate and overriding is a valid construal of the meaning of legitimate authority and provides at least a necessary condition for irregular war. Yet, this claim may smooth over a very complex problem. Acknowledging the permissiblity of the rising en masse does not by itself establish that particular guerrilla parties or insurgent movements are anything more than "a self-seeking, lawless gang of bandits."[25] Irregulars may well claim they are fighting on behalf of "the people" and invoke "the people" as the source of their authorization, but may nevertheless actually be "self-constituted" combatants. This possibility in part explicates Lieber's refusal to equate guerrilla war with the rising en masse as well as Walzer's qualification that guerrilla war is a "special form" of a people's war, and prominently poses the question of the moral relation between "the people" who are fighting and those who are not. Even if we accept the premise that authorization both to rule and to make war can come "from below," unless *all* the people are armed, it is necessary to ask *who* they have in fact authorized to fight.

In one of the few discussions that treats this issue, Walzer attempts to establish how "the war rights the people would have were they to rise en masse are passed on to the irregular fighters they support and protect." The essential condition of this transfer is that the "support" of the people be "voluntary"; at even this basic level, an implicit consent principle is a moral presupposition of irregular war. The degree of voluntariness can be determined by observing the extent to which the irregulars "live with the people they claim to defend" and "fight where they live." Walzer maintains that when "the guerrillas succeed . . . in fighting among the people" in these two senses, "it is best to assume that they have some serious political support among the people." When this threshold is attained such that it is no longer possible to isolate the irregulars from the people, then the "levee en masse is a reality and not merely a piece of propaganda," Walzer contends, and a conclusion implicit in Overton is made quite explicit: the government has no warrant, moral or legal, for fighting against the people and their authorized representatives.[26]

The difficulty with this argument from the standpoint of the just war tradition is one of temporality, for it implies that authorization *follows* rather than precedes the resort to violence. Walzer himself indicates that the "honorific name [a people's war] can be applied, however, only *after* the guerrilla movement has won very substantial popular support"[27] (my emphasis). But, if the popular support is "won" through an un-authorized resort to arms by what is initially a self-constituted guerrilla party, then it seems valid to question its "voluntariness." Walzer's ac-count then appears to allow for coercion as a means for the irregulars to obtain a foothold among the people, even if this feature of the rela-tionship diminishes over time.

This practical complication should not detract from the general point that in principle it seems possible to satisfy the condition of legitimate authority in the context of irregular war. The issue of determining actual consent for prosecution of a war, of course, is no less a vexing problem for recognized, constituted governments.

## JUST CAUSE AND COUNTERVIOLENCE

A seemingly less troubling issue in the tradition is whether circum-stances within a political entity can be so oppressive and morally abhor-rent as to validate a just cause for violent resistance. Historically, this seems not to be disputed even by those who have held an absolute prohibition against irregular war; they have simply denied that a just cause is a sufficient condition for revolt. Those who have permitted irregular war, meanwhile, have typically portrayed the denial of basic rights or needs necessary to a decent human existence as a violation of the principle of the protection of the innocent (the people) from an unjust "attack," "invasion," or "assault."[28] This way of framing the issue of just cause for irregular war can be controversial because it frequently relies on a disputed meaning of "violence."

We can, it is argued, distinguish two senses of violence: the intentional commission of an *act* that inflicts physical harm, including death, on another person, and a *condition* of pervasive injustice and oppression embedded in political, legal, economic, or social institutions, that is, "systemic violence." This latter conception of violence denotes that, whether from intention, omission, or neglect, basic needs are deprived or rights are violated; in particular, "premature" and "unnatural" death may be a widespread consequence of an *avoidable* condition of starvation, disease, economic exploitation, or industrial injury. Developing this rea-soning, John Harris claims that revolutionary movements are frequently generated by the "violence of normal times" afflicting the "innocent."[29]

It may be claimed that what Harris designates as "the Marxist con-ception of violence" is external to the just war tradition. But it is at least arguable that Marxist thought raised to prominence one meaning of

violence already embedded in some Western moral traditions. For instance, St. Thomas maintained that "unjust laws," in deviating from
right reason and human good, have "the nature not of law, but of
violence" and represent "acts of violence rather than laws." A similar
understanding seems presupposed in Richard Overton's and John
Locke's claim that even in the absence of the infliction of physical injury,
a government could become unjust (losing its authority) and create a
"State of War" against the people through "invasions" of fundamental
rights.[30] One need not embrace a Marxist paradigm, I would contend,
to incorporate a notion of "systemic violence" into Western moral reflection on war.

This definition of violence is not invulnerable to criticisms on conceptual grounds, but what I wish to focus on here are its very significant
moral implications when invoked in discourse about irregular war. First,
it places the established institutions, typically the government, in the
position of "aggressor" or "invader." The resort to arms by the people
and the irregulars who purport to protect the people can then be construed as *responsive* action; it is a necessary act of "self-defense" and
*"counter*violence," taken as a last resort to protect the innocent. Hence,
as John Langan suggests, "the notion [of systemic violence] shifts the
burden of proof from those who would resort to force to vindicate their
rights to those who would maintain an unjust order."[31] Moreover, this
portrayal presents irregulars as *conforming* to moral norms and legal
conventions permitting violence for reasons of self-defense. Finally, responsibility for *first* violating the moral immunity of the innocent is
placed on the government, a perception which may be used by the
irregulars to foment "support" and/or be cited as precedent should they
subsequently resort to indiscriminate measures in retaliation.

The concept of systemic violence, then, structures the burdens of proof
and responsibility in a way that reflects an effort to incorporate irregular
war under the normative moral reasoning about a conventional conflict.
From another perspective, however, it may well undermine the importance rightfully ascribed to justifying violence. For the claim that violence
is institutionalized in a socio-political system implies an interpretative
continuity between politics and violence: violence is described and
understood as a socially embedded and accepted means to achieve political and economic ends, and the "counterviolence" of irregulars is just
one more kind of violence in an already violent system. The need to
justify counterviolence may be minimized if violence is seen as politics
carried on by alternative, perhaps more effective, means.[32]

Nor is the notion of systemic violence morally innocuous with respect
to *jus in bello* limits; it instead may present a way of distancing irregulars
from moral suspicion of indiscriminate violence. For anyone, regardless
of role, function, or level of responsibility, who contributes to the main-

tenance of the oppressive status quo may be considered implicated in its violence and perceived as a legitimate object of attack. The moral complicity of all means there are no "innocent" to be distinguished from the "guilty."

The concept of systemic violence draws on a common understanding that the deprivation of basic needs or the violation of fundamental rights necessary to decent human life are injustices, but the crucial moral move is to designate these injustices as forms of "violence" against an innocent people. Without careful specification, however, it becomes a slippery, self-serving appeal that risks permitting too much violence and not imposing adequate limits. It contravenes the just war convention that "innocence" is to be assessed by objective lethal threat, not subjective support, a noticeable irony since the strategy of irregulars frequently raises questions about the "innocence" and moral complicity of their civilian supporters.

## EVENING THE ODDS: INTENTION, SUCCESS, PROPORTIONALITY, AND END

As Richard Shelly Hartigan has written, "the very essence of guerrilla conflict, the strength of the guerrilla, requires unrecognizability."[33] We might understand the practice of concealment by irregulars in part as an attempt to ensure that there is a reasonable chance of attaining success and realizing the objective of the conflict. The disproportionate advantage held by conventional forces in weaponry and personnel, James Turner Johnson has noted, means that at least in the initial stages of a conflict, "it would be suicide for the insurgents to attempt a conventional armed clash."[34] For many, this has been the decisive consideration against irregular conflict even in South Africa, where the justness of the cause for liberation from apartheid commands widespread consensus. A conventional fight in the open, away from civilian cover, seems certain to be a losing proposition; unrecognizability can even the odds, assisting irregulars to avoid the kind of armed clash that would be "nasty and short" for their side.

Historically, the laws of war have tried to impose visibility upon irregular fighters. In international conventions beginning with the Hague Conference in 1899 and 1907, irregulars could obtain the status of lawful belligerents only by meeting several conditions: they were to be answerable to a specific commander (a requirement that addresses Lieber's concern about the lack of discipline among irregulars), wear a distinctive badge, carry their weapons openly, and *in bello*, conform to the laws and customs of war. However, some modifications were introduced in Protocol I of the 1977 Geneva Convention, such that irregulars now must display arms openly only at the moment of attack, and the necessity of identifying markings was eliminated.[35]

The mode of unrecognizability may enhance irregulars' prospects of success, yet morally express illicit intentions by contravening the prohibitions of perfidy and treachery. As Lieber stressed, not requiring uniform dress in some circumstances is different from permitting irregulars to fight dressed as civilians. For unrecognizability not only culminates in fighting outside the "laws and customs of war," but is in fact subversive of those conventions: by using civilian clothing as a disguise, irregulars "violate the implicit trust upon which the war convention rests: soldiers must feel safe among civilians if civilians are ever to be safe from soldiers."[36] That trust not only is the condition for discriminate warfare, but also the prerequisite to achieving an end to war short of ending all civilian life. In this respect, when irregulars "fight the *only* way they can," relying on civilian rather than natural cover, the *jus ad bellum* and *jus in bello* converge to reinforce the presumption against irregular war. The morally important issue is whether there are other ways irregulars can fight to avoid suicide, *without* risking the lives of the civilians they purport to protect.

At a very practical level, irregular war seems to invite indiscriminate warfare. Moreover, ideological considerations not only confirm this practical dimension, but also press the boundaries of proportionality. The discourse of irregulars typically invokes very expansive notions of "success" and "end." "Success" may encompass not simply the overthrow of a government, but also "social transformation," which establishes ideological pressure to prolong the duration of the conflict and its violence. Moreover, if the "end" of the conflict is held to be the "birth" of a new order that will "succeed in ridding itself of all the muck of ages,"[37] restraints of proportionality on irregular violence will be susceptible to substantial expansion. The broadened criteria of success, proportionality, and end may, then, have substantial ramifications for the conduct of irregular war, including continuing violence beyond the period of assumption of political power or even sanctioning unlimited means for an unlimited duration.

## CIVILIAN DEATHS: WHOSE RESPONSIBILITY?

I have identified several asymmetries in irregular war that can converge to make it "intractably dirty" from a moral standpoint.[38] The initial disparity in military capability typically requires irregulars to adopt unconventional tactics, such as the discarding of identifying characteristics, to enhance their chances of a successful struggle. The consequences of unrecognizability, however, will be to place at greater risks the lives of their civilian supporters because of the inability of the regulars to differentiate adequately the people who are fighting from those who are not. This evening of the odds introduces an additional asymmetry, for then the burden of indiscriminate war seemingly is shifted to the conventional forces.

In an interesting way, then, the success of an irregular conflict does not necessarily depend on indiscriminate conduct by the irregulars. As Fotion and Elfstrom contend, "guerrillas are in a special position to fight a morally clean war." If they so choose, the guerrillas can be selective in their targeting since they "know where their enemy is, but the enemy does not know where they are."[39] This is not to say that in conflict, irregulars do not violate the laws and customs of war, but only that in principle the practice of unrecognizability, conditioned by the imperative of success, leaves open for the irregulars a morally crucial option, the choice to attack civilians directly, that appears foreclosed to the opposing army. Yet, even if the irregulars fight "cleanly," and avoid the raids, extortion, massacres, execution of prisoners, and gratuitous destruction commonly associated with irregular war, there remains a serious question about whether they are fighting "fairly." For *whoever* the agent, the strategy of irregular conflict seems premised on eroding the protection of noncombatants from direct attack.

It is for this reason that there is a consensus among several just war theorists that moral responsibility for the deaths of even those civilians killed by conventional forces falls on the irregulars: their hands are still dirty even if they are not bloody. Yet, within this consensus there are significant disputes about what this burden of responsibility implies for the conduct of the regular forces.

Paul Ramsey's argument on this issue is a classic illustration of how the formal principle of discrimination (it is never right to attack the innocent directly), which he defends as an absolute moral requirement, may be relativized by the kind of conflict to the extent that it has little or no practical bearing.[40] For Ramsey, "the decision of the insurgency to fight the war by means of peasants" means "the insurgents themselves have enlarged the target it is legitimate for counter-insurgents to attack, so far as the principle of discrimination is concerned." The moral limit on violence by the counterinsurgency forces is "mainly the principle of proportion." Indeed, it appears for Ramsey that civilians who support irregulars undergo a transformation of status, for whether "persuaded or terrorized" into support, such civilians may be considered "combatants without malice."[41]

The voluntariness of the irregular-civilian relation seems to make no moral difference to Ramsey. What seems crucial to consider, however complicated it may be in a particular circumstance, is whether the civilians are indeed being used as mere means or are using the insurgents to fight *their* war. That is, Ramsey's position on the *jus in bello* limits appropriate to counterinsurgents clearly seems to presuppose an arguable premise about the relevance of legitimate authorization for irregular war.

While Johnson and Walzer agree with Ramsey that the moral burden of the deaths of civilian supporters is the responsibility of irregulars, neither follows his move to classify the civilian as a kind of "combatant." That logic allows for seemingly indiscriminate conflict under the guise of the principle of discrimination, or at best conduct limited only by proportionality.[42] For both Johnson and Walzer, the moral immunity of civilian supporters remains intact: "The essential moral point is that the failure of the insurgents to observe fundamental moral restraints does not absolve the counter-insurgent forces from their duty to do so."[43] The stringency of these restraints may make the war against irregulars morally harder to fight and harder to win, given the feature of irregular unrecognizability. These dilemmas Ramsey avoids by effectively abandoning the principle of discrimination.

## ASSASSINATION

In the just war tradition, the distinction between "combatants" and "noncombatants" is typically a functional distinction: Combatants are soldiers who pose lethal threats or civilians who serve the fighting needs of the soldier, while noncombatants are those who serve human needs, such as medical care, food, or religious needs. Under this framework, what are we to make morally of a common method of irregular war, selective attacks on public officials who pose no objective threat but may have some degree of responsibility for a war effort or internal oppression? Can assassination or "selective terrorism" be compatible with the values and constraints on violence in the just war tradition?

One important context for discussion of this issue has been Albert Camus's account of "the fastidious assassins," members of the Russian terrorist Organization for Combat, who carried out assassinations in the early 1900s against officials implicated in the oppressions of tsarist rule.[44] Their self-interpretation as an order of "medieval knights" and use of the language of "chivalry" is suggestive, given the historically significant role of the knightly class and codes of chivalry in generating moral limits on violence for the just war tradition,[45] and indeed Camus indicates "these executioners . . . made attempts on the lives of others only after the most scrupulous examination of conscience." One consequence of this conscientious reflection was a "fastidious" observance of a principle of discrimination. In one incident, Ivan Kaliayev, whom Camus describes as "the purest image of rebellion," had been selected to assassinate the Grand Duke Sergei, who was involved in the suppression of revolutionary activity. At the crucial moment, however, Kaliayev failed to carry out the act for fear of killing two children accompanying the grand duke; this refusal, Camus indicates, met "with the full approval of his comrades." And these comrades exhibited similar constraints: Boris Savinkov opposed the assassination of an Admiral Dubassov on a train because "if there were the least mistake, the explosion could take place in the car and kill strangers," while Voinarovsky declares, "If Dubassov is accompanied by his wife, I shall not throw the bomb."[46]

Children, strangers, spouses—even among some terrorists, the narrative suggests, a distinction is made between legitimate and illegitimate targets of attack. But suppose we alter the situation somewhat and contemplate the morality of assassinating not merely the grand duke but the tsar himself? The involvement of the German pastor and theologian Dietrich Bonhoeffer in the conspiracy to assassinate Adolf Hitler provides an intriguing case study. Bonhoeffer, who was imprisoned and eventually executed for his role in the conspiracy, related to a prison companion his view that, "as a pastor, it was his duty not only to comfort the victims of the man who drove in a busy street like a maniac, but also to try to stop him." This duty prompted an "agonized participation" on Bonhoeffer's part and the development of "operative guidelines" for the assassination of Hitler that have been designated "adaptations of just war criteria."[47]

*There must be gross misrule by civil authorities that threatens irreparable harm to the political community and its citizens.* For Bonhoeffer, Nazism represented a triumph of moral degradation and nihilism that if left unchecked would destroy not only Germany but civilized society. The reign of the Third Reich, moreover, was that of a state that had lost its authorization to rule, had "ceased to be a true state." Implicit in this guideline are considerations of legitimate authority and just cause.

*The levels of political responsibility in society must be respected.* The first resort against tyranny must be legal and constitutional tactics and requests for redress from higher-placed authorities, who may be in a position to remove the tyrant short of a resort to violence. In Bonhoeffer's hierarchical order, private citizens could only assume such a grave responsibility after legal recourse had failed and both high public officials and the military were unable or unwilling to act on their behalf. Tyrannicide may then be contemplated as the ultima ratio in an "exceptional state of affairs." In this guideline encompassing authorization and last resort, Bonhoeffer's position differs markedly from the assassins extolled by Camus.

*There must exist a reasonable assurance that the tyrannicide will be successful.* Bonhoeffer's reasoning involved a broad meaning of "success" and makes this criterion particularly complex: Hitler's death would be a necessary but insufficient index of success, as the system he constructed could well survive him. Hence, "the ultimate question for a responsible man to ask is . . . how the coming generation is to live."[48] Several practical implications follow from this question. Successful tyrannicide could not be an act of a sole individual, but required a coordinated effort among many to the extent that Hitler's death would coincide with the assumption of critical civilian and military posts by fellow members of the resistance movement. Thus, it was essential that the conspirators formulate plans for takeover of the government and proposals for civil rule subsequent to its overthrow. Bonhoeffer's concern to ensure a reasonable expectation of success also involves proportionality considerations: inadequate attention to process might make the tyranny even more oppressive (Hitler, if the plan failed, or his successor, if it worked, might well impose an even harsher regimen on daily life, in part to prevent such an event from recurring) or, alternatively, plunge the society into the abyss of anarchy. In either case, the "coming generation" would not live well.

*The minimal amount of violence requisite to ending the Hitler regime must be applied.* The collaborators drew up a "General Order to the Armed Forces of the State" that precluded "arbitrary or revengeful" acts so that the liberated citizenry might witness "the difference from the wanton methods of their former rulers."[49] For Bonhoeffer personally, the "agony" of complicity in an act that he perceived as defying both positive and divine law also imposed limits on the extent of violence. If Augustine's just war was also "mournful," to Bonhoeffer, just assassination was "agonizing," and indeed considerably more ethically problematic than war.

But let us alter the scenario again somewhat and consider the case when the assassin is not a member of the nation under tyrannical rule. Bonhoeffer's heightened reservations about assassination relative to war are given moral intelligibility in James Turner Johnson's reasoning on why the United States should forgo assassination of contemporary leaders "we" consider a particular threat to international order, such as Muammar Qaddafi.[50] Western moral reflection, Johnson holds, passes different judgments on killing *by* assassination and killing *in* war. Assassination differs morally from war in its ends—the killing of one person rather than the achievement of specified political objectives—and in its calculated singling out of an individual for execution as distinct from the "random quality" of death in war. In these respects, assassination bears moral similarities with murder, and the moral prohibition on it is "nearly absolute" because it "strikes at the very fundaments of human life in community."

Moreover, Johnson follows the Augustinian conception that the fundamental wrong in killing is the presence of evil intentions, such as "implacable animosity" and personal hatred, which can be avoided in war but are the likely dispositive traits of an assassin. On several grounds, then, "there are the right and wrong ways to act even in the struggle against evil: assassination is wrong; yet military force can be right."

Still, the wrong is "nearly," but not *absolutely* prohibited. There are instances, Johnson concedes, where "assassination loses its moral stigma," particularly when an assassination attempt comes from "within a [tyrant's] community." Such reasoning seems to reflect something like Bonhoeffer's second guideline, respect for the levels of political responsibility.

Johnson opens the door to assassination just slightly, but more than Lieber allowed. Admittedly, Lieber was immediately confronted with the likes of Jefferson Davis, not a Hitler, or even a Qaddafi, though interestingly enough, he had as a young man taken an oath to assassinate Napoleon, invoking proportionality grounds: "[T]he idea of sacrificing two armies while the sacrifice of one life might stop all misery, seemed to me preposterous."[51] As a scholar on the laws of war, though, Lieber prohibited assassination for reasons of cause and intention as well as proportionality. If permitted, assassination "would lead to deplorable evils which would greatly impede the ultimate end of war-*quod est Pax*."[52] In part, this is because implicit in assassination is the kind of deception involved in perfidy and treachery: assassination too threatens the trust necessary to human interaction. This bond of trust may provide the underlying rationale for Lieber's assertion that the law of war forbids proclaiming any individual an "outlaw" to encourage his assassination. Furthermore, Lieber contends, "The sternest retaliation should follow the murder committed in consequence of such proclamation, made by whatever authority. Civilized nations look with horror upon offers of rewards for the assassination of enemies as relapses into barbarism."[53]

There are good reasons for following Lieber in making the prohibition of assassination absolute. For while I would argue that it is possible to defend the kind of "exceptional case" assassination represented in Bonhoeffer's operative guidelines, which are derived from just war criteria, the problem, once exceptions are made, is setting limits on who is selected. There are different levels of political complicity corresponding with the levels of responsibility; a "brutal tyrant who deserves to die" is different from a grand duke, who is still different from the mayor of a village. Exceptions can risk a slippery slope that may expand the targets of assassins to "all or almost all government officials" of any "agent of oppression," inviting a widespread campaign of assassination reinforced by the fact that mayors of villages are commonly more exposed and vulnerable.[54] The chances of success are enhanced the lower in the political hierarchy the assassin strikes. Thus, in not drawing a sharp line against assassination by prohibiting the first instance altogether, one risks excesses and several fuzzy lines.

If assassination is allowed, it might be limited to tyrannicide by drawing a line of selection around those persons who are at once both formulators of a nation's political policies and activities, as distinct from those who function as instruments of their implementation, *and* symbols identified with those policies, as in the case of Hitler and Nazism. Their culpability for systemic criminal acts of war or repression surely is more extensive than that of an ordinary village mayor; indeed, it is their policies that most commonly cause the military to wage war or civilians to rebel.

Assassination is a very limiting case in the just war tradition, a greyish shade in the midst of black. Its status as at least a "near absolute" moral wrong is supported by legal conventions that refuse to grant assassins any rights of belligerents if they are captured, but instead permit their execution, a punishment that some of its practitioners, the fastidious assassins and Dietrich Bonhoeffer, acknowledged as fitting. Still, the perspectives of law (Lieber) and ethics (Johnson) on assassination are not identical: the highest political officials do not pose the immediate lethal threat soldiers do, and they have traditionally been classified as nonmilitary persons immune from legitimate attack. Moral reflection, meanwhile, may permit "just assassinations" in the exceptional case, and consider assassins "entitled to a kind of moral respect . . . because they set limits to their actions," even though under the law they are treated as murderers.[55]

## TERRORISM AND NECESSITATED MURDER

Just assassins might be characterized as murderers in a good cause, but the moral difficulty in permitting the line prohibiting assassination to be crossed is how to control one act of assassination so that it doesn't appear to condone or culminate in a practice of indiscriminate violence by irregulars against noncombatants. The just war tradition, however, has recognized the possibility of exceptional circumstances of "supreme emergency" or "necessity," in which, in the face of an "imminent" and "serious" danger, it is permissible to adopt extreme measures, including deliberate, direct attacks on noncombatants, as a last resort to stave off a disaster for a community and its values. Would such reasoning be applicable to situations in which irregulars engage in indiscriminate violence?[56]

It might be best to approach this question indirectly and consider why indiscriminate violence seems more the first resort norm than the last resort exceptional case in irregular conflict. One factor has to do with the slipperiness of targeting tactics, as exemplified in Northern Ireland by the IRA's policy of "selective bombing."

[The IRA] see these actions as a legitimate part of war, the targets chosen being military and police barracks, outposts, customs offices, administrative and government buildings, electricity transformers and pylons, certain cinemas, hotels, clubs, dance halls, pubs, all of which provide relaxation and personal comforts for the British forces; also business targets, e.g., factories, firms, stores . . . owned in whole or in part by British financiers or companies, or who in any way are a contributory factor to the well-being of Her Majesty's invading forces, and in certain instances residences of people known to be in league with espionage personnel.[57]

At one level, this pronouncement attempts to reflect discrimination in targeting: the "British forces" are the designated enemy. But any pretense of observing the core concept of the principle of discrimination, that persons may be distinguished in their functions by whether they serve the fighting or the human needs of the soldier, is completely missing. Instead, by defining as legitimate targets establishments that "in any way" are perceived to contribute to the British cause in Northern Ireland, the pronouncement clearly opens the way to fighting against uniformed soldiers by means of attacks against nonuniformed civilians, as well as against soldiers in various modes of relaxation, that is, in places when and where an attack would not be expected. Its implications closely parallel those contained in the concept of systemic violence: the culpability of contributing "in any way" expands the possible targets, so while it can be claimed that "legitimate" actions of selective bombing conform to the principle of discrimination, in practice, few if any persons will be presumed innocent. In an all-too-real sense, the targeting policy makes an enemy of anyone and everyone who does not share the goals of the IRA: during a two-year period in the 1970s when selective bombing was in effect, hundreds of civilians in Belfast, both Catholic and Protestant, were killed, but not a single British soldier lost his life.

The problem of whether violence by irregulars is indiscriminate is complicated not simply by who is defined as the enemy, but also how the enemy is perceived. The enemy is frequently dehumanized or demonized; tyrants are "cruel and raging beasts" (Aquinas), "monsters and pests" (Overton), or "mad dogs" (Qaddafi as described by Ronald Reagan), and these images can be generalized so that the entire enemy is seen as less than human or demonic. Moreover, as David Rapoport has observed in identifying the "different" moral logic of terrorism, "Terrorists . . . normally avoid speaking of their victims as persons. Depending on the context, the victims become symbols, tools, animals, or corrupt beings."[58]

As illustrated in Lieber's concern about designating an enemy an "outlaw," the exclusion of the enemy from the human community can have clear moral and practical ramifications, for some of the constraints traditionally acknowledged relative to the killing of a human being seem erased. Such reasoning is clearly displayed in John Locke's appraisal of those who by their violations of natural law have degenerated into "noxious creatures" or "wild savage beasts." "One may destroy a man who makes war upon him, or has discovered an enmity to his being, *for the same reason*, that he may kill a wolf or a lion, because such men are not under the ties of the common law of reason, have no other rule, but that of force and violence, and so may be treated as beasts of prey"[59] (my emphasis).

This "logic" of dehumanization likewise presents a method of morally distancing irregulars from violations of the principle of discrimination. The argument seems to assume the validity of a moral principle prohibiting indiscriminate killing of human beings (or perhaps *any* killing of "human" beings), but portrays the enemy as in crucial respects less than human. Killing a "savage beast" or a "mad dog," therefore, does not represent a violation of the discrimination principle. Such reasoning seems susceptible to abuse, of course, precisely because the power of definition and exclusion is in the hands of those who kill.

Both the methods of expansive targeting and dehumanization of the enemy can permit irregulars to claim, however specious it appears, that their conduct is not indiscriminate. Rather than accepting responsibility for a moral violation, the issue is reinterpreted or redescribed so that wrongdoing can be denied. This approach must be distinguished from arguments that appeal to "necessity," in which a moral violation is acknowledged but excused because of the extremity of the situation.

We might consider briefly one illustration of this appeal that is closely tied to the IRA's policy of selective bombing, a statement of a Protestant faction in Northern Ireland: "Once more in the history of our people we have our backs to the wall, facing extinction by one way or another. This is the moment to beware, for Ulstermen in this position fight mercilessly till they or their enemies are dead." That interpretation of the "position" parallels fairly closely those recognized in the just war tradition as occasioning a situation of necessity; the choices are perceived to be limited either to "extinction" or to breaking the moral rules. The intent to violate the moral limits of the tradition is clearly expressed in the prospect for "merciless" conflict, but this is itself conditioned by the circumstances of extremity: "We . . . are fighting for survival" against those "educated and dedicated to destroying a way of life."[60]

A major difficulty with excusing violations of moral norms on grounds of necessity is the possibility of abuse; are the options actually as limited as described, or is the portrayal simply self-serving? It would be realistic to expect almost any community, after all, to describe its situation in confronting imminent defeat as one of supreme emergency, even when the consequences will not be "extinction." Moreover, the perceived nature of the danger can depend on the value-priorities of the community.

For example, the preservation of physical life, a narrow but at least necessary condition of survival, can be attained without preserving a "way of life." Which value or do both provide sufficient warrant for indiscriminate violence as the means of preservation?

A further issue is how a community that does survive can incorporate sanctioning violence without limits (or mercy) into its system of values without its own way of life being irreparably harmed. In some views, moral responsibility requires an attempt to reaffirm the significance of fundamental norms that have been violated in the course of conflict. Camus's account of the fastidious assassins identifies one symbolically potent approach to this question, a recognition that such killing exacted a moral price. Part of the organization's "chivalric code" mandated that one "had to accept death, to pay for a life with a life," to acknowledge the wrongness of the "murders."[61] Such a requirement reflects not only an ethic of instrumental rationality—assassination as a means of striking at tsardom—but also an ethic of expressive rationality, the acceptance of one's own death as an expression of the evil of the antecedent deed. By contrast, many contemporary terrorists may indeed accept the risk of personal death accompanying their action but as a means to personal salvation, not as an expression that the rules have been violated.

This analysis suggests that the discourse of irregulars and terrorists to justify attacks on civilians or indiscriminate violence typically fails to acknowledge moral norms on violence, denies moral responsibility for their violation, and ignores the need to reaffirm the significance of such norms. The strategies of justification thus fail in crucial ways to conform to the conditions for a valid appeal to necessity in the just war tradition. There is thus good reason to agree with Johnson's assessment that terrorism is "inherently at odds with the values expressed in the [just war] tradition."[62]

## JUST AND IRREGULAR WAR

The just war tradition is not merely a philosophical construct, but has been substantially shaped over time by the actual experience of war. We now live in an era in which the regular, normative practice of war predominantly seems to have become what is designated in the tradition as "irregular." How will this type of conflict inform our moral reasoning about war, now and in the future? Out of the preceding analysis, I want to develop four related answers to this question in conclusion.

First, despite some arguments to the contrary,[63] we should continue to use the just war tradition as our primary resource for moral reflection on irregular conflict. The tradition articulates substantive requirements and a procedure for moral reasoning that are unavoidable for human beings conscious of the profound moral dimension of any resort to lethal violence. We do away with the values embedded in this tradition at the peril of our humanity.

Second, the "presumption" against irregular war defended by contemporary just war theorists should be retained. This general presumption, I have suggested, is supported by specific moral considerations about authorization, intentionality, success, conduct, and responsibility. The collective bindingness of these considerations needs to be strongly reaffirmed, lest irregular war be too easily justified.

Third, for the tradition to adequately account for the pervasive experience of irregular war in the contemporary world, the meaning of various just war criteria may need to be broadened or reinterpreted. The condition of legitimate authority could be informed by versions of moral sanction for a people's war, and that of just cause by different substantive conceptions of violence. Criteria concerned with the ends of war, such as intention, success, and proportionality, may need to incorporate not only immediate and proximate ends, such as military success or the overthrow of a government, but also distant and ultimate ends, such as societal transformation. The concepts and norms addressing the methods of war, such as noncombatantcy and the principle of discrimination, may be qualified by different images of the enemy. Such interpretations need careful formulation and moral scrutiny to avoid justifying too much or limiting too little.

Finally, more thorough consideration needs to be given to the conditions under which the presumption against irregular war can be justifiably overridden. This question can be addressed from within the moral boundaries of the just war tradition and should incorporate discussion over the *meaning* of just war criteria as well as their *status* and *priority*. We will then make progress in adapting this moral tradition to provide distinctions between just and unjust irregular wars, and permissible, exceptional, and forbidden conduct, and to ground judgments that participation in irregular conflict does not establish immunity from moral responsibility.

## NOTES

1. "Instructions for the Government of Armies of the United States in the Field" (hereafter *General Orders, No. 100*), §I.15, in Richard Shelly Hartigan, *Lieber's Code and the Law of War* (Chicago: Precedent Publishing, 1983), p. 48.

2. *General Orders, No. 100*, §I.20, p. 49.

3. Paul Ramsey, *The Just War: Force and Political Responsibility* (New York: Charles Scribner's Sons, 1968), pp. 427–28. While revolutionary war, guerrilla war, and insurgency war can be differentiated to some extent, the question of classification would take us far beyond the scope of my concerns. In this chapter, I will use "irregular war" as a generic concept to refer to these various kinds of

armed conflict, in part because I think it is fair to say that, for all their differences, a very similar set of problems for the just war tradition is raised by these conflicts.

4. James Turner Johnson, *Can Modern War Be Just?* (New Haven, CT: Yale University Press, 1984), p. 54.

5. Hartigan, *Lieber's Code and the Law of War,* p. 2. A century later, Halleck's inquiry became an "urgent" question for Ramsey: "How shall counterinsurgency war be conducted justly?" I have chosen to concentrate on questions about the justification and conduct for "insurgency" war, but occasionally issues about counterinsurgency war will surface in the discussion.

6. Francis Lieber, "Guerrilla Parties Considered with Reference to the Laws and Usages of War," in Hartigan, *Lieber's Code and the Law of War,* pp. 43–44.

7. Lieber, "Guerrilla Parties," pp. 33, 41.

8. Ibid., p. 38.

9. Ibid., p. 39.

10. Ibid., p. 42.

11. Ibid., p. 43.

12. Ibid., pp. 33–34, 41.

13. Ibid., p. 34.

14. *General Orders, No. 100,* §IV.82, p. 60.

15. These issues underlie Michael Walzer's observation that guerrillas "seek to place the onus of indiscriminate warfare on the opposing army." Michael Walzer, *Just and Unjust Wars* (New York: Basic Books, 1977), p. 180.

16. *General Orders, No. 100,* §I.29, p. 50; §V.101, p. 63. Lieber's use of the qualifier "modern" is again important.

17. Lieber, "Guerrilla Parties," p. 40; *General Orders, No. 100,* §I.15–16, §V.101, p. 48, 63.

18. *General Orders, No. 100,* §I.16, p. 48.

19. Lieber, "Guerrilla Parties," p. 37.

20. Ibid., p. 39.

21. The magisterial Protestant reformers Martin Luther and John Calvin were quite explicit in affirming such a position. For some of Luther's views, see "Against the Robbing and Murdering Hordes of Peasants" and "An Open Letter on the Harsh Book against the Peasants," in J.M. Porter, ed., *Luther: Selected Political Writings,* (Philadelphia: Fortress Press, 1974), pp. 88, 97. For some of Calvin's views, see John T. McNeill, ed., *The Institutes of the Christian Religion* (Philadelphia: Westminster Press, 1960), iv. xx. 10, and "Commentaries on the Acts of the Apostles," and "The First Epistle of Peter," in William Kyle Smith, ed., *Calvin's Ethics of War* (Annapolis, MD: Westminster Foundation, 1972), pp. 32, 36, 57. For contemporary exponents of this position, see G. E. M. Anscombe, *Ethics, Religion, and Politics* (Minneapolis: University of Minnesota Press, 1981), pp. 53–55, and Roland Bainton, "Congregationalism: From the Just War to the Crusade in the Puritan Revolution," *The Andover Newton Theological School Bulletin* 35, no. 3 (April 1943), pp. 1–20. For further discussion of the views of Anscombe in this volume, see the article by Jeffrey Stout.

22. Nicholas Fotion and Gerard Elfstrom, *Military Ethics: Guidelines for Peace and War* (Boston: Routledge and Kegan Paul, 1986), pp. 214, 218, 224.

23. Walzer, *Just and Unjust Wars,* p. 180. Walzer is here describing the self-image of guerrillas, not stipulating a normative understanding.

24. Richard Overton, "An Appeal from the Commons to the Free People," in *Puritanism and Liberty, Being the Army Debates (1647–1649)* A. S. P. Woodhouse, ed. (London: J.M. Dent and Sons, 1938), 326–31. John Locke systematically formulates and draws out the implications of this process of "devolution" of political authority in *Two Treatises of Government*, Peter Laslett, ed. (New York: Cambridge University Press, 1965).

25. Johnson, *Can Modern War Be Just?* p. 54.

26. Walzer, *Just and Unjust Wars*, pp. 184–87; 187, 195–96.

27. Ibid., p. 195.

28. For discussion of the content of "just cause" and its implications for revolutionary conflict, see Ralph B. Potter, Jr., "The Moral Logic of War," *McCormick Quarterly* 23 (1970), pp. 203–33.

29. On my reading of revolutionary literature of various traditions, "premature death" and "dying before one's time" is a prime index of the presence and extent of institutionalized violence. For example, liberation theology has concentrated on the plight and privileges of "the poor," and thus Gustavo Gutiérrez's identification of the poor as "those who die before their time" is invested with enormous theological and moral significance. See Gutiérrez, *The Power of the Poor in History*, trans. Robert R. Barr (Maryknoll, NY: Orbis Books, 1983), pp. 77–90. Compare John Harris, "The Marxist Conception of Violence," *Philosophy and Public Affairs*, 3, no. 2 (Winter 1974), pp. 192–220.

30. Thomas Aquinas, *Summa Theologiae* I.II.Q.93,A.3 and I.II.Q.96, A.4, in *The Biblical Ideas of St. Thomas Aquinas*, Dino Bigongiari, ed. (New York: Hafner Press, 1974); John Locke, *Two Treatises of Government*, esp. chs. 3, 18, 19, *Supra* note 24.

31. John P. Langan, "Violence and Injustice in Society: Recent Catholic Teaching," *Theological Studies* 46 (1985), p. 689.

32. These implications are clearly evident in one of the few discussions of "violence" in liberation theology, Ignacio Ellacuria's *Freedom Made Flesh*, trans. John Drury (Maryknoll, NY: Orbis Books, 1976), pp. 171, 199, 227.

33. Hartigan, *Lieber's Code and the Law of War*, p. 24.

34. Johnson, *Can Modern War Be Just?* p. 54. Fotion and Elfstrom put this point this way: "The guerrillas' strategy is dictated by the overwhelming strength of their enemy. The enemy controls the institutions of the society including the banks and businesses, the public means of transportation, the mass media, and the nation's formal military organization. . . . [A] fight in the open would, for [the guerrillas], be nasty and short." See *Military Ethics*, pp. 213–14.

35. Paul Wilkinson, "The Laws of War and Terrorism," in *The Morality of Terrorism: Religious and Secular Justifications*, David C. Rapoport and Yonah Alexander, eds. (New York: Pergamon Press, 1982), p. 319.

36. Walzer, *Just and Unjust Wars*, p. 182.

37. The phrase is taken from Karl Marx's "The German Ideology: Part I" in *The Marx-Engels Reader*, Robert C. Tucker, ed. (New York: W.W. Norton, 1972), p. 157. It reflects a very pervasive theme in modern revolutionary literature, the idea that revolution can bring "freedom from history." As Albert Camus once commented, "If there had ever been one real revolution, there would be no more history." Albert Camus, *The Rebel*, trans. Anthony Bower (New York: Alfred A. Knopf, 1954), p. 79.

38. Johnson, *Can Modern War Be Just?*, p. 54.

39. Fotion and Elfstrom, *Military Ethics*, pp. 214–18.

40. Ramsey, *The Just War*, pp. 397, 410. Ramsey holds there are "two ingredients" in the principle of discrimination. "One is the prohibition of 'deliberate, direct attack.' This is the immutable, unchanging ingredient in the definition of justice in war. . . . The second ingredient is the meaning of 'combatancy-noncombatancy.' This is relativistic and varying in meaning and application," based on military technology and the organization of military forces.

41. Ramsey, *The Just War*, p. 436.

42. Johnson, *Can Modern War be Just?*, p. 57; Walzer, *Just and Unjust Wars*, pp. 192–93.

43. Johnson, *Can Modern War Be Just?*, p. 59. For Ramsey, by contrast, "when war is planned and carried out by an opponent on the principle that the guerrilla lives among the people like a fish in water, we may be justified in accepting the destruction of an entire school of fish . . . incidental to the elimination of the guerrillas," provided the principle of proportionality is satisfied.

44. Camus, *The Rebel*, pp. 164–73.

45. For discussion of this source of *jus in bello* limits, see James Turner Johnson, "Historical Roots and Sources of the Just War Tradition in Western Culture," in *Just War and Jihad: Historical and Theoretical Perspectives on War and Peace in Western and Islamic Traditions*, John Kelsay and James Turner Johnson, eds. (Westport, CT: Greenwood Press, 1991).

46. Camus, *The Rebel*, pp. 168–69.

47. Larry L. Rasmussen, *Dietrich Bonhoeffer: Reality and Resistance* (New York: Abingdon Press, 1972), pp. 94–126, 134–46. There are also interesting parallels between the "operative guidelines" and Walzer's condition of "supreme emergency," when the validity of the cause can override the norms limiting violence. Compare Walzer, *Just and Unjust Wars*, pp. 251–68, as well as my discussion in this chapter.

48. Rasmussen, *Dietrich Bonhoeffer*, p. 140.

49. Ibid., p. 143. Compare Walzer's claim that in irregular war, "the guerrillas have to discriminate, if only to prove that they are really soldiers (and not enemies) of the people." *Just and Unjust Wars*, p. 180.

50. James Turner Johnson, "Why We Shouldn't Assassinate Muammar Qaddafi," *The Washington Post*, April 20, 1986, pp. C1, C2.

51. See James F. Childress, *Moral Responsibility in Conflicts* (Baton Rouge, Louisiana State University Press, 1982), pp. 107, 151.

52. Ibid., pp. 132, 151.

53. *General Orders, No. 100*, §IX.148. One hundred and twenty-five years later, Western nations would respond precisely this way to the order by the late Ayatollah Khomeini to assassinate Salman Rushdie, author of *The Satanic Verses*. For discussion in this collection of Khomeini's thought on war and revolution, see Ann Elizabeth Mayer, "War and Peace in the Islamic Tradition and International Law," in *Just War and Jihad*, Kelsay and Johnson, eds, *Supra* note 45.

54. Fotion and Elfstrom, *Military Ethics*, p. 220; Walzer, *Just and Unjust Wars*, p. 202.

55. Walzer, *Just and Unjust Wars*, pp. 201–03.

56. This approach to addressing terrorism as part of irregular war was sug-

gested to me by Walzer's comment that defenses of terrorism (which he believes all fail) "represent one or another version of the argument from military necessity." See *Just and Unjust Wars*, pp. 203–04.

57. "Freedom Struggle by the Provisional IRA," in *The Terrorism Reader*, Walter Lacqueur, ed. (Philadelphia: Temple University Press, 1978), pp. 132–34.

58. David C. Rapoport and Yonah Alexander, eds., *The Mortality of Terrorism* (New York: Pergamon Press, 1982), p. xiii.

59. John Locke, *Two Treatises*, ¶16, *Supra* note 24. Compare Locke's discussion at ¶11, 172, 182, 230.

60. "Ulster: The Counter Terror," in *The Terrorism Reader*, pp. 134–37.

61. Camus, *The Rebel*, p. 173.

62. Johnson, *Can Modern War Be Just?*, p. 63.

63. See especially the arguments presented by Jon P. Gunnemann in *The Moral Meaning of Revolution* (New Haven: Yale University Press, 1979), pp. 1–50, and Jon P. Gunnemann, "Revolution," in *The Westminster Dictionary of Christian Ethics*, 2d ed., James F. Childress and John Macquarrie, eds. (Philadelphia: Westminster Press), pp. 550–51.

# 6

## Irregular Warfare and Terrorism in Islam: Asking the Right Questions

*Tamara Sonn*

### OVERVIEW

Irregular warfare and terrorism, as those terms are commonly understood, are almost uniformly condemned in Islamic literature, both classical and contemporary. Yet both seem to figure highly in comtemporary
developments in the Islamic world. The purpose of this chapter is to
examine the relationship between Islamic judgments and these forms
of action.

The first task is to gain some historical understanding of the general
tendency to condemn rebellion against established Islamic governments.
In effect, one finds that Islamic law, formulated in an age of religiously
legitimated governments suitable to the socio-economic milieu of the
early medieval world, gave full legitimation to only one type of warfare—
the *jihad*—and that this type is by definition a war waged against non-
Muslims and apostates. This stands in contrast to the context in which
contemporary Muslims must address questions of war and statecraft.
The historical processes associated with modernization or secularization
indicate that the centrally organized, expansive, or imperialist, structure
characteristic of religiously legitimated governments tends to give way
to the geographically limited structures of nation-states. This development is still in process in the Islamic world. And, just as in Europe,
where such processes were accompanied by an age of religious warfare–
an age which saw, at the same time, the birth of nationalism—the transformation is taking centuries. An understanding of these processes is
essentially in discussing the current recourse to irregular warfare and
terrorism within a cultural tradition that generally condemns such
activities.

This chapter discusses specific examples of revolutionary activity within Islam and examines the response of official Islam in both the classical and contemporary periods. Such examples indicate that instances of zealot or extremist activity have their place in the Islamic world, particularly during periods of radical socio-political and economic change. The examples also show that there is often popular support among Muslims for the expressed motives of revolutionary movements. Nevertheless, terrorist activity remains opposed to both the spirit and the letter of Islam.

## THE HISTORICAL CONTEXT OF THEORIES OF WARFARE

There is a famous story about a king who asked his wise men to explain to him why the weight of a pail of water with fish in it is less than the combined weight of the fish and the pail of water, weighed separately. After some time the sages returned to the king with many and varied explanations of the phenomenon—none of which was accurate, of course. The weight of a pail of water with fish in it is exactly the same as the combined weight of the pail of water and fish, weighed separately. The point of the story is that if you ask the wrong question, you will most likely get the wrong answer.

The point is well taken in the present discussion of theories of irregular warfare and terrorism in Islam. As those terms are generally understood, the Islamic tradition by and large judges them negatively. Yet no one can deny that instances of irregular warfare and terrorism play an important part in contemporary developments in the Islamic world. The question to ask, then, is why? What is it about the contemporary Islamic world that can explain this tension—a normative reluctance to approve irregular warfare and terrorism, coupled with a practical engagement in those activities. The answer lies in an understanding of the history of Islam, particularly as it relates to the process of modernization or secularization.

Broadly speaking, irregular warfare may be described as war waged outside the guidelines formulated and/or accepted by established governments. Similarly, terrorism may be described as the attempt to achieve political or other goals through the creation of fear, especially by means of acts of violence that target nonmilitary personnel, or which make use of assassinations, kidnapping, and the like. Concern with such actions is hardly a modern phenomenon. Yet contemporary discussions of irregular warfare and terrorism presume a particular socio-political context.

Historian Joseph Strayer provides an appropriate description of this context when he notes that "modern" Europe begins with the age of nationalism. This age began when geographically limited states began to replace the potentially universal Church as the community of people's highest allegiance.[1] The process may be summarized as follows. The development of the modern European state occurred in conjunction with a separation of religious and political spheres of authority. This was in part motivated by the need for religious institutions to maintain their sanctity in a world governed by power politics and also their universality in a world of geographically limited states. In a world of (theoretically) universal nations, the union of religion and politics had been natural and appropriate. But when changing economic factors made it impractical to maintain the centralized administrations of the great imperial states, religion (and religious institutions) necessarily became detached from political power. The process of modernization (or secularization, or decentralization) began with the decline of the Roman Empire, continued throughout the feudal period, and culminated in the later Middle Ages with the Reformation and the Enlightenment. The modernization of Europe took over five hundred chaotic, war-filled years, from the erosion of imperial political and economic foundations in the tenth and eleventh centuries to the final relinquishing of power by the Holy Roman emperor in the sixteenth and seventeenth centuries.

By comparison, the Islamic Empire, begun in the seventh century, experienced a similar process, but with considerable chronological differences. One might say that the process is still ongoing. For Islam, modernization began in the tenth and eleventh centuries c.e., when regional powers began to exercise virtually autonomous control over limited areas of the central caliphate's domain. The economic basis of the Iraqi-based Abbasid caliphate had begun to erode, and from the mid-ninth century to the end of the dynasty in 1258, the Abbasid caliphs were almost entirely dependent upon the imperial guards (the *mamluks*), whose concerns were generally regional rather than universal. As local or regional potentates became economically and militarily independent, it became possible and desirable for them to declare political independence as well.

In a culture where political legitimacy depended on religious factors, this presented serious problems. From the Sunni point of view, the universality of the Abbasid caliphate was supported by religious warrants, and the claims of regional governors to independence was tantamount to heresy. In this less than ideal situation, the scholars of Islamic law were forced to adapt their theories to continually changing realities. Not least of these was the impact of several invasions. Coming at a time when the old system no longer had the resources to enforce Islamic unity or to muster a coordinated defense against invaders, the Crusades and the Mongol invasions reinforced the trend toward decentralization. From this time on, the Islamic world fell victim to foreign domination— even as the European nations regrouped and gained sufficient strength to exploit what would become the Third World. Finally, the Islamic lands fell under Ottoman Turkish control in the fifteenth and sixteenth centuries. The Ottoman willingness to cooperate with the scholars of the law and the scholars' desire to foster unity, led to a modus vivendi in which the Ottoman ruler received religious legitimation as the caliph. The final incursion of foreign power came with effective European control of the region following the abolition of the Ottoman caliphate in 1924. In the latter half of the twentieth century, the traditionally Islamic lands have witnessed a struggle for independence that is, in one sense, a part of the struggle of Muslims to be free from foreign domination that began in the thirteenth century. In another sense, the struggle is to come to grips with the historical phenomenon of decentralization in the Islamic world.

The current instability of governments in the Islamic Middle East in particular represents the final stages of decentralization. Above and beyond the turmoil caused by colonial interventions (for example, the partitioning of Syria and the creation of the states of Lebanon and Israel) the existing governments in this region are struggling to establish their legitimacy within the context of a religious tradition that still conceives of politics in terms of the ideal of a universal Islamic state. The conflict is between social and economic realities that favor nation-states and a religious tradition that thinks of a single, centralized government for the entire region. Although the various nation-states in this territory are the creation of the European powers, they have become sovereign political units with governments that have a vested interest in the status quo. These governments are now in a very delicate position. They must condemn the colonial interventions that brought them to power and present themselves as the upholders of Islam. Yet they cannot implement the Islamic ideal of a single, expansive state with one religiously sanctioned ruler. To do so would involve dismantling over a dozen states, ranging from North Africa to Central Asia. It would also involve arranging the abdication of several very determined leaders. As the failure of the United Arab Republic showed, such abdications are very unlikely. These difficulties weaken the claims of existing governments to Islamic legitimacy; this invites criticism of the governments, which in turn breeds repressive responses. All this is in the context of underdevelopment, widespread illiteracy, and the obvious difficulties attached to the political life of populations characterized by a vast gap between an educated ruling minority and a disenfranchised majority.

Clearly this is a situation that breeds instability within and among states. The contemporary resurgence or repoliticization of Islam can be seen as a reflection, in this context, of the struggle for stability in the new nation-states. On the one hand, the popularity of Islamic movements reflects the alienation of the general populace from the political culture of the established governments. The alienated public suffers from the underdevelopment and instability of the region, the causes of which it does not understand. This population does, however, understand that various leaders have espoused nationalism and secularism and it knows that neither has brought relief. It also regards the West as responsible for stifling hopes for a revitalized, unified Islamic nation, and it believes that the West and its collaborators continue to wage undeclared war in the region—for example, by supporting Zionist and Maronite governments that are widely viewed as illegitimate. It follows naturally that nationalism and secularism, as ideas connected with the West, are evaluated as sinister by large portions of the general Muslim populace and that Islam is understood as the sole hope for victory.

On the other hand, popular support for Islamic movements affects the established regimes—they too must accept the repoliticization of Islam, at least as a way to muster popular support. Even the avowedly secular leadership of Iraq and Syria speaks in Islamic vocabulary and carefully cultivates Islamic support.

From the standpoint of historical analysis, the contemporary repoliticization of Islam represents a last, desperate attempt to prevent the separation of religion and politics.[2] An awareness of contemporary socioeconomic realities suggests that the formation of nation-states is a reality with which the Islamic world will have to contend. Yet Islamic political theory does not as yet reflect any consensus on this issue.

## THE ISLAMIC TRADITION AGAINST REVOLUTION

Of course, there are a number of Islamic thinkers who have made efforts to address the questions raised for their tradition by the existence of contemporary nation-states. But as yet there is no generally accepted theory by which Muslims may approve such states. The central problem has to do with geopolitical boundaries: the Islamic tradition approved a universal political institution, a judgment that flowed from the universal tendencies of the religion. The limited boundaries of modern nation-states contradict this judgment and suggest that the only realistic approach for religious thought is to separate religion and politics, maintaining universality for the former while accepting that the latter is a sphere for more limited claims.

To this point, official Sunni theory has not developed past the stage of condemning revolution against an Islamic government, namely, the caliphate. It has not ever recognized the legitimacy of a geographically limited state. Even in the days of the Abbasid decline, when territorial governors assumed practical independence from the central regime, Sunni theorists only counted as legitimate those governors who maintained a nominal relationship with the caliphate. Those who declared themselves sovereign authorities were classified as heretics. Classic Sunni political thought recognized only one ultimate source of political legitimacy: religion. The religion in question being universal, there could only be one legitimate political power.

It may be granted that the caliph was not always an ideal ruler and that he was not always able to sustain his universal claims. For example, the Abbasid Caliph al-Ta'i' (974–91 C.E.) was forced to crown the Buyid leader Abud al-Dawla (949–83) *sultan* (ruler) in Iran. Nevertheless, the aura of Sunni legitimacy was retained. When the Seljuq Turks took over in Iran in the eleventh century, they retained the ceremony of caliphal investiture of the territorial *sultan*. The Seljuqs paid lip service to the caliph for the sake of political legitimacy; the weakened caliph actually had little choice but to recognize them. From the standpoint of the religious scholars, however, this was enough to preserve the universality of the Islamic community. A territorial ruler recognized by the caliph was legitimate, even if the relation was purely formal. According to al-Mawardi (d. 1058 C.E.), even a usurper must be obeyed, so long as he formally recognizes the authority of the caliph.[3] And according to Abu Yusuf (d. 798 C.E.), even undesirable rulers must be accepted:

If [the rulers] act badly, sin weighs on them and you are obliged to be patient. They are the scourge with which God afflicts whom he wants to afflict. Do not oppose this affliction with wrath and indignation but accept it with meekness.[4]

There was at least one voice of opposition among the official Sunni scholars, however. The renowned Hanbali jurist Ibn Taymiyya (d. 1328) addressed the disparity between the theoretical unity of the Islamic empire and its fragmented reality. He interpreted the weakness and disunity of the empire as the result of laxity in religious practice. Such laxity had, he argued, allowed incursions by Christians and Mongols, which had ruined Islamic unity. However, Ibn Taymiyya's notion of Islamic unity differed from the traditional view. For the Hanbali scholar, the unity of Islam lay primarily in a unity of doctrine rather than politics. Within the limits of true doctrine there can be a certain amount of diversity—for example, there have evolved four recognized schools of jurisprudence. But all schools must be united in encouraging goodness and denouncing iniquity. The ideal Muslim community is characterized by the mutual support of believers for just behavior, including the offer of correction when necessary. Within such unity it is acceptable for believers to vary on details.

This emphasis on doctrinal unity allowed Ibn Taymiyya to deviate from the pattern of most Sunni jurists and to justify the reality of political diversity within the Islamic empire. He did not condemn those who failed to offer formal submission to caliphal authority, although he did condemn active revolution against an Islamic government. Ibn Taymiyya's relegation of Islamic political unity to secondary importance was revolutionary. It was an attempt to accommodate the seemingly ineluctable forces of political decentralization without losing the essential characteristics of Islamic society.[5]

Unfortunately, Ibn Taymiyya's approach was not accepted. The forces resisting reform prevailed, and the Islamic world slipped into an age of stagnation that left it open to foreign exploitation—an age from which it is only now emerging. Since the eighteenth century various movements have attempted to understand and revive the moral strength of which Ibn Taymiyya spoke so forcefully. And the modern Islamic revivalist movements almost unanimously call Ibn Taymiyya the father of modern Islam. Even so, it is his call to Islamic solidarity, to a return to true Islam, that excites modern Muslims—not his concern with the separation of religious from political spheres of authority. The corpus of Islamic religious law still recognizes only the legitimacy of a single, universal Islamic ruler. And just as in the days of Ibn Taymiyya, revolution against such a ruler is condemned. There is, then, considerable weight in the Islamic tradition against any revolution or refusal to submit to an established, centralized Islamic authority.

## REVOLUTION IN THE ISLAMIC TRADITION

Nevertheless, there have been (and are) revolutionary movements in Islam. And they have found, or thought themselves to have found, Islamic justifications for their actions. Despairing of the established powers' ability or will to enforce a truly Islamic program, such groups have determined to undertake the task themselves and have rationalized the use of violence against other Muslims. I shall discuss two such groups: the Kharijis (al-Khawarij) and the Nizari Isma'ilis (the infamous "Assassins").

The Kharijis were the first Muslim dissidents, their origins dating to the third decade of the Islamic calendar (i.e., 660s c.e.). The group included those who insisted that the leadership of the Islamic community should be by members of the Prophet's family (i.e., the early Shi'a) and also those who stressed simply that the leader should be a pious Muslim. The latter view made the Kharijis attractive to those whose status or ethnic origin placed them outside the circle of power in the early Islamic community—for example, non-Arabs and women. According to the Kharijis, piety rather than status was the factor that differentiated persons in Islam. Although very little is known of Khariji beliefs apart from the allegations of later Muslim heresiographers (who actually employed the label for a number of groups), it does seem possible to say that the group agreed that deviation from the norms established by the Prophet

was intolerable. Anyone who disagreed was declared an apostate. This
was so whether "disagreement" was active (demonstrated through inappropriate behavior) or passive (demonstrated by a refusal to condemn
those engaging in inappropriate behavior).

The Kharijis became known for the ferocity of their tactics. Whether
out of conviction or a feeling that they had little to lose, various groups
labeled as Kharijis sowed terror throughout the Islamic world for nearly
a century. They organized in small bands, struck quickly and without
warning, and practiced assassination without regard for age or gender.
Such tactics were justified in their view by the conviction that true religion demanded absolute rectitude, and that it was the responsibility
of true believers to excise impure persons from the Islamic community.
As opposed to mainstream Sunni doctrine, the Kharijis argued that right
belief was insufficient as a criterion to distinguish Muslims from non-
Muslims. Right action was also required. Anyone who claimed to be a
Muslim but committed forbidden acts forfeited that claim. Further, the
Khariji groups believed such a person could never reenter Islam and
should therefore be killed along with his immediate family.[6]

The term used by the Kharijis to describe such killing in legal discussion was *isti'rad*, "religious execution." Originally the term implied in-
terrogation or inquisition regarding one's religious beliefs, but since
those subjected to it were usually found guilty of behavior unbecoming
to a Muslim and put to death, the term came to include killing.[7] Again,
records indicate this included women and children, and willingness to
participate in *isti'rad* seems to have been a criterion for testing the sin-
cerity of Khariji recruits.

Similarly famous for ferocity were the Nizari Isma'ilis, specifically the
Syrian branch of the Isma'ili movement, known as the Hashishin (corrupted to English "assassin"). The Isma'ilis were a group of diverse
subsects of Shi'i Islam who split with other branches over questions of
leadership in the mid-eighth century. At first they seem to have been a
relatively cohesive group, but the leadership disputes that distinguished
them from other Shi'i groups continued within the Isma'ili movement
and led to further splits. The general Isma'ili orientation toward the
esoteric conveyance of truth through divinely chosen savants did little
to promote doctrinal continuity. Antirevolutionary measures taken by
the central Abbasid caliphate in the tenth century drove the group un-
derground, resulting in further splintering. As a result there is little
reliable information concerning later developments.

The Nizari Isma'ilis were particularly active in Persia during the eleventh century. Under the leadership of Hasan-i-Sabbah they established
a series of mountain fortresses and carried on revolutionary activities
against the Seljuq rulers. They became famous for their use of assassination. The Persian Nizaris gained a following in Syria (and also in

Egypt, though the Fatimid Isma'ili rulers there held the group in check). By the twelfth century there were reports of similar tactics being used by Muslim groups, particularly against the Crusaders. The Syrian Nizaris seem to have developed relatively independently, separated by distance and language barriers from other Nizari groups. They are the ones who came to be called Hashishin, most probably as a term of derision. There is little evidence that their behavior resulted from the use of hashish, although that is the story brought back to Europe by the Crusaders.[8]

Like the Kharijis, the Nizari Isma'ilis were intent on religious reform. Their view of Islam prevented them from accepting the form of leadership practiced by the caliphs and their *sultans*. Unlike the Kharijis, they did not take it upon themselves to punish personal transgressions; instead, their assassinations were directed against political and religious leaders. They seemed to believe that, once freed of less than righteous leadership, the Muslim community would turn toward true belief. But they were wrong. Instead, they (and the Kharijis) encountered widespread resentment and condemnation, for at least two reasons.

In the first place, the spirit of Islam holds that human life is sacred. This is consistent with its Arab heritage. In the pre-Islamic period, raiding was common. But the deliberate and unjust taking of human life was forbidden, even in the context of such raids. Anyone who took life without cause was subject to a harsh vengeance, which put not only the killer but his family in jeopardy. The stakes for unjust killing were therefore quite high, reflecting Maxime Rodinson's judgment of Arab ethics: "Man was the highest value for man."[9] It is true, as Rodinson continues, that this concern for life was limited by considerations of tribe or clan. It was one of the chief accomplishments of Islam that it introduced a universalizing tendency into Arab ethics. Islam thus extended concern about unjust killing by inculcating concern for human life as such. Therefore, the Khariji and Isma'ili tactics went against the mores of Arab society and Islamic belief regarding the sanctity of human life.

Beyond that, the result of such tactics was to destablize the general community. This was so even with the Nizaris, whose assassinations were in some sense discriminate:

The assassinations [by the Nizaris] were aimed at single prominent enemies who caused them special damage (or at turncoats) and were seemingly calculated to avoid bloodshed among ordinary people, whose champions, in the name of justice, the Isma'ilis felt themselves to be . . . . The Isma'ili assassinations were made as public and dramatic as possible, as warnings, and zealous Isma'ili youths gladly sacrificed their lives in such acts.[10]

Still, the Nizari campaigns sowed terror among the general populace, who had no way of knowing the rebels' pious motives. The caliph and the territorial governors were therefore able to muster sufficient support to defeat the dissidents. As Hodgson concludes, "Perhaps the chief political result of the Isma'ili revolt . . . was to discredit the Shi'i opposition generally, and to assure the allegiance of moderate men, even of Twelver Shi'is, to the amirs [established rulers] and the Jama'i-Sunni society they maintained."[11]

As these examples demonstrate, instances of revolutionary behavior involving assassinations and other "irregular" tactics, while obviously present in the Islamic tradition, were not usually supported by the Muslim community at large. They were deviations from the accepted norms. Fazlur Rahman claims that the general antirevolutionary tendency of Islamic law is a direct result of the terror sown by Khariji activity in the first century of Islam.[12] This was reinforced during the various Isma'ili revolts and is reflected in the rejection of Ibn Taymiyya's views on the Islamic state. On the other hand, the existence of such groups as the Kharijis, and even more so the Nizaris, was a reflection of changing historical conditions, in particular the pressure toward decentralization. Had it not been for the cumulative effect of the Crusaders' and the Mongols' invasions, the domination of the Islamic territories by the Ottoman Turks, and European imperialism, it seems probable that the Islamic world would have developed geographically limited states, with some appropriate mechanism to confer political legitimacy. In any event, there is no doubt that the present turmoil in the traditionally Islamic lands, and the emphasis on revolution and irregular tactics, is an indication that the Islamic world has resumed its struggle to develop effective political structures.

## THE CONTEMPORARY CONTEXT

The first rumblings of modern Islamic discontent were connected with the Wahhabi movement in Arabia during the eighteenth century. Not surprisingly, Ibn Taymiyyah provided the inspiration for the movement, whose idea was to restore true Islam as the basis of social solidarity and, as a consequence, political strength. But the impact of the Wahhabis was limited to the Arabian peninsula—at least until the turn of the present century, when it became clear that Ottoman control of the Islamic lands was weakening, and Arab desires for independence began to assert themselves.

Such thinkers as Tahtawi (1801–73), al-Afghani (1839–97), and Muhammad Abduh (1849–1905) had begun to lay the foundation for an Islamic theory of the nation-state, particularly insofar as they implied that a particular populace should judge the legitimacy of its political leadership. To this they added the provision that the judgment concerning political order belonged to the people as a unit, without regard to distinct religious affiliations. A negative judgment by the citizens of a state would become the instrument for alterations in political authority—even, the basis for notions of just revolution. Again, however, the development of such ideas was stifled—this time by European imperialism. In the turmoil that followed the First World War, the European division of the Islamic lands created an opportunity for some Muslim theorists to develop further the theories of popular sovereignty advocated by Abduh and others. Ali Abd al-Raziq (1888–1966), for example, argued for a secular political order. Abd al-Raziq's revisionist thought received little support, however. Given the fact of European hegemony, popular sentiment mitigated against a change in traditional Islamic theory and favored instead the argument of those advocating a rejection of foreign influence in favor of traditional Islam. Notions of a return to "pure Islam" became the order of the day, especially as articulated by the Muslim Brothers' spokesman Hasan al-Banna' during the mid to late 1920s. In recent years (i.e., since the disastrous defeat of Arab forces in the 1967 war with Israel), this tendency has accelerated, the desire being to develop a kind of Islamic self-sufficiency.

In this context the various forms familiar to modern politics (nationalism, secularism, and the like) are viewed as foreign and devoid of religious or moral value. The goal of Islamic movements in the Middle East is to reinstate Islamic models in the region, some movements going so far as to call for a dismantling of the boundaries between existing states. For example, the 1985 Muslim Institute Conference asserted that

modern nationalism is a peculiar product of western political development and has been introduced to the lands and people of Islam through colonialism. . . . [T]he major goal of the ummah in the next phase of history is to abolish and dismantle the nation-states that now govern the Muslim areas of the world and to create a unified dar al-Islam.[13]

Yet there remain strong antirevolutionary tendencies in Islamic thought, leading one scholar to claim that the Islamic tradition has a "clear tendency toward an almost unconditional submission to the authorities, a theologically justified quietism."[14] Given such a tendency, it has proven difficult to develop approved means for alterations in political order. Thus the Islamic world—in the throes of socio-economic and political developments—is in turmoil. Some people and groups within this world resist revolution, while others foment it. All the while, massive change in social structures is the rule for almost every part of the Islamic world. This is the context for developing an understanding of the renewed interest of Muslims in *jihad*, the symbol of approved warfare in Islam.

## REVIVING AND REVISING *JIHAD*

A glance at the names of contemporary revolutionary groups in the Middle East reveals that there is currently a surge of interest in *jihad* as a possible justification for antiestablishment activity. Consider the following list: al-Jihad ("The Struggle"), Junud al-Rahman ("Soldiers of the Merciful"), Munazzamat al-Jihad ("Jihad Organization"), Talia al-Muqatila li'l-Mujahidin ("Combat Vanguard of Fighters"), Mujahidin ("Strugglers"), and Jihad al-Islami ("Islamic Struggle"). During the early part of this century, there was little attention paid to *jihad*, and when the issue was addressed it was in a tone very different from that used by today's movements. At the turn of this century *jihad* was officially described as war fought in self-defense against attacks by non-Muslim states. The stress was on *jihad* as effort, the supreme struggle to spread the religion of God. According to this line of thought *jihad* goes far beyond military efforts. Teaching and exemplary personal conduct are at least as important as military means of struggle. And *jihad* as warfare can be justified only as a last resort, as a response to external military attack.[15]

Contemporary Islamic revivalists, by contrast, have revived the *jihad* of the high caliphal period. Hasan al-Banna', founder of the Muslim Brotherhood, provided an early example of contemporary thinking when he attacked the notion that there was a "spiritual" *jihad* that should be considered superior to the military one. Hasan al-Banna' argued that the popular tradition depicting Muhammad saying upon his return from a raid that he and his companions had "returned from the lesser *jihad* to the greater *jihad*," i.e. to the struggle for self-control, should not be considered authentic, since it is not found in the authoritative collections of *ahadith* (reports concerning the Prophet's words and deeds). According to al-Banna' this report had been spread in a deliberate attempt to weaken the will of Muslims in the struggle against European colonizers.[16] Sayyid Qutb (1906–66), al-Banna''s ideological successor, furthered this argument, reminding Muslims that the Qur'an enjoins them to "establish the kingdom of God on earth and bring all humanity from the worship of created things to the worship of God alone."[17] Muslims must fight until they regain political dominance, he says, reminding them of the Qur'anic words: "God has promised those of you who believe and do good works that he will make you his viceregents on earth as he has made others before you. He will surely establish for them their religion . . . and exchange their fear for security." (24:55) That is, Islam must be reestablished as the sole basis of political legitimacy. Until Islamic governments are established, Muslims must take up the struggle to change the status quo:

Islam . . . has to deliver blows at the political forces that make men the slaves of something that is not God, i.e., that do not rule them according to Islamic law and the authority of God, those forces that prevent them from hearing the elucidation and from freely embracing the creed, without being hindered by any authority.[18]

Abu'l A'la Mawdudi, Pakistani founder and chief ideologue of the "Islamic party" (*Jama'at-i Islami*) agrees. Islam, he says, "is an all-embracing order that wants to eliminate and eradicate the other orders which are false and unjust so as to replace them with a good order and a moderate program that is considered to be better for humanity than [all] others."[19] The Islamic order, "a practical program," must be made "victorious" throughout the world, "irrespective of who carries the banner of truth and justice or whose flag of aggression and corruption is thereby toppled. Islam wants the whole earth and does not content itself with only a part thereof."[20] In order to achieve this "lofty desire," Islam has established and demands *jihad*:

Islam wants to employ all forces and means that can be employed for bringing about a universal, all-embracing revolution. It will spare no efforts for the achievement of this supreme objective. This far-reaching struggle that continuously exhausts all forces and this employment of all possible means are called jihad.[21]

For Mawdudi, as for Sayyid Qutb, Islam demands *jihad* to relieve the world of its miserable condition. But the key point for this discussion is that they imply that *jihad* applies to all unjust rulers—even those who claim to be Muslims. This was in fact the justification used by Anwar Sadat's assassins, who declared: "To the leaders of Islamic groups today: Kill every leader who looks for fame, wealth, power, and social station."[22] This was despite Sadat's conspicuous displays of Muslim piety.

Ayatollah Khomeini sounded the same theme in his program of revolutionary Islam. Expounding at length on the West's exploitation of the Third World, he called upon all Muslims, and especially religious scholars, to struggle against Western domination. This effort is the "sacred jihad."[23] For Khomeini, *jihad* means overthrowing "Muslim" rulers:

Give the people Islam, then, for Islam is the school of jihad, the religion of struggle; let them amend their characters and beliefs in accordance with Islam, and transform themselves into a powerful force, so that they may overthrow the tyrannical regime imperialism has imposed on us and set up an Islamic government.[24]

To further support his position, Khomeini pronounced a series of legal opinions dealing with revolutionary activities. For example, he said that if the evil [that is to be prevented] is of a kind accorded great importance by the Sacred Legislator, one that he in no wise wishes to occur, it is permissible to prevent it by any means possible. If someone wishes to kill another, for example, in the absence of legal justification, he must be prevented. If the killing of the wronged party cannot be prevented except by killing the wrongdoer, then it is permissible, even necessary to do so.[25]

And he specifically included leaders of Muslim countries as prime candidates for this action: "If certain heads of state of Muslim countries . . . permit foreigners to expand their influence . . . they automatically forfeit their posts. . . . Furthermore, it is the duty of the Muslims to punish them by any means possible."[26]

## ISLAMIC REJECTION OF EXTREMISM

The growth of revolutionary rhetoric is a significant development within a religious tradition that is generally conservative. It is in opposition to the spirit of Islam, which holds human life sacred and personal culpability a matter for God alone to determine. There is no denying that there is broad sympathy in traditionally Islamic lands for calls to revive the tradition as a political force or for contemporary interpretations of *jihad* as a struggle to establish an Islamic state. Yet it would be a mistake to equate such sympathy with a general acceptance of terrorism or irregular tactics. Despite the undeniable personal charisma of some revolutionary leaders, terrorist tactics are condemned by scholars of Islamic religious law and are generally viewed by Muslims as repugnant.

Consider the response to the assassination of Anwar Sadat. There can be no doubt that Sadat's popular support faded (almost to the point of oblivion) in the wake of the Camp David Accords and the continuing economic and social problems of Egypt. Yet the act of assassination was condemned by al-Azhar, the institution representing "official" Islam in Egypt. Considering the fact that al-Azhar has been publishing opinions dealing with *jihad*, sometimes even with positive references to the military of the Isma'ilis since the beginning of Nasser's regime (1952), it might be expected that the legal opinions of the institution's scholars would reflect sympathy with the revolutionaries.[27] Yet al-Azhar has also condemned dissension among believers and socially disruptive behavior. The tendency of the institution has been to praise the perseverance of activists, but to warn that actions leading to public disorder are dangerous and even sinful.[28] Domestic conflict, whether among Muslims or between Muslim and non-Muslim Egyptians, is rejected. Truly Islamic behavior is said to promote social order, not to undermine it.[29]

In response to the assassination of Sadat, al-Azhar did not condemn activism. Instead it mourned the confusion of zealous believers. Just after the assassination, an editorial in al-Azhar's official journal condemned extremism and argued that it was a mistaken interpretation of *jihad* that connected it with the attempt to destroy society.[30] As the source of official Islam, al-Azhar seemed to take responsibility for the confusion. It set up new committees of leading Muslim scholars that were to be dedicated to "correction and elucidation of the interpretations of certain traditions which certain persons have attempted to exploit by incorrect explanations."[31]

Following these initial responses, the rector of al-Azhar, Shaykh Jadd al-Haqq, issued a detailed refutation of the assassins' self-justification (issued in a pamphlet entitled "The Neglected Duty.")[32] Shaykh al-Haqq began by restating the traditional Islamic position on apostasy. The assassins believed they could judge Sadat as an apostate and that he therefore deserved death. But the Shaykh argued that a Muslim becomes apostate only if he or she renounces monotheism. In support of this position, he quoted the Qur'an (4:116): "God will not forgive the association of anything with Himself, though He forgives anything short of that."[33] In particular, calling a professed Muslim an apostate is forbidden. The Shaykh argued that killing the leader of an Islamic country cannot be a part of *jihad*, even if that leader be a tyrant. Sadat's assassins had presented Qur'anic verses that they interpreted as calling for tyrannicide. But the Shaykh countered with a reiteration of the traditional prohibition of such an act in Islamic law, a prohibition that is especially strong in the case of a leader who is a practicing Muslim. "How can anyone legalize . . . the murder of a Muslim who prays, pays religious taxes, and recites the Qur'an?"[34] In conclusion, Shaykh al-Haqq claimed that the assassins' "Testament" cannot be considered a religious document. Instead, it is an incitement to social disorder and must be considered as nothing more than a misguided political manifesto. He compared the assassins to the Kharijis, whose conviction that sin renders one an apostate deserving of the death penalty served no purpose but to destroy the Islamic community.

There are those who believe that the Azhar scholars' position in Egypt compromises their objectivity, and that they are subsequently not free to speak their minds. Yet Shaykh al-Haqq's articulation of Islamic principles is authoritative and based on well-established interpretations of Islamic sources. His position was generally supported throughout the Islamic world despite Sadat's unpopularity and the widespread sympathy with the assassins' desire for strong and pious leadership.

The isolation of national leaders who openly advocate revolution is another indication of mainstream Islamic sentiment against terrorism and irregular tactics. Col. Muammar Qaddafi of Libya, for example, bases his claims to legitimacy on the interpretation of Islam contained in the three volumes of his *Green Book*. There he specifically states that, although his theory is based on religious and nationalist ideas, it is "an international ideology, not a national movement."[35] Qaddafi's meaning is that any national entity has the right to establish its own political and religious identity. For that reason he supports revolutionary movements around the world. Nevertheless, his own claims to Islamic purity are a form of religious legitimacy and are (understandably) considered a threat by other leaders in the Islamic world. If Qaddafi is a true Islamic leader, then by implication, they are not. The colonel's operations in Egypt, the Sudan, and Chad are therefore taken as convincing evidence of Qaddafi's expansionist plans. As a result, Qaddafi is considered a destabilizing element in the Islamic world. The failure on the part of Islamic leaders to come to his aid when the United States launched its attack in 1986 is itself evidence of the unpopularity of his revolutionary rhetoric.

The response of the Arab League to the Ayatollah Khomeini is if anything even more revealing. At the November 1987 Amman Summit the Arab League, for the first time in its history, did not focus on Palestine and did not identify Israel as the major threat in the region. Instead, the league turned its attention to Iran and the threat of revolution emanating from the Islamic republic. The league denounced the "bloody and criminal acts perpetrated by the Iranians" in Mecca during the summer of 1987. In July and August, Iranian pilgrims had begun a demonstration during the annual pilgrimage; the demonstration turned into a riot which lasted several days. Iranian pilgrims carried pictures of Khomeini, demonstrated against the United States and Israel, and burned effigies of Ronald Reagan, despite the traditional injunction against political activity and violence of any sort during the pilgrimage and the prohibition of religious images. When the Saudi security forces attempted to suppress the demonstration, violence erupted. Operating on an order of Khomeini entitled "Charter for Revolution," the "splendid demonstration" of the Iranian pilgrims resulted in over 400 deaths and 650 injuries. When the leaders of the demonstration were arrested, they informed the Saudi forces that the Ayatollah had called on his followers to rally in Mecca and to demonstrate their "deliverance from infidels." Khomeini had told them, they said, that pilgrims should "not refrain from giving expression to their hatred of the enemies of God and man." More distressing still to the Arab leaders, the leaders of the demonstration declared that their goal was to make the Ayatollah Khomeini the leader of all Muslims.[36] This, combined with heightened activity by Iranian revolutionaries throughout the region, led to the pronouncement by the Arab League.

There is no question about the popularity of contemporary Islamic movements. The Muslim Brotherhood, for example, has become a part of the mainstream in Egypt. Its members act openly, leading the parliamentary opposition to Husni Mubarak's ruling National Democratic Party. They reportedly receive regular support from the region's most conservative nation, Saudi Arabia. Yet it is important that the Brotherhood has ceased to call for violent revolution; Brotherhood representatives even joined in the denunciation of Sadat's assassins. The groups that practice terrorism, on the other hand, have relatively low membership. Their motivations are respected, but their tactics are considered by many to be unacceptable.

## CONCLUSION

It is difficult to find support for the use of irregular or terrorist tactics in the Islamic tradition. Both are condemned under the rubric of Islam's general reticence concerning revolution, its respect for life, and its insistence that God has exclusive rights in judging the piety of believers. There have certainly been instances of revolutionary, even irregular activity in Islamic history, especially during periods of adjustment or when the leadership of the community has been particularly decadent or tyrannical. Many Muslims have supported condemnations of impiety and calls for a revival of authentic Islam. Yet irregular and terrorist tactics have generally been rejected in Islamic religious law and by Islamic popular opinion.

However, the contemporary revival of interest in *jihad* provides a unique opportunity to understand the dynamic of development in the Islamic world. It is true that there is a spirit of revolution—in the sense of social and moral change—at the heart of the Islamic message. That sense of mission is what gave Islam its initial success; its dissipation no doubt contributed to stagnation in the Islamic world, while the revival of that sense is the goal of contemporary Islamic movements. The revival of a sense of mission is not, however, to be equated with terrorism or irregular tactics in armed revolutions. Instead, such revival is the shibboleth of those committed to revitalizing the political, economic, social, moral, and general cultural strength of the classical Islamic world, in forms compatible with contemporary realities. When that process has been completed and stability returns to the Islamic world, no doubt *jihad*'s more militant connotations will lose their pride of place.

## NOTES

1. Joseph Strayer, "The Historical Experience of Nation-Building in Europe," in *Nation Building*, ed. Karl W. Deutsch and William J. Foltz (New York: Atherton Press, 1963), p. 22.

2. For a complete discussion see Tamara Sonn, *Between Qur'an and Crown: The Challenge of Political Legitimacy in the Arab World* (Boulder, CO and London: Westview Press, 1990).

3. In his *al-Ahkam al-Sultaniyya*. This position is also affirmed by al-Ghazali (d. 1111); see the discussion in Gerhard Endress, *An Introduction to Islam*, trans. Carole Hillenbrand (New York: Columbia University Press, 1988), p. 72.

It should be noted that this discussion generally refers to Sunni Islam, although with modifications it could apply to Shi'i Islam as well. For while Shi'i Islam began as an opposition movement, once it became the established religion of Safavid Persia, Shi'is introduced structures designed to foster political accommodation. As Bassam Tibi puts it:

They encouraged the promulgation of the doctrine which permits political power to be delegated to secular rulers prior to the return of the Mahdi. . . . Through this maneuver Shi'i Islam was employed as the religious legitimization of political authority. . . . The ruler is supposed to be controlled by the Shi'i scholars of Qum, although the latter are also part of the ruling authorities. Thus, the oppositional character of Shi'i Islam was lost.

See Bassam Tibi, *The Crisis of Modern Islam: A Preindustrial Culture in the Scientific-Technological Age*, trans. Judith von Sivers (Salt Lake City: University of Utah Press, 1988), p. 108.

4. Cited by Fritz Steppat, "Der Muslim und di Obrigkeit," *Zeitschrift fur Politik* 12 (1965), p. 325.

5. By way of comparison, Ibn Taymiyya's solution differed significantly from the attempt of the Holy Roman Empire to deal with similar forces some three hundred years later. The Augsburg formula employed by Europe to deal with its conflict kept religious solidarity tied to political control. Whoever had such control also determined religious policy. Ibn Taymiyya placed religious unity above politics. Rather than sacrifice the ultimate ideal of religio-cultural unity, he justified the parceling out of political control.

6. See G. Levi Della Vida's article on "Khawarij" in *Encyclopedia of Islam*, new ed. (henceforth *EI2*), IV: 1076–77 (London: E. J. Brill, 1978). As G. Levi Della Vida says:

Outside of general principles and a few particular cases, the law and dogmatic of the Khawariji are not known to us in their totality except for the Ibadiyya, whose survival to the present day has preserved in its integrity their religious tradition.

7. See Charles Pellat's discussion in "Isti'rad," *EI2*, IV: 269. In fact, since most of the Muslim community disapproved of these executions, the term came to mean "religious murder."

8. See Bernard Lewis, "Hashishiyya," *EI2*, IV: 267–68.

9. Maxime Rodinson, *Mohammed*, trans. Anne Carter (New York: Vintage Books, 1974), p. 21.

10. Marshall G. S. Hodgson, *The Venture of Islam*, vol. 2 (Chicago: University of Chicago Press, 1974), p. 61.

11. Ibid.

12. Fazlur Rahman, "The Law of Rebellion in Islam," in *Islam in the Modern World: 1983 Paine Lectures in Religion*, ed. Jill Raitt (Columbia, MO: University of Missouri-Columbia, 1983), p. 3.

13. Quoted in *Inquiry*, 2, no. 9 (September, 1985) p. 63.

14. Steppat, "Der Muslim und di Obrigkeit," p. 325.

15. See, for example, Sir Sayyid Ahmad Khan, *Review on Dr. Hunter's Indian*

*Musulmans: Are They Bound in Conscience to Rebel Against the Queen?* (Benares, India: Medical Hall Press, 1872); Syed Ameer Ali, *A Critical Examination of the Life and Teachings of Mohammed* (London: Williams and Norgate, 1983); Muhammad Abduh, *Al-Islam wa'l Nasraniyyah wa'l-ʿilm wa'l-Madaniyya,* 8th ed. (Cairo: Dar al-Manar, 1373/1954).

16. Hasan al-Banna', "Risalat al-Jihad," in *Majmu'at Rasa'il al-Imam al-Shahid Hasan al-Banna'* (Beirut: Dar al-Nur, n.d.), p. 58; cited by Rudolph Peters in *Islam and Colonialism: The Doctrine of Jihad in Modern History* (The Hague, Paris, New York: Mouton Press, 1980), p. 193, n. 39.

17. Sayyid Qutb, *Fi Zilal al-Qur'an,* vol. 10 (Beirut: Dar al-Shuruq, 1973–74), p. 117; cited by Muhammad Tawfiq Barakat, *Sayyid Qutb* (Beirut: Dar al-Daʿwah, n.d.), p. 64.

18. Sayyid Qutb, *Fi'l-Tarikh: Fikrah wa Minhaj* (Beirut: n.p., 1974), pp. 310–11.

19. Abu'l A'la Mawdudi, *Al-Jihad fi Sabil Allah* (Beirut: Dar al-Fikr, n.d.), pp. 27–28.

20. Ibid., pp. 12–13.

21. Ibid.

22. See Michael Youssef, *Revolt Against Modernity: Muslim Zealots and the West* (Leiden, Netherlands: E.J. Brill, 1985), p. 177.

23. Imam Khomeini, "The Form of Islamic Government," in *Islam and Revolution,* trans. Hamid Algar (Berkeley: Mizan Press, 1981), p. 116.

24. Imam Khomeini, "Program for the Establishment of an Islamic Government," in *Islam and Revolution,* p. 132.

25. Imam Khomeini, "Legal Rulings," in *Islam and Revolution,* p. 438.

26. Ibid.

27. See Hasanayn Muhammad Makhluf, *Fatawa Sharʿiyyah wa Buhuth Islamiyya,* vol. 1 (Cairo: Mustafa al-Babi al-Halabi, 1965), pp. 81, 182. See also the discussion in Johannes J. G. Jansen, *The Neglected Duty: The Creed of Sadat's Assassins and Islamic Resurgence in the Middle East* (New York and London: Macmillan, 1986).

28. Jansen, *The Neglected Duty,* pp. 45–46.

29. *Majallat al-Azhar,* 54/1 (Muharram 1402/November 1981): 104; cited by Jansen, *The Neglected Duty,* p. 49.

30. *Majallat al-Azhar,* 54/2 (Safar 1402/November 1981): 180; compare Jansen, *The Neglected Duty,* p. 50.

31. *Majallat al-Azhar,* 54/2 (Safar 1402/November 1981): 304; compare Jansen, *The Neglected Duty,* p. 51.

32. For the complete discussion, see Jansen, *The Neglected Duty,* pp. 35–62.

33. Jadd al-Haqq Ali Jadd al-Haqq et al, *Al-Fatawa al-Islamiyyah min Dar al-Ifta' al-Misriyya* (Cairo: Al-Majlis al-A'la i'l Shu'un al-Islamiyya, Wizarat al-Awqaf, Jumhuriyyat Misr al-ʿArabiyyah, 1983), p. 3733; Jansen, *The Neglected Duty,* p. 54.

34. Ibid.; Jansen, *The Neglected Duty,* p. 56.

35. Lisa Anderson, "Religion and State in Libya: The Politics of Identity," *The Annals of the American Academy of Political and Social Science,* 483 (January 1986), p. 61–72.

36. Reported by Michel Jansen, "After the Mecca Tragedy," *The Middle East International,* 306 (August, 1987), p. 4.

# 7

# *Ahkam Al-Bughat*: Irregular Warfare and the Law of Rebellion in Islam

*Khaled Abou El Fadl*

## INTRODUCTION

Irregular or insurgency warfare poses immense practical and ethical problems for the just war tradition. Courtney Campbell's chapter provides an extensive discussion of the many ethical dilemmas irregular warriors present to traditional thinking about the rules of war.[1] For example, "irregulars" rely on surprise, deception, and disguise. Indeed, in certain cases, such warriors proclaim that the justice of their cause renders the rules of conventional warfare irrelevant. Alternatively, irregulars measure guilt and innocence in nonconventional ways, so that notions such as noncombatant immunity are altered to suit the ethical considerations of their cause.

From the perspective of those responding to irregulars, the insurgents lack "right authority." It is simple, at least in theory, for one government to recognize the authority of another to declare war, and thus to treat an enemy nation on a reciprocal basis. But irregulars seem to lack the authority to engage in armed conflict. Their alterations of the conventional rules for military engagement are thus rendered problematic. Finally, irregulars are often viewed as armed bandits whose aim is simply to undermine the foundations of the established order. They therefore lack a "just cause" to legitimate their resort to armed force. The challenge for serious moral and legal thinking is to distinguish between insurgents who are merely criminals and those who are soldiers.

In spite of the problems posed by irregular warfare, Western thought considers irregulars, and the conflicts involving them, to be subject to the criteria of the just war tradition.[2] According to James Turner Johnson, the just war tradition presumes that irregular war is not legitimate; nevertheless, the pressure "has been toward defining the parameters within which an insurgency movement can be treated as having political legitimacy (that is, enjoying right authority or having *competence de guerre*) and its armed forces as an organized military body rather than as a self-seeking, lawless gang of bandits." In fact, the parameters are often set so as to transform irregular warfare into something more similar to conventional military conflict and thus to make it more manageable.[3]

The purpose of this chapter is to provide a comparative view of irregular warfare from the perspective of classical Islam. The criteria of the just war tradition are Western. As such one should not force a comparison between the Islamic and Western traditions. Nevertheless, one often finds that diverse cultures are forced to deal with similar problems and that the responses of these cultures are informed by similar ethical considerations. As John Kelsay persuasively argues, both the just war tradition and the Islamic tradition reflect a moral concern that the just and the unjust not be equally subject to the damage of war.[4] In this respect, the two traditions share common moral foundations. Indeed the essential question in both traditions relates to the justice of the end pursued and the justice of the means used to serve the end.

Muslim jurists saw that irregular warfare, especially rebellion, poses a number of difficulties for the Islamic order of justice. Those difficulties are similar to the ones confronted by the just war tradition. And, in a manner not unlike that of the West, the pressure in the Islamic tradition has been to define the parameters within which an insurgency movement can be treated as having political legitimacy and to require that insurgents act, in certain respects, like a conventional army. The Islamic response, however, has been largely guided by religious criteria. As Kelsay argues, the content of justice or injustice, guilt or innocence, in the Islamic as well as in the just war tradition, is often specified in accord with religious or ideological considerations.[5] The Islamic treatment of irregular warfare, particularly in the context of rebellion, is indicative of this process.

Muslim jurists dealt with a particular brand of insurgency warfare in *Ahkam al-Bughat*. *Ahkam al-Bughat* is not coextensive with the broad issue of irregular warfare. It is, in essence, the law that regulates rebellion by Muslims living under an Islamic order. As a practical matter, the rebels will very likely be a group of irregulars; therefore *Ahkam al-Bughat* addresses many of the same concerns that preoccupy Western writers reflecting on irregular warfare.

This chapter is divided into two main parts. The first part provides a systematic exposition of *Ahkam al-Bughat* as developed by Muslim jurists. This portion of the chapter is descriptive, and very few interpretative comments will be made. The second part of this chapter is more evaluative. I will make an effort to point out the moral choices that Muslim jurists struggled with in dealing with irregular warfare. Naturally, one has to be cognizant of the fact that a modern scholar's evaluation of a medieval doctrine should not be allowed to distort the doctrine. But one cannot ignore the fact that Islamic jurisprudence, for Muslims, is not merely a historical phenomenon but is an everlasting legal and moral code of conduct. Hence the issue of discerning the moral implications of a medieval doctrine like *Ahkam al-Bughat* is ultimately a critical, practical question for modern Muslims.

The limitations of this chapter should be stated outright. The main focus here will be on *Ahkam al-Bughat* as a legal and moral teaching. No attempt will be made to relate the theoretical doctrines to actual practices in Islamic history. There will be occasion to mention certain practices that influenced the development of the Islamic doctrines, but the extent to which Islamic law concerning the subject influenced political practices in the Islamic civilization must be left for someone else to explore. Additionally, the focus here is on Sunni jurisprudence. Other schools of thought (for example, the Shi'i), will not be discussed.[6]

## *AHKAM AL-BUGHAT* IN SUNNI THOUGHT

### The Sources of *Ahkam al-Bughat*

*Ahkam al-Bughat* indicates the rules that regulate the treatment of those who rebel against the *Imam* of the Islamic state.[7] As such, these rules deal with the treatment of political or religious dissidents. There will be occasion to comment extensively on the precise type of dissent covered by *Ahkam al-Bughat* later in this chapter.[8] But as a general proposition, this area of Islamic law considers those legal and moral notions that are to govern cases of irregular warfare between Muslims. As such, *Ahkam al-Bughat* is a very particular area of Islamic law. It is to be distinguished from *Ahkam al-Hiraba* (judgments that relate to those at war with the Islamic state) or *Ahkam Qat' al-Tariq* (laws relating to highway robbery). The former deal with non-Muslims at war with Muslims, while the latter deal with common criminals motivated by private gain. The treatment of such groups in Islamic law is far less generous than that accorded to those who qualify as *bughat* or "rebels." *Ahkam al-Bughat* is also to be distinguished from *Ahkam al-Ridda* (laws relating to apostasy), which will be briefly discussed.[9]

*Ahkam al-Bughat* originated from the attempt of Muslim jurists to codify the practices of Ali Ibn Abi Taleb (the fourth of the "rightly guided" caliphs, who reigned from 656 to 661) in resisting those who dissented from his rule. Shortly after Ali ascended to power, his reign was challenged; the challenge became a civil war. Several factions challenged

Ali's reign, among them one led by the Meccan aristocrats Talha and Zubayr and the Prophet's wife A'isha. Ali's most formidable opponent, however, was Mu'awiya, a former governor of Syria. (Mu'awiya would eventually defeat Ali and reign from 661 to 680.) Finally, Ali was opposed by the Khawarij, "secessionists" who made use of insurgency tactics, and who eventually succeeded in assassinating Ali. Hence Ali's treatment of these factional opponents, especially the Talha and al-Zubayr faction in the Battle of the Camel in 656, set a precedent for most of the principles or rules adduced in *Ahkam al-Bughat*.[10]

Ali was not the only one of the early caliphs to deal with insurgents or rebels. Uthman, Ali's predecessor (reigned from 644 to 656), was killed by a group of rebels from Fustat, Egypt. Additionally, the very first rightly guided caliph, Abu Bakr (reigned from 632 to 634), became engulfed in the Riddah wars in which he defeated secessionists among some of the Arab tribes. Nonetheless, Muslim jurists spent very little space in discussing the examples of Abu Bakr and Uthman as precedents for *Ahkam al-Bughat*. This is probably due to historical and/or political reasons that are beyond the scope of this chapter.

Besides the practices of Ali, Muslim jurists occasionally cited the practices of the caliph Umar Ibn al-Aziz (717–20), considered by some to be a fifth rightly guided caliph.[11] In any case, *Ahkam al-Bughat* emerged, to a great extent, out of the attempt to deduce legal judgments from historical precedents. In certain respects, this gave the Islamic approach to rebellion a rather technical and absolute character, with normative value assigned, not to theoretical principles, but to specific historical precedents. Nevertheless, there is an important sense in which Muslim jurists based their opinions on doctrinal sources. These are somewhat conflicting, and the jurists had to strike a balance between several competing principles and dictates.

One such source is found in the exemplary practice of the Prophet (*sunna*). There is an abundance of reports (*hadith*) in which the Prophet calls for order and stability in the Islamic state. Often this brand of *hadith* calls upon Muslims to obey and support the ruler and to kill those who contest the ruler's power.[12] Such reports place a premium on the unity of Muslims and tend to play down other considerations. While the general emphasis of these reports (i.e., unity and stability) always permeated the treatment of rebellion, it was the special focus of those jurists writing from the thirteenth to the sixteenth centuries.[13] Even these relatively "late" jurists did not adhere fully to this type of report, however. For example, they did not hold that rebels against the *Imam* or *sultan* should be executed. Rather, they often cited such reports in order to emphasize the illegality of rebellions, but then cited other considerations in support of leniency toward rebels.

A second source influencing the formulation of *Ahkam al-Bughat* was the injunction to "enjoin good and forbid evil."[14] As interpreted by Muslim jurists, this means that Muslims generally have a duty to promote whatever is just and right, for example by insuring that Islamic norms are enforced. The Prophet said, "If people see an oppressor and they do not enjoin him then God will punish all of them."[15] Arguably, this *hadith* is advocating a notion that the whole nation may be doomed if ordinary people fail to resist injustice. Some jurists used this notion to argue that the *Imam* must enjoin the good and forbid the evil by suppressing any rebellion, thus protecting the nation from the evils introduced by rebels.[16] Other jurists used this principle to legitimate rebellion against an unjust *Imam*.[17]

In connection with the injunction to "enjoin good and forbid evil" the jurists also considered the well-established principle that "no obedience is owed to a created (human being) if [it entails] disobeying the Creator." The Prophet is reported to have said, "To hear and obey [the *Imam*] is obligatory, so long as one is not commanded to disobey God for if one is commanded to disobey God, he shall not hear or obey."[18] This was understood by certain jurists to mean that it is not legal to rebel against a sinful command even if ordered by an *Imam* or, in the terminology of some jurists, a *sultan*.[19] But, as will be shown, this understanding has not been consistently followed. Rather, it became a general principle, to be followed more or less strictly depending on the school of thought and circumstances.

Finally, the most important factor taken into consideration by Muslim jurists is the Qur'anic injunction on the subject. The Qur'an states:

> If two parties among the believers fall into a quarrel, make ye peace between them: but if one of them transgresses beyond bounds against the other, then fight ye [all] against the other, then fight ye [all] against the one that transgresses until it complies with the command of God. But if it complies, then make peace between them with justice, and be fair; For God loves those who are fair [and just]. The Believers are but a single Brotherhood: so make peace and reconciliation between your two [contending] brothers. And fear God, that ye may receive mercy.[20]

The jurists deduced two principles from these verses. First, they argued that the *bughat*, or rebels, remain Muslims despite their rebellion. And second, they argued that the primary purpose of *Ahkam al-Bughat* is the reconciliation of the contending parties and not the punishment or elimination of the dissenters. In Islamic legal terminology, the object of *Ahkam al-Bughat* is *al-Daf'a* or *rad al Sa'il* (meaning to end the controversy) and not *al-qatl* (to kill).[21] Therefore, Muslim jurists state that vengeance or oppression should play no role in suppressing the rebellion of *al-Bughat*.[22]

To recapitulate: the Qur'an imposes a requirement of reconciliation between contending parties, but this injunction is complemented by three other principles: (1) the duty of imposing order, (2) the duty to enjoin the good and forbid the evil, and (3) the duty to obey God. These are the ideas most often cited by the jurists in dealing with the question of rebellion. Before turning to the specific rules defining the *Baghy* and the treatment due to the *bughat*, a few additional prefatory remarks placing *Ahkam al-Bughat* in context are necessary.

### Ahkam al-Bughat in Context

Despite its obvious political connotations, *ahkam al-Bughat* is a doctrine of law rather than political theory. All the major books of Islamic jurisprudence contain a chapter on the subject. Political theorists like Ibn Taymiyya (1328/726 c.e./a.h.) and al-Juwayni (1085/478) do not treat this subject. They do, however, refer to it in passing. In fact, al-Juwayni advises his readers to pursue the subject in the books of *fiqh* (law) if they so desire.[23] Those who wrote books advising the *sultan* on the administration of political affairs (e.g., Ibn Jama'a (1331/732), al-Mawardi (1058/450) and Abu Ya'la ibn al-Farra (1065/458) also dealt with the subject.[24] However, their treatment tends to be cursory, no more than a general exposition of the relevant principles and rules.

The specific content of *Ahkam al-Bughat* has been relatively constant throughout Islamic history. Thus, the specific rulings of al-Shafi'i (820/204) or Malik (795/179) are echoed in substantially the same language by jurists writing several hundred years later.[25] This may be due in part to the fact that the later works are commentaries upon commentaries that were written on the original works. But it may also be an indication that *Ahkam al-Bughat* were not a part of the actual practice of statecraft in Islam. This could arguably be attributed to the formal, technical character of this area of law; a character which rendered it, in a sense, impractical for its day. This hypothesis is further supported by the fact that although the technical aspects of *Ahkam al-Bughat* remained constant through the ages, the political aspects (such as when, if ever, is rebellion justifiable) were reinterpreted and altered by later jurists.

Although there is a general consensus among the different schools of Sunni jurisprudence on the content of *Ahkam al-Bughat*, there is no agreement on its categorization. Some jurists discussed *Ahkam al-Bughat* as a branch of *al-qanun al-jina'i (criminal law)*. For them, a discussion of *al-baghy* is followed by apostasy, then adultery, then highway robbery and so on.[26] Other jurists discussed the topic under the chapter on *juruh* (torts)[27] or, alternatively, in a chapter between those on *juruh* and *al-jinayat*.[28] Still other jurists discussed *Ahkam al-Bughat* as a branch of *siyar* (the conduct or practice of the Islamic government) or as a topic within a chapter on *jihad*.[29] The vast majority of jurists entitled their chapters, *"Ahkam qital al Bughat"* (rules for fighting rebels) while a few discussed the topic under the title of *"al-Khawarij."*[30]

## Content of Ahkam al-Bughat

A *baghi*, according to most Muslim jurists, is someone who commits a *khuruj* (an act of rebellion) with a *ta'wil* (interpretation or reason) while enjoying *shauka* (power). If *ta'wil* or *shauka* is lacking, then the party in question is treated as a common criminal, and is not a *baghi*.[31] The *baghi* is not a common criminal; in fact, those who come under this classification are to be treated in ways which clearly set them apart from apostates or highway robbers. With the possible exception of those associated with the Hanafi school, Muslim jurists did not consider the *bughat* to be *fussaq* or *fusaqa* (iniquitous). Although rebelling against an *Imam* is not permitted, there is no sin that attaches to an act of *baghy*.[32] Some Shafi'i jurists went further; they asserted that *al-baghy* is not an *ism zamm* (i.e., not a name implying blame).[33] This should not be understood to imply that rebellion was sanctioned or condoned per se. In fact, jurists who assert this view are very careful to emphasize that rebelling against even an unjust ruler is illegal. Rather, the jurists are simply emphasizing that *al-baghy* is an objective, legal issue, and not a political matter. This is supported by the fact that the requirements of *khuruj*, *ta'wil*, and *shauka* are formal and technical. If a group satisfies the legal requirements it is entitled to be treated under *Ahkam al-Bughat*, and political considerations do not matter. The concepts *khuruj*, *ta'wil*, and *shauka* may be summarized as follows.

## Al-Khuruj

*Al-Khuruj* is an act of resistance to the *Imam* or his *wali* (agent). Such resistance might involve the use of force; alternatively, it would involve acts of noncompliance. Generally, any act that carries the intention of deposing the *Imam* or that involves disobedience to the orders of the *Imam* constitutes *khuruj*. The *khuruj* requirement is not a demanding one; basically, it only requires that there be a conflict between the established order and a particular group and that the conflict involve the violation of a legal or social obligation. Hence a refusal to pay *kharaj* (tax or land taxes) or to hand over fugitives from justice, or even a refusal to pay one's debts constitutes a *khuruj*.[34] Of course, simply because *khuruj* exists does not mean the offender has become a *baghi*. It only means that one of the criteria of *baghy* has been fulfilled.

Political criticism or advocacy unaccompanied by an illegal action does not rise to the level of *khuruj*, and, therefore, cursing or vituperating the

*Imam* is not considered *khuruj*.[35] However, some jurists held that the *Imam* might punish a person who curses him because the *Imam* as a private individual is entitled to the same protections from abusive language afforded to other private individuals.[36] Other jurists argued that abusive language directed against public officials is not punishable.[37]

Once there is an illegal act (and not mere talk) there is a *khuruj*. Nonetheless, there are two remaining questions. First, can an act of *khuruj* be committed against any *Imam*—just or unjust? Or to put the question in a different way, does *Ahkam al-Bughat* apply to rebellions against *sultans* as well as *Imams*, just or unjust?[38] Second, if the *Imam* orders a person to commit an unjust or sinful act and that person refuses to comply, is such refusal considered *khuruj*?

Early jurists, for example al-Shafi'i, specifically stated that *Ahkam al-Bughat* is invoked if the *khuruj* is directed against a just *Imam* or a true *Imam* (*Imam adil* or *Imam haq*).[39] This implies that if the *Imam* is not "just" or "true" then *khuruj* is not illegal. Later, some Muslim jurists dropped the words *adil* or *haq*, simply stating *Imam*[40] or used the words *sultan* and *Imam* interchangeably.[41] However, the majority of late Muslim jurists reiterated that *Ahkam al-Bughat* applies to the *Imam al-haq*. At the same time, they argued that *al-Imam al-haq* could be just or unjust, and, in either case, must be obeyed. They then asserted that the true *Imam* could attain power by a proper *bay'a* (vote) or *istikhlaf* (inheritance or by the choice of the *Imam* preceding him) or *istila* (usurpation). Thus, whether the *Imam* is a rightful one (for example, Ali) or a usurper (one who does not fulfill the requirements of the caliphate[42]), *Ahkam al-Bughat* still applies. In short, according to the later jurists, a *khuruj* could be committed against a rightly guided caliph or a usurper, or against a *sultan* or an *Imam*.[43]

Even if a *khuruj* may exist in relation to an unjust *Imam*, one still must deal with the issue of whether an illegal or sinful command by an *Imam* could excuse a *khuruj*. More specifically, how does the principle "that no obedience is owed to the created if it entails disobeying the Creator" factor into *Ahkam al-Bughat*?

The majority of Maliki jurists (including those writing in the thirteenth to eighteenth centuries) insisted that an illegal order excuses the *khuruj*. If the *Imam* orders the people to pay an unjust tax, they argued, then the people are justified in not complying.[44] The Zahiri Ibn Hazm goes a step beyond this judgment; in his view, if the *Imam* issues an illegal order then those who resist him are not *bughat*; rather, the *Imam* is the *baghi*.[45]

Later jurists (from schools of thought other than Maliki and Zahiri) refused to excuse a *khuruj* if the *Imam*'s order was sinful or illegal.[46] As a legal matter, they argued that the question of an excused *khuruj* need not be raised. *Khuruj* is always illegal. Nevertheless, this judgment could be qualified. If the *Imam* is just, these jurists argued, then all people have to assist him in fighting the *bughat*. But if the *Imam* is unjust or if his command is sinful then people should refrain from assisting the *Imam* or the *bughat*—so some argued. In the opinion of others, if the *Imam* is unjust then people should assist the *bughat* against the *Imam*, but only if it is expected that the *Imam* will respond to such pressure and the dissenters have clearly been wronged.[47]

### Al-Ta'wil

Most Muslim jurists required that the *khuruj* be based on a *ta'wil*. This means that the *bughat*, as a group, must adhere to a point of view or interpretation. This is best viewed as a control factor; people who break the law for purposes of private gain are not entitled to preferential treatment.[48] On the other hand, if the dissidents' rebellion is based on an interpretation of an Islamic source they cannot be treated as common criminals.[49] As Ibn Qudamah al-Hanbali (1146/541) stated, *Al-Bughat* "are not dissolute but they are wrong in their interpretations (opinions) and the *Imam* [the leader] and *ahl al-adl* [the people supporting the *Imam*] are right in resisting them. They [the *bughat*] are like *al-mujtahidin* [those who exercise independent interpretation]," and the *mujtahid* cannot be treated as a common criminal if his crime is based upon *ijtihad* (interpretation of recognized Islamic sources).[50]

Nonetheless, the exact nature of the *ta'wil* is not clear. Does the *ta'wil* have to be religious or does a *ta'wil* based on social or political interests suffice? The answer to this question really depends on whether *Ahkam al-Bughat* was designed only to cover religious schismatics and conflicts, or whether it was also intended to extend to rebellions committed by Muslims who do not represent a particular religious school of thought. There is no clear answer to this question, and one can only venture a tentative response.[51]

Most jurists agreed that Talha and al-Zubayr (led by A'isha) and Mu'awiya were *bughat*. Talha and al-Zubayr and Mu'awiya advanced as a justification for their rebellion against Ali the claim that Ali assisted in the assassination of Uthman (the third rightly guided caliph) or alternately, that he knew the identity and whereabouts of Uthman's assassins yet refused to punish them. The claims of Talha and Zubayr and Mu'awiya were considered by Sunni jurists to be an acceptable *ta'wil* even though they were primarily political rather than religious.[52]

The other case discussed by jurists in this regard is the rebellion of the Khawarij, whose "secession" from the party of Ali made reference to religious claims—in particular, they claimed that Ali submitted to the judgment of human beings rather than to God. The majority of Muslim jurists agreed that the Khawarij had an acceptable *ta'wil* and, thus, were *bughat*. A few jurists argued that since the Khawarij advocated the indiscriminate slaughter of Muslims they were apostates rather than *bughat*.[53] For most, however, the Khawarij were classified as rebels whose claims were based on religious ideas rather than on purely political grievances. In certain ways, the Khawarij could be considered a school of thought equal in status to the Shi'i or Mu'tazili sects.

Finally, a commentary on Ibn Abidin's work indicates that the Wahhabi movement could be considered *bughat* in relation to its uprising against the Ottomans (1233/1803).[54] The Wahhabis were a reformist movement heavily influenced by Ibn Taymiyya and the Hanbali school of thought. But they were also influenced by ethnic (i.e., Arabist) ideas. One can only surmise that the historical precedents cited by Muslim jurists, while inconclusive, seem to lend credence to the notion that a legitimate *ta'wil* could be political as well as religious.

The specifically doctrinal arguments on this subject are equally inconclusive. Some jurists, e.g., Malik, specifically stated that the *ta'wil* must be religious (*ta'wil dini*). Others referred to the *bughat* as *mujtahidin*, thus implying that their *ta'wil* is necessarily religious.[55] Still other jurists discussed *ta'wil* as if it could be either politically or religiously founded.[56] In short, one may conclude that *Ahkam al-Bughat* was only intended to apply to religious schismatics or that the *Ahkam* extends to political rebellions. Both points of view are plausible. My personal view is that *Ahkam al-Bughat* applies to all dissenters, whether their dissension is based on religious or political reasons.

At any rate, most jurists agreed that, whether the *ta'wil* is religious or political, it is immaterial whether such *ta'wil* is right or wrong. Stated in modern terms, there is no inquiry about the correctness of the *ta'wil*. Consequently, the rebels are not to be denied the protection of *Ahkam al-Bughat* simply because their *ta'wil* is incorrect.[57]

The jurists of the Shafi'i school provide a notable exception to this general rule. They argued that the *ta'wil* of the rebels *has* to be wrong but cannot be so in a frivolous sense.[58] The reason for this requirement is as follows: if the interpretation of the *bughat* is right and the *Imam* concedes this, then the *Imam* should be liable—not the dissenters. If the *bughat* are in the right and the *Imam* is in the wrong, then the *Imam* has no legal or moral right to harm the *bughat* until and unless he addresses the cause of their complaint. If he does that, the *bughat* are no longer dissenters or if they continue to resist, they are unjustified. Therefore, the *bughat* must have a wrong *ta'wil* or at least a *ta'wil* considered false by the majority of the Muslims. Otherwise the legitimacy of the *Imam* is undermined.

The requirement of such jurists that the *ta'wil* not be frivolous is somewhat obscure. What they seem to be saying may be phrased as follows: if a rebellious group seeks the corruption of religion and society by denying a tenet of religion (like praying) or by advocating indiscriminate slaughter of Muslims (like the Khawarij) then they should be treated as apostates not *bughat*. Thus while there is a desire by these jurists to recognize the legitimacy of the rebels' *ta'wil*, even if it is supported by weak evidence, there is a concern that the *ta'wil* does not verge on apostasy.[59]

This brings into focus the distinction between apostasy and *baghy*. In brief, a frivolous *ta'wil* may not only deny a group the protection of *Ahkam al-Bughat*; it may even make them apostates. A clear case of apostasy (*irtidad*) occurs when a person publicly disavows belief in Islam. Additionally, if a person vituperates the Prophet or blasphemes God, or physically destroys or soils a Qur'an that is also an act of apostasy. An apostate is asked to repent for three days and nights. If he does not do so, he is killed.

Apostasy comes very close to *baghy* when the latter involves a denial of *ma'lum min al-din bil darura* (something recognized as a part of religion by necessity). Things that fall in this category are fundamentals of religion, such as *salat* (prayer), *hajj* (pilgrimage), or *zakat* (almsgiving). For example, if a person denies that praying five minutes a day is an Islamic requirement, he becomes an apostate. This is to be distinguished from a person who does not pray because he is lazy, yet does not deny the requirement of prayer itself.[60]

Most of the rules on apostasy were taken from the practices of Abu Bakr (the first rightly guided caliph) in fighting *al-Murtadin* in 633 C.E.[61] Certain Arab tribes refused to pay *zakat* to Abu Bakr, and this in itself presented a conceptual difficulty for the jurists: how does one distinguish an act of apostasy from an act of *baghy*? It is clear that the tribes in question were refusing to perform a basic tenet of Islam; but did they become apostates by their refusal?

Muslim jurists divided the *murtadin* into two groups. The first group refused to pay the *zakat* because they denied that it was an Islamic requirement or because they intended to defy Islam. This group were apostates, and if they did not repent, they should have been executed. The second group did not pay the *zakat* because of its interpretation of the Qur'an rather than because of defiance. The Qur'an states, "Of their goods take alms so that thou mightest purify and sanctify them; And pray in their behalf. Verily thy prayers are a source of security for them."[62] This second group of *al-Murtadin* argued that the *zakat* should have been paid to the Prophet when he was alive, but that Abu Bakr should not receive the *zakat* because his (i.e., Abu Bakr's) prayers were not a "source of security to them." Since the second group relied on the above-mentioned Qur'anic interpretation, the jurists argued that its members did not have a frivolous *ta'wil*. Consequently, they were *bughat* and they should not have been executed.[63]

From a modern perspective, one has to admit that the doctrine of a "frivolous" *ta'wil* compounds the potential for abuse already abundant in the laws of apostasy.[64] Distinguishing a wrong *ta'wil* from a frivolous one seems to involve such intricate distinctions that the notion is not amenable to coherent application.

### Al-Shauka

*Al-Shauka* (also referred to as *al-hawza* and *al-min'a*) means that the rebellious group must possess some power in the form of organization, leadership, and membership. Thus a "group" of one, two, or ten dissenters cannot be treated as *bughat*; some further demonstration of strength is required.[65] The justification for this numerical requirement is given by several jurists. Ibn Qudamah (1223/620), for example, affirms the generally accepted proposition that the *bughat* are not responsible for the destruction of property or life if such destruction occurs in the course of a rebellion. Then he argues that if the status of *bughat* is given to groups regardless of the strength of their support, suffering will increase. Other jurists argue that the requirement of *shauka* is necessary to guard against encouragment to "anarchy and lawlessness" (*hatta la tafsad al-siyasat*). Without this requirement, every corrupt person will fabricate a *ta'wil* and claim to be a *baghi*.[66]

The Zahiri school of thought and the majority of jurists from the Maliki school rejected the requirement of *shauka* altogether, however. The Maliki jurists argued that one person could be a *baghi* because the requirement of *ta'wil* provides a sufficient guarantee against lawlessness.[67]

The discussion of *khuruj*, *ta'wil*, and *shauka* form the heart of the content of *Ahkam al-Bughat*. But a complete description requires attention to two more items: the concept of *al-mughalaba*; and the rules governing the treatment of *al-Bughat*.

### The Concept of Mughalaba

If the dissenters commit an act of rebellion (or disobedience) based on *ta'wil*, and they commit the act as an organization (rather than as private individuals) then they are *bughat*. Nevertheless, there are further legal and moral difficulties associated with the concept of *mughalaba* or "revolt by force."

Some of the Maliki jurists argued that *Ahkam al-Bughat* only apply when there is a revolt by force. In other words, they considered *al-mughalaba* a part of the definition of rebellion; without revolt by force, there is no rebellion. However, these jurists disagreed about the precise meaning of *mughalaba*. Some asserted that it means "combat" or "struggle" while others maintained that it means "strife" or "contest." In justifying this position (that *mughalaba* is necessarily a part of rebellion) such jurists argued that a person who refuses to give his *bay'a* (vote) to an *Imam* is not a rebel because there is no *mughalaba*: no law has been broken, therefore there is no *baghy*.[68]

Certain modern jurists have claimed that Islamic law requires the existence of *mughalaba* for the application of *Ahkam al-Bughat*. Unlike some of the earlier Maliki jurists, however, these scholars argue that *mughalaba* means actual combat, and not merely strife or contest. This means that *Ahkam al-Bughat* can only apply if the dissenters engage in revolt by force.[69]

There are several difficulties inherent in the concept of *mughalaba*, in particular as interpreted by the aforementioned contemporary jurists. If *mughalaba* means contest or strife then what does it add to the concept of *khuruj*? As indicated, *khuruj* involves an act of rebellion or disobedience; laws are thereby broken. Once laws are broken, a contest or strife necessarily (i.e., by definition) exists. If that is so then the concept of *mughalaba* (as contest or strife) is superfluous.

Alternatively, if *mughalaba* means combat, there are other difficulties. The medieval discussions seem to assume that *Ahkam al-Bughat* apply, for the most part, to cases of violent rebellion. Nonetheless, most of the jurists (the Malikis are the main exception) did not go on to make *mughalaba* part of the concept of *baghy*. Violent rebellion, for the earlier jurists, was one type of *khuruj*. *Khuruj* could also, however, take the form of passive disobedience (*al-imitina*, or abstention). The addition of *al-mughalaba* negates a portion of the discussion of *khuruj*, and frankly seems to create unnecessary confusion.[70]

### Treatment of the Bughat

Most jurists agreed that if the *bughat* only discuss rebellion and do not make a firm decision to rebel (*qiyam al-azm*), the *Imam* cannot interfere. If they reach a decision to rebel and begin to mobilize, organize, and purchase weapons, then the *Imam* must warn them and, if time permits, debate them. Some jurists from the Hanafi school of thought held that a warning or debate is recommended but not required. If the *bughat* ignore the warning and refuse to abide by the orders of the *Imam*, then the *Imam* can take action. But the jurists were divided on the type of action that would be appropriate. Most jurists from the Hanafi school held that the *Imam* could commence combat. The majority of jurists from the other schools asserted that the *Imam* could imprison the *bughat* until the conspiracy was aborted, but could not commence combat until the *bughat* attacked.[71] In all cases, the use of force should be a last resort; if it is possible to repel the *bughat* without the use of force then nonviolent means must be taken. If the *bughat* themselves do not intend to use force then the *Imam* must not use force either.[72]

If fighting does occur, the Shafi'i and Hanbali jurists held that the

*Imam* may not use destructive weapons, such as fire or mangonels, unless absolutely necessary to defeat the *bughat*. The other schools permitted the use of such weapons, but the Maliki and Zahiri schools added that the use of destructive weapons is forbidden if it would lead to the death of children or women.[73] If, in the course of a violent rebellion, a *baghi* is wounded or captured, he may not be killed. This rule applies even if the *bughat* execute the prisoners of *ahl al-adl* (the people supporting the *Imam*). Some jurists, most notably those from the Hanafi and Maliki schools, held that a prisoner from the *bughat* may be executed if there is a fear that the *bughat* will liberate their prisoners. Nevertheless, once the *bughat* are defeated no further killing is permitted (including executions).[74] All Muslim jurists, except the Hanafis, maintained that, unlike the apostates, the dead from *al-bughat* are granted the privilege of an Islamic burial. The Hanafis argued that even though the *bughat* were Muslims, they should be denied an Islamic burial as a form of punishment. The other schools responded that a dead person should not be punished.[75]

These rules have the greatest applicability if a rebellion is violent. If it is not and the *bughat* are not armed then, as stated earlier, the *Imam* does not have the option of resorting to violence. There are some additional rules, however, that apply whether or not the rebellion is violent.

In all cases, the property of the *bughat* and their money may not be confiscated.[76] Those *bughat* who are prisoners must be released after the rebellion has ended. There is, however, disagreement among Muslim jurists as to whether the prisoners have to be released immediately after the rebellion has subsided. Most jurists chose this option.[77]

The *bughat* are not responsible for any destruction of property or life if such destruction occurs in the course of the rebellion. If the *bughat* destroy any property or life before or after the general act of rebellion then they are to be held responsible. This means that, unless the destruction occurs in the course of the rebellion, the *bughat* are treated as common criminals. If the rebellion is nonviolent (e.g., refusal to pay taxes) there would seem to be no occasion for the destruction of property or life. But if there is such destruction, the *bughat* are exempted from liability only if the destruction occurs in the course of the rebellion.[78] Should one or two members of the *bughat* destroy property or life while the rest of the group remains inactive then they, i.e., the one or two, are held liable because they acted without *shauka*. A case in point, often cited by the jurists, involves the Khariji Ibn Muljam, who assassinated Ali in 661. Since Ibn Muljam did not kill Ali in the course of a general rebellion by the Khawarij, he was held liable and was executed.[79]

In the Maliki and Zahiri schools of thought (for which *shauka* is not necessary), one or two members can be exempted from liability as long as the crimes are committed in the context of an act of rebellion by the individual. However, it is not clear how and when an individual can commit a general act of rebellion or defiance.

## AHKAM AL-BUGHAT IN A MODERN PERSPECTIVE

*Al-Baghy* is not a crime of thought. In other words, *Ahkam al-Bughat*, unlike apostasy, does not deal with heretical ideas or ideas that negate well-established Islamic principles. Rather, *Ahkam al-Bughat* deals with the objective act of rebelling against the *Imam* or refusing to obey a law for political reasons. While *Ahkam al-Bughat* was designed to deal with Islamic dissent, that does not necessarily mean that its relevance is limited to cases of religious dissent. The jurists could have said that the rules of *Ahkam al-Bughat* are only designed to deal with sectarian dissenters (e.g., Shi'a or the Khawarij). But they did not do so. As I have argued, the Sunni jurists understood *Ahkam al-Bughat* to cover rebels such as Mu'awiya—that is, Muslims who rebel, but not necessarily for sectarian reasons.[80]

The problems posed by the *bughat*, if their rebellion is violent, are similar in many respects to the problems posed by insurgency movements. Insurgency or irregular warfare usually arises in the context of individuals challenging the authority of an established government. As a matter of practice, governments often assert that the insurgents lack legitimacy and, thus, the authority to use lethal force. Even more frequently, irregulars are criticized on *jus in bello* grounds: the means they employ make it difficult to establish irregulars as belligerents, in the legal sense. Article 3 of each of the four Geneva Conventions (1949) and the 1977 Second Protocol respond to this problem by extending many of the rules applicable to international conflicts to civil wars. The 1977 First Protocol to the Geneva Conventions goes further by treating most internal conflicts as international conflicts. However, the fact that only a limited number of nations have ratified the First and Second Protocols clearly exemplifies the gravity of the problem that insurgency warfare poses to established governments.[81]

From a legal and moral point of view, the questions are whether insurgents ought to be recognized as belligerents instead of criminals, and if so, what type of treatment to afford such insurgents. Alternatively, one could inquire as to the justice of the insurgents' ends (*jus ad bellum* inquiry) and the justice of the insurgents' means (*jus in bello* inquiry).

The inquiry into the justice of the insurgents' ends is a very difficult one. Dealing with the insurgents as anything but as criminals threatens the legitimacy of an established government. The majority of Muslim jurists chose a practical approach to this problem. They did not seriously discuss whether it is morally justified for the *Imam* to fight the *bughat*, nor did they discuss whether the *bughat* are authorized to rebel. Clearly there are authoritative sources that appear to address the second of these issues. One notes, for example, the principle that no obedience is owed to a created if it entails disobeying the Creator. But the majority of Sunni jurists did not use this principle to grant rebels the right to revolt. Some, for example Ibn Hazm, held that an unjust *Imam* has no right to fight the *bughat*. Others combined moral theory with practical considerations and maintained that a rebellion is justified if the *Imam* is unjust and there is a good chance that the rebels might succeed in deposing him.[82] The majority, however, asserted that the primary concern, regardless of who is at fault, is to reconcile the contending parties and reestablish order.

For such jurists, the *bughat* could not be classified simply as criminals because a government does not seek reconciliation with criminals; rather, it punishes them. Therefore, to insure that the *bughat* could not simply seek pillage and plunder, Muslim jurists imposed *ta'wil* as a minimum requirement. Interestingly, however, no inquiry was made into the just-ness of the *ta'wil*. Rather Muslim jurists seemed willing to concede that the *bughat*, as *mujtahids*, might ultimately be correct in their *ta'wil*. In this sense, truth is relative and only God knows what is just. This is not dissimilar to Franciscus de Victoria's concept of invincible ignorance or, as Johnson calls it, "simultaneous ostensible justice."[83] Since the truth is unknown, Victoria argued, each party should treat the other as if it had just cause. Muslim jurists added the notion of reconciliation, which acts to protect the rights of the insurgents not only during the conduct of warfare but even after the hostilities have terminated.[84]

The Islamic response to rebellion is significant precisely because it is a religious response. It provides a powerful demonstration of the ways in which religious criteria might supplant or compliment moral consid-erations. By way of contrast, one might consider certain aspects of West-ern cultural history. The pre-nineteenth century Western world treated rebels with extreme hostility. Only after the French Revolution, and under the influence of theorists such as Francois Guizot, did political rebels become entitled to preferred treatment as a special brand of "hon-orable" criminals. The vice of the rebels became the violent means they chose rather than the goals they pursued.[85] As Pierre Papadatos wrote:

The crime against the state is now looked upon as an infraction, conditioned by the circumstances in which it was produced, by the legitimacy or illegitimacy of the power it is attacking, and whose anti-social character is relative; its author, generally driven by noble motives, witnesses by his deeds a turbulance rather than a corruption of the spirit, an audacity rather than perversity, fanat-icism rather than vice. Also, he seemed worthy of indulgence, and they thought that the punishments they inflicted on him should only be light and not dishonorable.[86]

Prior to the French Revolution, the established churches in Europe often provided the state with more legitimacy. However, after the French Revolution the moral dominance of Christian churches weakened and political truths became relative as the state lost its absolute claim over morality.[87] The interesting comparison here is that, in the Islamic tradition, notions of the relativity of political truth developed within the structure of normative religious thought.

Muslim jurists dealt with the issue of rebellion solely by reference to Islamic principles and injunctions. The highest moral value for them was the protection of the Islamic order. Therefore, as long as all the contending parties remain within the bounds of Islam, a decision about who is ultimately correct in a specific interpretation is immaterial. Jurists such as Ibn Qudamah could go further and insist that the *bughat* were engaged in a type of *ijtihad*. In this way, the Sunni jurists endowed insurgents with a certain degree of legitimacy. Both the government and the *bughat* stand as equals before God. This type of argument seems quite unique, especially in a religious context where truth is supposed to be absolute and uncompromising. The development was due in part to the absence of a church in Islam; to the competing ideas contained in the authoritative sources of Islam (enjoining the good and forbidding the evil, etc.); and the central role of *ijtihad* in Islamic thought. This suggests, in my opinion, that it is difficult to make generalizations about the role of religion in law and society. Islam has its own very particular and unique frame of reference. The example of the jurists' application of Islamic norms to the question of rebellion provides an important counterexample for theories that understand religion primarily as a legitimating feature for authoritarian regimes. One has to admit, of course, that the fact that Muslim jurists state their conclusions by way of legalistic deductions and without theoretical systematization makes their ideas of political relativity a kind of extrapolation. But it is an extrapolation with significant roots in Islamic sources.[88]

In effect the Muslim jurists who developed *Ahkam al-Bughat* deemphasized *jus ad bellum* criteria in favor of the *jus in bello*. Their emphasis was on the procedural problems that insurgency warfare poses and on the treatment due to insurgents rather than the justice of the insurgent's cause. They were therefore interested in the visibility and recognizability of the insurgents. Insurgents do not wear uniforms, and they often act as individuals, attacking where one least expects them. While there is no evidence that Muslim jurists were concerned with the issue of military uniforms, it is clear that they expended much effort on the issue of the *bughat*'s recognizability. Hence, they insisted that the *bughat* have a *shauka* and that the *khuruj* be by the group as a whole at a specific time. Presumably, the rationale is that if the group has a leadership and an organization, and if the group acts as a whole, then it becomes easier to recognize and to distinguish from the population at large. Consequently, attacks that require disguise, for example assassinations or acts of terrorism, would not qualify under *Ahkam al-Bughat*. Perhaps there is an exception to this rule in the Maliki position, since it does not require a *shauka*, but can recognize a single rebel as a *baghi*.

The treatment Muslim jurists afforded the *bughat* was unusually lenient. As Courtney Campbell argues, it is very difficult to justify lenient policies towards insurgents. Muslim jurists, however, insisted that the contending parties be reconciled with the least amount of bloodshed possible. Therefore, limits were placed on the use of destructive weaponry. Additionally, a notion of benevolent quarantine was imposed where a *baghi* promises to stop fighting in exchange for safety pending the termination of the war and even afterwards.[89] Furthermore, the slaughtering of women, children and noncombatants was prohibited. Nevertheless, these prohibitions, for the most part, were not absolute. As indicated, the majority of Muslim jurists did permit the use of destructive weapons and the killing of prisoners if there was an overriding necessity.

In certain aspects, the Islamic treatment calls to mind the concepts of "proportionality" and "discrimination" in the *jus in bello*.[90] Proportionality basically prohibits the use of destructive weapons if such use will result in an inordinate destruction of human life and value. The principle of discrimination holds noncombatants to be immune from direct attack. The moral and practical difficulty, both in the Islamic and Western traditions, is in giving those concepts specific content. Especially in the modern era, it is not easy to define which weapons cause disproportionate destruction and in what context. Similarly, distinguishing combatants from noncombatants or defining a direct attack is far from clear. But one has to note that the Western tradition has debated and, to an extent, clarified these concepts. The Islamic tradition, beyond the classical juristic discussions, has not attempted to develop these concepts within a systematic theoretical framework. Medieval Muslim jurists wrote *Ahkam al-Bughat* as a set of general legal injunctions. They left a number of particular questions with ambiguous answers, at best. It will remain for modern Muslims to resolve these ambiguities.

One of the most notable ambiguities in the *Ahkam al-Bughat* is whether the *bughat* themselves are restricted, in some fashion, in the way they conduct their rebellion. It is fairly clear that the government is not free to resist the *bughat* by disproportionate or indiscriminate means. But it is not clear whether the *bughat* are similarly restricted. Perhaps more important, one may ask whether *Ahkam al-Bughat* protect insurgency warfare only when it targets state interests or also protect those who target private interests. A few examples will illustrate. Assume that a particular group is opposed to the showing of foreign films in movie theatres. In its view such films are promiscuous and, therefore, un-Islamic. Consequently, the group, in an act of general revolt, attacks and destroys several of those movie theatres. Here the question is: Was the destruction of private property an act of *khuruj*? What if all movie theatres are publicly held? Similarly, consider that the group attacks a military school, killing several students. Or consider a case in which a government uses its state-controlled television station to broadcast political propaganda. A group then attacks this television station, harming the government, but also killing several broadcast workers in the process.

The initial difficulty in all three examples is to determine what is a governmental target and what is a civilian target. Then one may ask: even if the target is governmental are the rebels justified in killing innocent civilians? Finally, one must ask who is an "innocent civilian" and who is not.

My own inclination is to say that the *bughat* can only attack government personnel who distinguish themselves from the general population by a uniform, badge, or the carrying of a weapon. Additionally, the *bughat* are excused if they attack an interest that is specifically engaged in enforcing the government's laws (for example, the ministry of the interior). Therefore, the attack on the military school is excused, while the attacks on the movie theatres and television station are not. Damages to private interests are excused only if such damages occur incidentally and in the course of targeting the governmental interest. However, I will freely admit that such an inclination is in itself still very vague, and I will also admit that my inclinations are not supported by an explicit Islamic text. Nevertheless, if Muslim jurists thought it permissible to limit the government in its conduct of war there is little sense in not imposing some limitations on the *bughat*. Furthermore, there is some precedent for my inclinations, for certain jurists did refuse to recognize the Khawarij as *bughat* because the Khawarij engaged in indiscriminate slaughtering of Muslims. In the terminology of those jurists, this is a form of corruption on the earth (*ifsad fi al-ard*) that cannot be consistent with Islamic morality.[91]

In conclusion, it seems that Muslim jurists intended *Ahkam al-Bughat* to serve as an active guide to the conduct of statecraft. As such, *Ahkam al-Bughat* contain a definite practical and legal dimension as well as a theoretical and moral dimension. The significance of *Ahkam al-Bughat* for modern organizations like the Muslim Brotherhood is evident. One might note two contemporary cases as an indication of what might materialize in the future.

In 1989 several defendants stood accused of committing terroristic acts in Kuwait. The attorney for the defendants argued to the court that according to Islamic law his clients were *bughat*, and therefore he argued that they should not receive the death sentence. After pronouncing the death sentence on several of the defendants, the judge chided the attorney for arguing outside his brief; then the judge noted that he was bound by the Kuwaiti criminal code and not Islamic law. In any case, the judge commented, *Ahkam al-Bughat* was designed to cover crimes committed in the course of rebellion, and not general acts of terrorism. In another case, in 1982 the attorneys representing those accused of assassinating President Anwar al-Sadat argued that pursuant to Article 2 (as amended on 22 May 1980) of the Egyptian constitution, a sentence pronouncing the death sentence on political criminals would be unconstitutional. The argument was that those who assassinated President Sadat were *bughat*, and since Article 2 provides that "the principles of the Shari'a are the main source of legislation in the Arab Republic of Egypt" the court could not assess the death penalty without contravening the Shari'a. The military tribunal ignored this argument in passing the death sentence on certain defendants.[92]

Of course it remains to be seen how *Ahkam al-Bughat* might be interpreted in a modern state that does adhere to Islamic law, particularly insofar as it is a legal doctrine. What is clear, and of considerable interest, is that classical jurists did not think that the irregularity of certain armed conflicts placed such conflicts outside the realm of moral and legal discussion. The cost and challenges are very high in irregular warfare, but it is precisely when the stakes are so high that it is important for moral and legal restraints to discipline the zeal for victory and the fear of defeat.

## NOTES

1. Courtney Campbell, "Moral Responsibility and Irregular War," in the present volume.

2. See James Turner Johnson, "Historical Roots and Sources of the Just War Tradition in Western Culture," in *Just War and Jihad: Historical and Theoretical Perspectives on War and Peace in Western and Islamic Traditions*, ed. John Kelsay and James Turner Johnson (Westport, CT: Greenwood Press, 1991), for a discussion of *jus in bello* and *jus ad bellum*. See also his discussion in *Can Modern War Be Just?* (New Haven and London: Yale University Press, 1984), pp. 53–63. See Michael Walzer, *Just and Unjust Wars* (New York: Basic Books, 1977), pp. 176–206 for a discussion of the ethical considerations that should guide irregular warriors and those responding to guerrilla warfare.

3. Johnson, *Can Modern War Be Just?* pp. 54–55.

4. John Kelsay, "Religion, Morality and the Governance of War: The Case of Classical Islam," forthcoming in *Journal of Religious Ethics*; also "Islam and the Distinction Between Combatants and Non-Combatants," this volume.

5. Ibid.

6. See Etan Kohlberg, "The Development of the *Imami* Shi'i Doctrine of Jihad," *Zeitschrift der Deutschen Morgenlandischen Gessellschaft*, 126 (1976), pp. 69–78 on the *bughat* in Shi'i thought.

7. The use of the word "state" does not refer to the modern concept of statehood. Rather it is a convenient term used in this chapter to refer to a territory governed by an *Imam*, whether it be an *ummah*, nation, empire or any other territorial entity.

8. The terms *bughat* (rebels), *baghi* (rebel) or *baghy* (rebellion) will consistently be used in this essay.

9. For a brief statement on the difference between *Ahkam al-Ridda, Ahkam al-Hiraba, Ahkam Qat' al Tariq* and *Ahkam al-Bughat* see Abu Ya'la, *al-Ahkam al-Sultaniyah* (Beirut: Dar al-Kutub al-ilimiyah, 1985) pp. 51–64; al-Mawardi, al-Ahkam al-Sultaniyah (Beirut: Dar al-Kutub al-ilmiyah, 1985), pp. 61–81; Ibn Taymiyya, *al-Siyasa al-Shari'a* (Beirut: Dal al-Afaq) 1983, pp. 74–84; and Majid Khadduri, *War and Peace in the Law of Islam* (Baltimore: Johns Hopkins University Press, 1979), pp. 76–80.

10. For example, see al-Shafi'i *al-Umm*, vol. 4 (Cairo: Kitab al-Sha'ab, n.d.) pp. 133–39; al-Nawawi, *al-Majmu Sharh al-Muhazab*, vol. 17 (Cairo: al-Imam, n.d.) pp. 516–42; al-Sarakhsi, *Kitab al-Mabsut*, vol. 9 (Cairo: al-Sa'adah, 1324 Hijra) pp. 125–32; and Ibn Qudamah, *al-Mughni*, vol. 8 (Cairo: Maktabat al-Qahira, 1969), pp. 424–28. Some Shafi'i jurists specifically state that *Ahkam al-Bughat* were taken from Ali's practices. See al-Ramli, *Nihayat al-Muhtaj*, vol. 7 (Cairo: Mustafa al-Halabi, 1967), p. 403 and al-Jamal, *Hashiyat al-Jamal*, vol. 5 (Cairo: al-Maktaba al-Tujariya al-Kubra, n.d.), p. 113.

11. See for example, Malik, *al-Mudawwana al-Kubra*, vol. 2 (Baghdad: al-Muthanna Library, 1323 Hijra), p. 47.

12. One such *hadith*, for example, says, "That [person] who comes to you while you have all agreed upon one *Imam* [and] advocates the dismantling of your unity and the dispersion of your group, kill that person." Another *hadith* states, "He who dislikes an order of an *amir* should withhold himself from opposition, for he who rebels against the *sultan* by a span dies a death of *jahiliyya*." For a list of similar *hadiths* on the subject see al-Bayhaqi, *al-Sunan al-Kubra*, vol. 8 (India: Da'erat al Ma'aref, 1304 Hijra) pp. 168–72.

13. Compare for example al-Shafi'i's treatment of the subject (*supra* note 10) with that of al-Jamal, *supra* note 10, p. 114. See also Ibn Qudamah, *supra* note 10, p. 423 and al-Buhuti, *Kashaf al-Qina an Matn al-Ina*, vol. 6 (Riyad: Maktabat al-Nasr al-hadithah, n.d.) pp. 158.

14. See on this principle Hamid al-Ghazali, *Ihya ulum al-Din*, vol. 2 (Beirut: Dar al-Ma'aref, n.d.) pp. 306–12. Also see Qur'an 3:104, 9:71, 9:112; 22:41; 3:114; 7:157; 9:67, 31:17.

15. In Abi Zakariya al-Nawawi, *Riyadd al-Salihin* (Beirut: Dar al-hadith, n.d.) pp. 109.

16. For example, see al-Buhuti, *supra* note 13 at p. 158.

17. For example, see Ibn Hazm, *al-Muhala*, vol. 11 (Beirut: al-Maktab al-Tujari, n.d.), p. 98.

18. For this *hadith* and similar injunctions, see Ibn Hajar al-Asqallani, *Fath al-Bari*, vol. 13 (Beirut: Dar al-Ma'aref, n.d.), pp. 121–23.

19. See for example Ibn Abidin, *Hashiyat Radd al-Muhtar*, vol. 4 (Cairo: al-Halabi, 1966), p. 261 and al-Sawi, *Bulghat al-Salik ila Arab al-Masalek*, vol. 3 (Cairo: Dar Ih'ya al-Kutub al-Arabiyah, 1978), p. 442.

20. Qur'an 49:9–10. Translation of Yusuf Ali.

21. al-Bayhaqi, *supra* note 12 at pp. 189–93; al-Sarakhsi, *supra* note 10 at p. 270; Ibn Qudamah, *supra* note 10 at p. 423 and 527; Ibn Muflih al-Maqdisi, *al-Mubd'i fi Sharh al-Mughni*, vol. 9 (Damascus: al-Maktab al-Islami, 1979), p. 161; al-Buhuti, *supra* note 13 at p. 158; al-Nawawi, *al-Majmu*, *supra* note 10 at p. 524; al-Hattab *Mawahib al-Jalil* and printed with it, al-Mawaaq *al-Taj wa al-iklil*, vol. 6 (Beirut: Dar al-Kitab, n.d.), p. 227; al Shafi'i, *supra* note 10 at pp. 237 and 144; and Ibn Jama'a, *Tahrir al-Ahkam fi Tadbir ahl al-Islam* (Qatar: al-Shu'uon al-Diniyah, 1985), p. 243.

22. See for example Ibn Abidin, *supra* note 19 at p. 265; Ibn al-Humam, *Sharh Fath al Qadir*, vol. 4 (Cairo: al-Matba'a al-Qubra, 1316 Hijra), p. 214. See also all sources cited in note 21.

23. See Ibn Taymiyya, *Minhaj al-Sunna*, vol. 2 (Beirut: al-Maktabah al-ilmiyah, n.d.), pp. 232–33 and al-Juwayni, *Fada'ih al-Batiniyya* (Qatar: Matba'at Nahdat Misr, 1401 Hirja), pp. 109–10, 126, 214–15, and 254.

24. Abu Ya'la, *supra* note 9 at p. 54; al-Mawardi, *supra* note 9 at p. 73; and Ibn Jama'a, *supra* note 21 at p. 239.

25. Compare al-Shafi'i, *supra* note 10 to al-Jamal (writing about 1,000 years later), *supra* note 10; compare al-Sarakhsi, *supra* note 10 to Ibn Abidin (writing about 700 years later) *supra* note 19; compare Malik, *supra* note 11 to al-Sawi (writing nearly 1,100 years later) *supra* note 19; compare Abu Ya'la, *supra* note 9 to Ibn Qudamah (writing about 200 years later) *supra* note 10 and to al-Buhuti (writing about 400 years later) *supra* note 13.

26. For example, see al-Sawi, *supra* note 19 at p. 442; al-Dasuqi, *Hashiyat al-Dasugi ala al-Sharh al-Kabir*, vol. 4 (n.p.: Dar ihya al-Kitab al-Arabi, n.d.), p. 298; and Ibn Muflih, *supra* note 21, table of contents of volume 9.

27. For example, Ibn Hazm, *supra* note 17, table of contents of volume 11.

28. For example, al-Haythami Ibn Hajar, *Tuhfat al-Muhtaj*, vol. 3 (Damascus: Dar al-fikr, n.d.), p. 424 and Malik, *supra* note 11 at p. 47.

29. See al-Shafi'i, *supra* note 10 at pp. 133–39; al-Samarqandi, *Tuhfat al-Fugaha*, vol. 3 (Damascus: Dar al-Fikr, n.d.), p. 424; and Malik, *supra* note 11 at p. 47.

30. Malik, ibid., and al-Sarakhsi, *supra* note 10 at p. 124. Most jurists, with the Malikis as the notable exception, do not justify their organizational rationale. But this lack of consensus over whether *Ahkam al-Bughat* is a crime, tort, or merely an issue of administrative conduct reflects the underdeveloped status of this area of the law. Additionally, it symbolizes the fact that *Ahkam al-Bughat* is a combination of specific laws and moral exhortations that do not always easily coexist.

31. See Abd al-Rahman al-Jaziri, *Kitab al-fiqh ala al-Mazahib al-Arba'ah*, vol. 5 (Beirut: Dar Ihya al-Turah al-Arabi, n.d.), p. 417; al-Kasani, *Kitab Bada'i al-Sana'i*, vol. 7 (Beirut: Dar al-Kitab al-Arabi, 1973), p. 140; al-Sarakhsi, *supra* note 10; Ibn Hazm, *supra* note 17 at p. 97; al-Dardir, *al-Sharh al-Saghir*, vol. 4 (Cairo: Dar al-Ma'arif, 1972), pp. 426–27; al-Kharashi, *al-Sharh al-Saghir ala Khalil*, printed with it al-Adawi, *Hashiyat al-Adawi*, vol. 7 (Cairo: al-Matba's al-Kubra, 1317), p. 60 and al-Nawawi, *Minhaj al-Talibin*, vol. 3 (Batavia:

Imprimerie du Gouvernement, 1884), p. 198. The Hanbali and Hanafi jurists had a typically archaic method of stating those three requirements. They divided those who rebel against the *Imam* into three main groups. Group one are those who commit *khuruj* without either a *ta'wil* or *shauka* and those who are treated as common criminals. Group two are those who commit *khuruj* with *ta'wil* and *shauka* but their reasoning advocates the indiscriminate slaughter of Muslims; for example, the Khawarij. Group three are those who commit *khuruj*, and they have a *ta'wil* and *shauka*; these are *bughat*. See Ibn Qudamah, *supra* note 10 at p. 424; Iban al-Humam, *supra* note 22 at pp. 408–9; and Ibn Abidin, *supra* note 19 at p. 262.

32. Ibn Qudamah, *supra* note 10 at p. 536; al-Sawi, *supra* note 19 at p. 443; and al-Mawaq, *supra* note 21 at p. 278. But see al-Sarakhsi, *supra* note 10 at p. 130. Al-Ramli, a Shafi'i jurist, reports the unpopular opinion that no sin attaches to the *baghy* in this life, but the *bughat* might be held accountable in the final day, *supra* note 10 at p. 404.

33. Al-Ramli, ibid., and al-Jamal, *supra* note 10 at pp. 113–14. Also see Ibn Jama'a, *supra* note 21 at pp. 240–41 and Ibn Hajar, *supra* note 28 at pp. 66 and 68.

34. Al-Jaziri, *supra* note 31 at p. 418; al-Sawi, *supra* note 19 at p. 442–43; al-Dasuqi, *supra* note 26 at p. 298; al-Mawardi, *supra* note 9 at p. 73; Ibn Hajar, *supra* note 28 at p. 66; Ibn al-Humam, *supra* note 22 at pp. 408–9; al-Kasani, *supra* note 31 at p. 140; Ibn Muflih, *supra* note 21 at p. 159; and Ibn Qudamah, *supra* note 10 at p. 423. A few writers argued that *Khuruj* cannot exist without the dissenters mobilizing in a particular area (*tahayyuz*). See Abu Ya'la, *supra* note 9 at p. 52 and al-Mawardi, *supra* note 9 at p. 73. However, this requirement has been rejected by the majority of Muslim jurists. Additionally, from a modern perspective, it is quite archaic in nature and pointless.

35. See Najati Sanad, *Nazariyat al-Jarima al-Sayasiya fi al-Islam* (Cairo: Top Guy, n.d.), pp. 362–73 for a useful study of this matter.

36. Ibn Qudamah, *supra* note 10 at p. 530.

37. See al-Sarakhsi, *supra* note 10 at p. 126 and Al-Bayhaqi, *supra* note 12 at p. 184. Al-Bayhaqi, who is a Shafi'i jurist, relies on the following precedent: Bin al-Khatab (the governor of Kufa) found a person cursing the Caliph Umar Bin Abd Al Aziz in the market. Bin al-Khatab wrote to the caliph asking if he should kill or whip the offender. The caliph answered back saying, "If you would have killed him I would have killed you [referring to the governor] and if you would have severed one of his limbs or whipped him, I would have done the same to you. You can either [verbally] insult him back [as he has done to me] or forgive him."

38. Western scholarship, as opposed to modern Islamic scholarship, is fond of distinguishing between the terms *"caliph," "Imam," "sultan"* and *"amir."* See for example Ann Lambton, *State and Government in Medieval Islam* (Oxford: Oxford University Press, 1981) and W. Montgomery Watt, *Islamic Political Thought* (Edinburgh: Edinburgh University Press, 1968). I am not sure these sharp conceptual distinctions hold much merit. Late Muslim writers such as al-Mawardi and Abu Ya'la used the terms *"sultan"* or *"Imam"* interchangeably. Additionally, in several *hadith* the words *"amir"* or *"Imam"* are used interchangeably. See Hafiz al-Munziri, *Mukhtasar Sahih Muslim* (Kuwait: al-Dar al-Kuwaitiyah, 1966), pp. 87–

94. In fact, Umar Bin al-Khattab was called *amir al-mu'minin* and *caliph* simultaneously.

39. al-Shafi'i, *supra* note 10 at p. 135.

40. See al-Samarqandi, *supra* note 29 at p. 423.

41. See Ibn Jama's, *supra* note 21 at pp. 239–40. Ibn Hazm, *supra* note 17 specifically states that no distinction should be made between an *Imam* or *sultan* at pp. 98–99.

42. The requirements for a rightful caliph are usually (1) moral and religious probity (*adala*), (2) religious learning that qualifies a person to perform *ijtihad*, (3) full physical and mental health, (4) probity in political matters, (5) courage, (6) Qurayshi lineage.

43. al-Nawawi, *supra* note 31 at pp. 198 and 203; al-Nawawi, *supra* note 10 at p. 516; al-Jamal, *supra* note 10 at pp. 114–19, 121; Al-Ramli, *supra* note 10 at pp. 66 and 78–79 (also see the commentaries on his work by al-Abadi and al-Sharwani printed in the same volume and the same pages); Ibn Abidin, *supra* note 19 at pp. 263–64 (also see the commentary on his work—name unknown—same reference); al-Sawi, *supra* note 19 at p. 442; al-Kharashi and al-Adawi, *supra* note 31 at p. 60; al-Dardir, *supra* note 31 at pp. 426–27; al-Dasuqi, *supra* note 26 at p. 298; al-Buhuti, *supra* note 13 at p. 158; and Ibn Qudamah, *supra* note 10 at p. 526–27.

44. al-Sawi, *supra* note 19 at pp. 442–43; al-Dardir, *supra* note 31 at pp. 426 and 428; al-Dasuqi, *supra* note 26 at p. 299; and al-Hattab, *supra* note 21 at p. 277. But for a contrary opinion from a Maliki see al-Kharashi, *supra* note 31 at p. 60.

45. Ibn Hazm, *supra* note 17 at p. 98.

46. Both the commentators to Ibn Abidin's work, *supra* note 19 at p. 261, and Ibn Hajar's work, *supra* note 28 at p. 66, explicitly state that at the early stage of Islamic history refusing to obey what is thought to be a sinful command is excused. But in light of the fact that injustice has become widespread in their age, disobedience could never be excused.

47. Ibn al-Humann, *supra* note 22 at p. 441; Ibn Abidin, *supra* note 19 at p. 265; al-Juwayni, *supra* note 23 at p. 115; al-Kasani, *supra* note 31 at p. 140; and Ibn Muflih, *supra* note 21 at p. 161.

48. This is particularly obvious in the thought of Ibn Hazm, *supra* note 17 at p. 98. Also see Ibn Abidin, *supra* note 19 at p. 267; Ibn al-Humam, *supra* note 22 at pp. 408–9; al-Sawi, *supra* note 19 at p. 443; and al-Jaziri, *supra* note 31 at p. 417.

49. See al-Bayhaqi, *supra* note 12 at p. 175 and Ibn Qudamah, *supra* note 10 at p. 536.

50. Ibn Qudamah, *supra* note 10 at p. 536; also see al-Bayhaqi, *supra* note 12 at pp. 172–74.

51. Several modern Muslim scholars examining the question have concluded that *Ahkam al-Bughat* were designed to apply to cases of political rebellion as well as religious rebellion. See Medhat Abou El Fadl, "*Jarimat al-Baghy fi al-fiqh al-Islami*," *al-Mohami* 69 no. 79 (April-May-June 1982); Abd al-Qadir Awda, *al-Tashr' al-Jina'i al-Islami*, vol. 1 (Beirut: Dar al-Kitab al-Arabi, n.d.), p. 100 and Sanad, *supra* note 35 at p. 412.

52. See al-Tamimi al-Baghdadi, *Usul al-Din* (Beirut: Dar al-Hilal, 1980), p. 290; Ibn Muflih, *supra* note 21 at p. 159; Ibn Hajar, *supra* note 28 at pp. 66–67; Ibn

Qudamah, *supra* note 10 at p. 423; Adawi, *supra* note 31 at p. 114; see al-Tabari, *Tarikh al-Tabari*, vol. 4 (Beirut: Iz al-Din, 1987), pp. 525–27 and 552–54 for the claims of Talha and Zubayr against Ali.

53. Ibn Qudamah, *supra* note 10 at pp. 524–25; al-Buhuti, *supra* note 13 at p. 161; Ibn Muflih, *supra* note 21 at p. 160; Malik, *supra* note 11 at p. 47; Ibn Abidin, *supra* note 19 at p. 262; al-Kasani, *supra* note 31 at p. 140; Ibn al-Humam, *supra* note 22 at p. 408; al-Ramli, *supra* note 10 at p. 403; see also Ibn Taymiyya, *supra* note 23 at p. 232–33 for a virulent attack on those who claim that the Khawarij are *bughat* and not apostates.

54. Ibn Abidin, *supra* note 19 at p. 262.

55. See Malik, *supra* note 11 at p. 47; Ibn Muflih, *supra* note 21 at p. 166; Ibn Qudamah, *supra* note 10 at p. 536; and al-Sarakhsi, *supra* note 10 at p. 132. Both Abu Ya'la, *supra* note 9 at p. 54 and al-Mawardi, *supra* note 9 at p. 73, equate a *ta'wil* to a *madhab* (a religious school of thought).

56. Ibn Hazm, *supra* note 17 at p. 98; al-Adawi, *supra* note 31 at p. 60; al-Dardir, *supra* note 31 at p. 403; and Zakariyah al-Ansari, *Sharh al-Manhaj*, printed with al-Jamal, *supra* note 10 at p. 114.

57. al-Sarakhsi, *supra* note 10 at p. 132; Ibn Abidin, *supra* note 19 at p. 267; Ibn al-Humam, *supra* note 22 at pp. 414–15; Ibn Muflih, *supra* note 21 at p. 159; and al-Nawawi, *supra* note 10 at p. 523.

58. al-Jamal, *supra* note 10 at pp. 113–14; Ibn Hajar, *supra* note 28 at pp. 66–67; al-Ramli, *supra* note 10 at p. 403; Ibn Muflih, *supra* note 21 at p. 159; and Abu Yihya al-Ansari, *Asna al-Matalib fi Sharh Raud al-Talib*, vol. 3 (Cairo: al-Mayminyah) at p. 111. Modern jurists have reported this proposition, advanced by particular jurists from the Hanafi and Shafi'i schools of thought, as though it were a well-established principle. See Abou El Fadl, *supra* note 51 at p. 72; and Sanad, *supra* note 35 at pp. 420–21. I cannot agree that it is a well-established requirement because it is not mentioned by a great many Muslim jurists. It cannot be assumed that the lack of such mention is simply an oversight.

59. See al-Jamal, *supra* note 10 at p. 114; al-Ramli, *supra* note 10 at p. 403; Ibn Hajar, *supra* note 28 at pp. 66–67; and Sanad, *supra* note 35 at p. 422.

60. On the laws of apostasy see Abu Ya'la, *supra* note 9 at pp. 51–53; al-Buhuti, *supra* note 13 at pp. 168–74; al-Dasuqi, *supra* note 26 at pp. 301–6; al-Hattab, *supra* note 21 at pp. 280–90; al-Dardir, *supra* note 31 at pp. 434–40; al-Sarakhsi, *supra* note 10 at pp. 98–124; al-Kasani, *supra* note 31 at pp. 134–40; al-Jamal, *supra* note 10 at pp. 121–24; and al-Ramli, *supra* note 10 at pp. 413–20.

61. al-Jamal, *supra* note 10 at p. 113 and al-Ramli, *supra* note 10 at p. 403.

62. Qur'an 9:103, translation of Yusuf Ali.

63. Ibn Muflih, *supra* note 21 at p. 159; Ibn Qudamah, *supra* note 10 at p. 423; al-Dardir, *supra* note 31 at p. 427; Adawi, *supra* note 31 at p. 60; Ibn Hajar, *supra* note 28 at pp. 66–67; Ibn Jama'a, *supra* note 21 at p. 240; al-Ramli, *supra* note 10 at p. 403; and al-Jamal, *supra* note 10 at p. 114.

64. This is especially so in light of the fact that Muslim jurists consider that a *zindiq* is an apostate who hides his true beliefs. So even if a person accused of being a *zindiq* vehemently denies any heretical beliefs, he might be executed.

65. Ibn Qudamah, *supra* note 10 at p. 424; Ibn Muflih, *supra* note 21 at pp. 159–60; al-Shafi'i, *supra* note 10 at p. 135; Ibn Jama'a, *supra* note 21 at pp. 239–40; al-Nawawi, *supra* note 31 at p. 198; al-Jamal, *supra* note 10 at p. 114; al-Sa-

marqandi, *supra* note 29 at pp. 425 and 427; and al-Sarakhsi, *supra* note 10 at
p. 128. A few Hanafi jurists argued that *shauka* exempts the *bughat* from liability
because the coercive sovereignty of the *Imam* ceases (*li suqut wilayat al-ilzam*); al-
Kasani, *supra* note 31 at p. 141; and Ibn al-Humam, *supra* note 22 at p. 415.

66. Ibn Qudamah, *supra* note 10 at p. 424; al-Buhuti, *supra* note 13 at p. 161;
al-Ramli, *supra* note 10 at p. 405; and Ibn Hajar, *supra* note 28 at p. 70. Al-Ramli
relies on *shauka* to such an extent that he argues that if *shauka* exists liability is
negated even if there is no *ta'wil*.

67. al-Dardir, *supra* note 31 at p. 427; al-Dasuqi, *supra* note 26 at p. 299; al-
Kharashi, *supra* note 31 at p. 60; al-Sawi, *supra* note 19 at p. 442; and Ibn Hazm,
*supra* note 17 at p. 99. In Ibn Hazm's opinion, a *baghi* could be a single person
because if the dissenters are right and the caliph, as a single individual, could
be a *baghi*, by necessity, one person could be a *baghi*.

68. al-Hattab, *supra* note 21 at p. 277; al-Kharashi, *supra* note 31 at p. 60; al-
Sawi, *supra* note 19 at p. 443; al-Dasuqi, *supra* note 26 at p. 299; and al-Dardir,
*supra* note 31 at p. 427.

69. Abou El Fadl, *supra* note 51 at pp. 71 and 74; Sanad, *supra* note 35 at
pp. 436–38; and Awda, *supra* note 51 vol. II at pp. 674 and 687. Both Sanad and
Abou El Fadl seem to have relied on Awda's opinion in reaching this conclusion.
Another modern scholar, Wahba al-Zuhayri, *al-fiqh al-Islami wa adilatuh*, vol. 6
(Damascus: Dar al-Fikr, 1984), p. 142, who wrote independently from Awda did
not list *al-mughalaba* as a definitional requirement for *Ahkam al-Bughat*.

70. The difficulties of *al-mughalaba* are illustrated by the following example,
often used by medieval jurists. A group of Muslims refuses to pay taxes. Clearly
their action constitutes a *khuruj*. Assuming that the group satisfies the conditions
of *ta'wil* and *shauka*, there are (legally speaking) two possible responses. In the
first scenario, the *Imam* forces the group to pay taxes, and applies *ahkam al-
Bughat*. In the second, he forces them to pay taxes but does not apply the *ahkam*.
In the latter case, the group may be imprisoned and the property of its members
may be confiscated. In other words, the group's decision not to use violence
renders the application of *ahkam al-Bughat* discretionary. If *al-mughalaba* is applied, *ahkam al-Bughat* becomes a provision according to which a group that
undertakes armed rebellion is treated more leniently than one whose *khuruj* is
nonviolent. Such a distinction in treatment makes little sense. In the end, the
fact that most medieval jurists did not explicitly require the use of violence as
a prerequisite for the application of *ahkam al-Bughat* indicates that there is no
need to introduce the confusing and contradictory notion of *mughalaba*.

71. See al-Sarakhsi, *supra* note 10 at pp. 125–26 and 128; Ibn al-Humam, *supra*
note 22 at pp. 409–11; Ibn Abidin, *supra* note 19 at pp. 261–64; al-Kasani, *supra*
note 31 at p. 140; al-Shafi'i, *supra* note 10 at pp. 143–44; al-Mawardi, *supra* note
9 at pp. 74–75; al-Nawawi, *supra* note 31 at p. 200; Ibn Jama'a, *supra* note 21 at
p. 240; al-Bayhaqi, *supra* note 12 at pp. 178–81; Ibn Hajar, *supra* note 28 at pp. 70–
71; al-Ramli, *supra* note 10 at p. 406; al-Dardir, *supra* note 31 at p. 428; al-Sawi,
*supra* note 19 at p. 443; al-Dasuqi, *supra* note 26 at p. 299; Ibn Qudamah, *supra*
note 10 at p. 527; Ibn Muflih, *supra* note 21 at pp. 160–61; al-Buhuti, *supra* note
13 at p. 55; and Ibn Hazm, *supra* note 17 at p. 99.

72. Al-Shafi'i, *supra* note 10 at p. 144; Ibn Abidin, *supra* note 19 at p. 264; al-

Sarakhsi, *supra* note 10 at p. 128; Ibn Qudamah, *supra* note 10 at pp. 527–28; and cites ibid.

73. Ibn-Qudamah, *supra* note 10 at p. 529; al-Buhuti, *supra* note 13 at p. 163; Ibn Muflih, *supra* note 21 at p. 162; Ibn Hazm, *supra* note 31 at p. 60; Ibn al-Humam, *supra* note 22 at p. 41; al-Kasani, *supra* note 31 at p. 141; al-Shafi'i, *supra* note 10 at p. 72; and al-Ramli, *supra* note 10 at p. 407; al-Sawi, *supra* note 19 at p. 443; al-Kharashi and Adawi, *supra* note 31 at p. 60.

74. Ibn Abidin, *supra* note 19 at p. 265; al-Samarqandi, *supra* note 29 at p. 424; al-Kasani, *supra* note 31 at p. 140; Ibn al-Humam, *supra* note 22 at pp. 412 and 414–15; al-Sarakhsi, *supra* note 10 at p. 129; al-Hattab, *supra* note 21 at p. 278; al-Kharashi, *supra* note 31 at p. 61; al-Dardir, *supra* note 31 at p. 429; Ibn Qudamah, *supra* note 10 at pp. 532–33; al-Buhuti, *supra* note 13 at p. 164; Ibn Muflih, *supra* note 21 at pp. 162–63; Ibn Hazm, *supra* note 17, pp. 100–103; al Shafi'i, *supra* note 10 at p. 137; al-Ramli, *supra* note 10 at p. 406; and al-Bayhaqi, *supra* note 12 at p. 181. Al-Bayhaqi complains that the rule not permitting the killing of the prisoners of the *bughat* has caused much hardship in his day.

75. al-Shafi'i, *supra* note 10 at p. 140; al-Bayhaqi, *supra* note 12 at p. 185; al-Mawardi, *supra* note 9 at p. 77; Ibn Qudamah, *supra* note 10 at p. 535; Abu Ya'la, *supra* note 9 at p. 56; al-Buhuti, *supra* note 13 at p. 165; al-Sarakhsi, *supra* note 10 at p. 131; and al-Samarqandi, *supra* note 29 at pp. 425–26. Muslim jurists disagreed as to whether those killed from *Ahl al-Adl* are considered martyrs or not. See Ibn Hazm, *supra* note 17 at p. 108 and all sources cited in note 74.

76. al-Sarakhsi, *supra* note 10 at p. 126; Ibn Abidin, *supra* note 19 at p. 265; al-Kasani, *supra* note 31 at p. 141; Ibn al-Humam, *supra* note 22 at p. 412; Ibn Qudamah, *supra* note 10 at p. 534; al-Bayhaqi, *supra* note 12 at pp. 181–82; al-Mawardi, *supra* note 9 at p. 75; Ibn Hazm, *supra* note 17 at p. 102; al-Sawi, *supra* note 19 at p. 444; and al-Jaziri, *supra* note 31 at p. 421.

77. al-Jaziri, *supra* note 31 at p. 422; Ibn Hazm, *supra* note 17 at pp. 100–101; al-Dardir, *supra* note 31 at p. 429; Ibn Qudamah, *supra* note 10 at p. 532; al-Buhuti, *supra* note 13 at p. 165; Ibn Hajar, *supra* note 28 at p. 72; al-Ramli, *supra* note 10 at p. 407; Ibn Jama'a, *supra* note 21 at pp. 244–45; al-Nawawi, *supra* note 10 at p. 532; and Ibn al-Humam, *supra* note 22 at p. 412. Some jurists like Ibn Abidin, *supra* note 19 at p. 265 and Ibn Muflih, *supra* note 21 at p. 163 argued that the *Imam* can imprison *bughat* until they repent and promise not to return to rebellion again.

78. al-Sarakhsi, *supra* note 10 at pp. 127–28; Ibn al-Humam, *supra* note 22 at p. 414; Ibn Abidin, *supra* note 19 at p. 267; Ibn Hazm, *supra* note 17 at p. 105; Ibn Qudamah, *supra* note 10 at p. 532; Ibn Muflih, *supra* note 21 at p. 164; al-Buhuti, *supra* note 13 at p. 165; al-Kharashi, *supra* note 31 at p. 300; al-Dardir, *supra* note 31 at p. 429; and al-Sawi, *supra* note 19 at p. 444. Some Shafi'i jurists disagreed and said that *al-Bughat* should always be *financially* liable for the destruction of property or life. See Ibn al-Humam, *supra* note 22 at p. 414 and Ibn Qudamah, *supra* note 10, vol. 10, at p. 61, refuting this opinion. al-Shafi'i himself first refused to except the *bughat* from liability. Later, he changed his opinion. See al-Shafi'i, *supra* note 10 at p. 134 and al-Jamal, *supra* note 10 at pp. 116–17. Some late Shafi'i jurists argued that liability is negated only if the destruction that occurred was a result of the necessities of combat. Therefore, if the *bughat*

engaged in a pointless rampage, they were held liable. See al-Ramli, *supra* note 10 at p. 405 and Ibn Hajar, *supra* note 28 at p. 72.

79. See al-Shafi'i, *supra* note 10 at p. 135 and 136–37; al-Kasani, *supra* note 31 at p. 141; Ibn Hazm, *supra* note 17 at p. 414; al-Sarakhsi, *supra* note 10 at pp. 134–35. In addition to the story of Ibn Muljam, the following story is a precedent for this rule. During the reign of Ali Ibn Abi Taleb a group of al-Khawarij resided at the al-Nahrayan region. Ali appointed a governor over the area who was eventually assassinated by the group. Ali, as caliph, demanded that the group turn over the murderer for prosecution. However, the group refused to do so insisting that they, as a group, collectively killed the governor. Ali then fought the whole group and subdued it. This story is in al-Mawardi, *supra* note 9 at p. 74 and al-Bayhaqi, *supra* note 12 at p. 185. *Ahkam al-Bughat* did not protect the group because the crime was not committed during an act of general rebellion by the Khawarij. Rather one person killed the governor and subsequently the group claimed responsibility.

80. Modern Muslim jurists, relying on this type of rationale, argue that *Ahkam al-Bughat* is equivalent to the Roman and Western concept of the political crime. As such, *Ahkam al-Bughat* might not only protect clearly religious/political rebels like the Muslim Brotherhood, but might even protect Muslim rebels who are not specifically religiously oriented (perhaps an organization that seeks democratic reforms or the like). See Sanad, *supra* note 35; Awda, *supra* note 51; and Abou El Fadl, *supra* note 51.

81. See on this subject Michael Akehurst, *A Modern Introduction to International Law* (London: George Allen and Unwin, 1984), pp. 240–47.

82. This type of argument is remarkably similar to the notion of proportionality in the Western *jus ad bellum*, by which the resort to force might be justified if the total good outweighs that total evil anticipated. See Johnson, *supra* note 2 at pp. 25–27.

83. See Johnson, *supra* note 2, pp. 20–21.

84. The notion of reconciliation eventually surfaced in Western thought in the twentieth century. See Otto Kirchheimer, *Political Justice* (Princeton: Princeton University Press, 1961), pp. 398–99.

85. Robert Ferrari, "Political Crime," *Columbia Law Review* 20 (1920), pp. 311–13.

86. Pierre A. Papadotas, "Le delit politique: Contribution a'letude des crimes contre l'etat." These no. 507, Librarie E. Droz, Geneve, 1954. First part, p. 2 quoted in B. L. Ingraham and Kazuhiko Tokoro, "Political Crime in the United States and Japan: A Comparative Study," *Issues in Criminology* 4 no. 2 (1969), p. 145.

87. Ingraham and Tokoro, "Political Crime," p. 159.

88. See Fahmi Howeidi, *Al-Qur'an wa al-Sultan* (Cairo: Dal al-Shuruq, 1981).

89. Campbell, *supra* note 1. See Walzer *supra* note 2 at p. 177 for a discussion of benevolent quarantine in the Western war tradition.

90. See Johnson, *supra* note 2 on these concepts in the just war tradition.

91. See Ibn Taymiyya, *supra* note 23 at pp. 232–33.

92. Case no. 7 for the year 1981, High Military Court for National Security. See the book on this case by Shawqi Khaled, *Muhakamat Fir'aun* (Cairo: Sina Lil Nashr, 1986). Also see on the trial of the *Jihad* members Omar Abd al-Rahman, *Kalimat Haq* (Cairo: Dar al-itisam, n.d.), especially pp. 32–80.

# III

Combatancy, Noncombatancy, and Noncombatant Immunity

# 8

## Combatancy, Noncombatancy, and Noncombatant Immunity in Just War Tradition

### Robert L. Phillips

#### I.

The tradition of just war thinking intends to stand as the moral and prudent choice over two unacceptable alternatives—pacifism and realism. The pacifist alternative is rejected primarily because it elevates a single value (life) to a position of paramountcy. The version of just war theory espoused in this chapter follows an essentially Aristotelian approach to ethics, arguing that there are many fundamental goods and that these goods are incommensurable. This means that while life is indeed a value, it is not reasonable to think that all other values (liberty, friendship, etc.) must always be downgraded in favor of life whenever there is a conflict between life and one of the other values. The pacifist's single minded commitment to preserving life at all costs radically downgrades other values.

It can also be argued that the pacifist does not provide convincing justification of his claim that saving life *is* paramount and that even if pacifism were adopted there is no guarantee that it would have the ethically desirable consequences that its proponents advertise. Nonviolent resistance may be an appropriate tactic under some circumstances, but under others it may involve negating the very values it seeks to preserve. Thus pacifism may have been appropriate against the British in India in 1946 or as part of the American civil rights movement of the 1960s but hardly against a Hitler or a Stalin. Indeed, for these tyrants the very nonviolence of the pacifists would be confirmation of their inferiority.

Pacifism is an essentially "other-worldly" doctrine which, despite some domestic successes, is irrelevant in the area of international relations. It is for this reason that many states are willing to exempt pacifists from military service. The pacifist objection to all war, regardless of the causes and conditions, is no real threat to the political policies of any state, unlike the possibility of selective objection built into just war theory.

The polar alternative to pacifism is realism (realpolitik), the view that state interest predominates and overrides moral considerations in calculations about the use of force. For realists, state interest is in no way constrained by moral considerations or any other "inherent" principles. States may do whatever they conceive to be in their interests. In Hobbesian terms, international society is a "state of nature" or the "war of all against all." Thus in the absence of a universal sovereign, international law is always superseded by domestic law. For realists, just war theory is self-contradictory in admitting that states have interests but in denying them the means to defend those interests.

Just war theorists do indeed grant that states have their own interests, but will deny that moral restraints are incompatible with such interests. Rather, the very notion of a "state interest" entails that if force is used it will be in pursuit of some policy that seeks the good of that state. To that extent, force will be restrained by the aims of the policy itself. Indeed, war as a social activity is itself a restraint on absolute force. This is surely part of the meaning of the Clausewitzian dictum that war is a continuation of statecraft by other means. As a political program with any reasonable claim to be serving the interests of its constituents will not be usefully advanced by means that are likely to counter the policy, the use of force will be constrained by the shape of the policy and by the long-term effects of any use of force. Moreover, war itself is a purposive social activity (unlike riot), which is internally and externally rule governed and thus is inherently a restrained use of force. The emergence historically of conventions governing the initiation and prosecution of war, such as declarations of war, armistice, prisoner of war conventions, etc., attests to the recognition that war ought to be as restrained as possible and that the best way of restraining war is to insist that it be justified and that it be fought by armed and uniformed combatants. In short, the just war tradition argues that while states may well be the final judges of their interests, states cannot be said to *have* any interests that can be satisfied only by resort to *any* means whatever. A "policy" entails a political society, a moral community guided by reason and prudence. If war is an act and an instrument of policy, then it will be minimally restrained by those underlying principles. A realism that understands war simply in terms of available means is, moral questions aside, ultimately unrealistic. Bernard Brodie has succinctly put this point in a discussion of morality and state interests:

While morality by its very nature must be finally justified entirely on its own terms, it is not amiss to remind ourselves that especially in this world of rapid and abundant communications, any of our policies abroad that are either conspicuously immoral to begin with or likely to lapse into behavior that can easily be so labelled, whether justly or not so justly, is likely to prove quite inexpedient and ultimately self-defeating.[1]

The futility of detaching war from political aims is fairly obvious. But once political aims become the guiding principle behind the use of force, then we inevitably begin to think beyond the battlefield to the shape of things after the fighting, of what sort of world we want to live in as a result of our decision to go to war. We will also be brought, for prudential reasons, to reflect upon the way our conduct of hostilities will be perceived by other nations (including our enemies). And we will adopt a flexible response with respect to escalation as well as a willingness to maintain a degree of diplomatic contact. In other words, to adopt the viewpoint of political realism will be to find ourselves asking the kinds of questions raised by the just war tradition. State interest and morality are not always identical, but when rulers begin to think about statecraft in terms of their long range interests (with respect to war) they will inevitably articulate these interests using a set of questions like those that make up the just war tradition. In addition, the essential features of the just war tradition have passed into the usages of international law and into the rules for warfare of the various civilized states. And so for those wishing to participate in the public debate on international violence, there really is no alternative to articulating these issues in terms of some version of just war thinking.

If we reject pacifism and if political realism entails ultimate moral considerations, then we will be left to understand questions of international violence from the perspective of justice in war. That is, in addition to justifying the use of force as a defense of life and rights we are also required to exercise that force with due regard to discrimination and proportionality, the two principles that together define the *jus in bello* of just war tradition.

## II.

The *jus in bello* provisions of just war theory center upon the principles of discrimination and proportionality and the doctrine of double effect. I begin with a brief summary of these ideas.

*Discrimination*. The principle of discrimination is an application to war of the categorical prohibition of murder. While the deaths of innocent persons may be accepted incidentally to an attack upon a legitimate military target, innocent persons may never be directly attacked or targeted. Both murderous attack and murderous intent are ruled out. The doctrine of double effect is employed here to articulate the moral difference between intending the death of an innocent person and accepting the death of an innocent person as a collateral effect of attempting to bring about a good. This distinction relies heavily upon the intention of the agent, as double effect excuses agents from blame even though they may have foreknowledge of the death of innocent persons. Just war theory claims that the distinction between murder and acceptable or collateral civilian damage is moral and reasonable. If we are never allowed to place innocent lives at risk for a good cause, then most social activities would be impossible. For example, the activities of police, fire, and rescue services presuppose foreknown accidents where innocent people will be the victims of efforts by these services to save lives. While one knows with a statistical certainty that these deaths will occur, it would be unreasonable to claim that these inadvertent killings were the equivalent of murder. The principle of discrimination, then, prohibits direct attacks upon or targeting of innocent people but permits a degree of incidental or collateral damage.

*Proportionality.* Complementing the principle of discrimination is the principle of proportionality. Proportionality specifies that even after reasonable efforts are made to practice discriminate targeting, if the means used are sufficiently crude to cause the death of noncombatants out of proportion to the threat to the attacker, such means are not permitted. The principle holds that in cases where the use of force is justified it cannot be employed in absolutely *any* measure. If a war has the aim of justice, then the level of force cannot be such that new and greater injustices are created. It is critically important to note that in the just war tradition judgments of proportionality are not the "greater good/ lesser evil" calculations characteristic of the position known as ethical consequentialism. Consequentialists seek to ground ethics in such calculations, not recognizing that human goods are incommensurable. Judgments of proportionality, by contrast, are made in light of already existing ethical principles, such as the equality principle, which holds that there is to be no arbitrary choice among persons. Thus a decision to undertake a military action that risks civilian casualties will be done in light of a judgment that one is not imposing upon these civilians any risks that one would not be willing to have imposed upon oneself in relevantly similar circumstances.

*Double Effect.* Double effect is a refinement of a more general set of conditions having to do with the discriminating use of force. If the use of force by legitimate authority is to be justified, then obviously it cannot be administered in any quantity whatever or directed at any and every target. The most widely discussed aspect of double effect has been in connection with noncombatant immunity, and one of the key issues raised is how to make such immunity compatible with the foreknowledge that we will normally possess of the certain death of noncombatants incidental to military operations.

Double effect is derived from a quite general criterion of moral judgment enunciated by Aquinas: "Now moral acts take their species according to what is intended and not according to what is beside the intention, since this is accidental."[2] Aquinas is not claiming that the consequences of actions are morally irrelevant but, rather, that when one raises questions about the morality of a particular action (as opposed to its beauty, utility, and so on) one is inevitably making reference to the agent's intentions. "Accidental" is here used to mean not only the unforeseen but also the foreseen but undesired consequences of the action.

By emphasizing intention as the defining feature of moral behavior, supporters of *bellum justum* attempt to mark a difference between killing in war and murder in two different cases. First, the killing of enemy combatants in a justified war may be morally acceptable under certain specified circumstances. Second, the killing of noncombatants incidental to the prosecution of a necessary military operation in a justified war may also be morally acceptable under some circumstances. Finally, a direct attack upon noncombatants is morally prohibited.

There are at least two senses in which it is sometimes claimed that there is no relevant distinction between killing in war and murder. First is the view that all killing is murder, and that it is always wrong to deliberately take the life of another human. This would mean that in war it would be wrong to kill both combatants and noncombatants, and, indeed, that there is really no moral difference between these two classes. This is a version of pacifism that holds that under no circumstances may the death of another human being be willed; killing is wrong even if one's own life is placed at grave risk and even if the other person is the agresssor.

In the second view, the killing of noncombatants is murder even though the death of an aggressor combatant in war is morally acceptable. Thus if a war could be fought exclusively between combatants it would be, in principle, possible to avoid injustice. However, in actual combat where there is foreknowledge that operations will cause the death of noncombatants, there is, according to this view, no relevant difference between killing and murder. This view has generated two rather strikingly different conclusions with respect to what a moral agent ought to do faced with the possibility of combat.

On the one hand, since modern weaponry tends to be indiscriminate or to lend itself to indiscriminate use and since foreknowledge of the death of noncombatants cancels whatever good intentions we may offer by way of exculpation, we end up as pacifists by default. While admitting the theoretical possibility of a just war, the disproportionate use of force that seems a feature of modern war makes us pacifists, as it were, war by war.

On the other hand, starting from the same premises, it has sometimes been argued that since there are no relevant differences between killing and murder with respect to noncombatants, war may be fought without any restraint at all. That is, if a war is justified, then the absence of criteria for distinguishing between killing and murder is a permission to employ any means necessary to bring about victory. This argument is usually found embedded in a larger consequentialist framework that, in extreme cases, would permit the killing of noncombatants as a means of securing peace. This seems to have been the line taken by Sir Arthur Harris over the British bombing of German cities in World War II. When reproached with the indiscriminate and/or disproportionate character of area bombing, Harris replied, "It is war itself which is evil," thus implying the pointlessness of attempting to make distinctions between combatants and noncombatants. These then are the two main lines of criticism directed against the moral significance of the principle of double effect and, consequently, of the distinction between killing in war and murder.

As to the pacifist charge that combatancy is murder: if force is ever to be justified it must be directed against a target other than the person as such. One way of understanding this is that in war we are not precisely seeking the death of another person either as such (punishment) or as a means to some further end (deterrence). Therefore, the purpose or intention of an act of force in combat must be toward restraint or incapacitation of the aggressor. In this sense, the pacifist and the just war theorist might agree on the intrinsic value of human life, and so acts of force would target the person only in his role as combatant, or would target the combatant in the person. The purpose of combat and the intention of discrete acts of combat would carry the general intention merely to stop aggression, not to kill.

It may be objected that it is a logical impossibility to separate out the totality of actions plus the underlying rationale for such behavior that together constitute the combatant in the man. That is, to speak of a particular man or of "man" in general apart from particular behavior patterns is to speak of a nonentity. Hence the combatant in the man is not a possible target. Furthermore, to kill one is to kill the other. A soldier going into combat with the general intention of restraining or incapacitating must know before he ever lifts a weapon that combat will result in the death of a great many persons.

A consequentialist might put the objection in the following way: Two soldiers go into combat. Jones carries with him the intention to restrain, Smith intends to kill as many of the enemy as he can to avoid being killed now or in future. They both kill several of the enemy. What difference do their intentions make from the moral perspectives? In both cases an act of force causes the death of another person. No amount of "intentional" redescription can alter the brute fact of these corpses.

In trying to explain the centrality of intention in the just war tradition and in classical ethical writings, there are two points to make. The first has to do with the way in which awareness of an agent's intentions is crucial to understanding the meaning of any action and consequently to knowing how to describe it correctly. Setting moral questions entirely aside, we would be unable to make intelligible whole classes of human behaviors if we supposed that they could even be described as human actions without making intention central to the descriptions. That is, there are many cases where two sets of behaviors are identical with respect to result, observable bodily movements, and foreknowledge of result or effect. In such cases the only way to distinguish them as different *actions* is with reference to intention. As an example, take the case of suicide. If we follow the consequentialist suggestion and consider as relevant only foreknowledge of result, behavior patterns, and end results (a dead body), then suicide would be effectively defined as *any* action that the agent knew would bring about his own death. This is clearly absurd, for it would not permit us to distinguish between, for example, an officer who shoots himself to avoid a court-martial and another officer who courageously fights a rearguard action in such a way that he knows he will not survive. In both cases there is foreknowledge of one's own death, there are objective behavior patterns leading to that result, and there is the result itself. They differ importantly only with respect to intention. Intention is what makes them different actions. To put the point in a general way, failure to take account of intention means that we are unable to mark the difference between doing x in order that y shall result and doing x knowing that y will result.[3]

The second point about intention is its moral significance. The crucial difference between the Smith and Jones of our earlier example is that Jones is committed to behaving differently from Smith toward those of the enemy who have removed themselves from the role of combatant (or been removed through wounds). The belief that force must be directed against the combatant and not the man is the only presupposition that could provide a moral basis for taking prisoners.[4] Smith would have no reason to observe this distinction. He might, on a whim or for immediate reasons of prudence, decide to spare the life of the enemy, but he is not logically committed by his beliefs to doing so. The belief that a combatant who voluntarily restrains himself or who is restrained by being wounded ought to be immune from further attack is only intelligible as a moral injunction on the basis of the distinction between the man and the man as combatant. The moral principle that prisoners ought to be taken and well treated also accords with the equality principle that one should not impose upon others burdens that one could not reasonably impose upon oneself.

To summarize: to those who argue that there is no relevant difference or distinction between combat killings and any killings, we may reply that given that the provisions of *jus ad bellum* apply, force may be directed in such a way that the death of the enemy combatant is foreknown but not willed in the sense that his death could reasonably be described as a murder. As Paul Ramsey and others have argued, the purpose of combat as expressed in the actions of individual soldiers is the incapacitation or restraint of an enemy combatant from doing what he is doing as a soldier in a particular historical situation; it is not the killing of a person. This is the essence of the distinction between killing in war and murder in the case of combatants, and the moral relevance of the premise is exhibited in the obligation to respect prisoner immunity, an obligation not incumbent upon someone who fails to observe the central distinction between the man and the man as combatant. Thus, an action may have an unintended but foreknown consequence for which the agent will not be culpable. The intention to restrain or incapacitate the combatant from doing what he is doing is compatible with the foreknowledge that he will be killed.

The intention to incapacitate will entail that soldiers provide the enemy with reasonable opportunity to remove themselves from the role of combatant and, if wounded, with facilities for humane treatment. Finally, it should not be supposed that the intention to incapacitate entails any naive restrictions with respect to targeting or other purely tactical matters; for example, soldiers cannot be required to avoid firing at vital areas of the body, etc., or otherwise to place themselves at unreasonable risk. That is, a soldier will routinely take actions that will cause the death of the enemy. Soldiers will not be understood as killing *in order* to incapacitate but as using their weapons with the intention to stop the enemy, while knowing that in most circumstances the only available weapons and tactics will cause death. A soldier fighting in a justified war ought to intend the former but be prepared to accept the latter if given no choice. At the same time, states do have an obligation to seek agreements prohibiting weapons that tend to create unnecessary damage, as in the case of the Hague convention banning the dumdum bullet, poison bullets, and bullets containing glass.

We turn now to the second of our questions regarding *jus in bello*: noncombatancy and the principle of noncombatant immunity. In the modern era the problem of noncombatants is frequently thought to center upon the supposed difficulty of distinguishing a separate class of noncombatants. A typical example is the following comment of Joseph Margolis.

One of the favorite issues that the genteel discussion of war has insisted on concerns the treatment of innocent parties. Miss Anscombe, registering the prevailing view, says that it is murderous to attack innocent people. She also says that innocence is a legal notion but if it is then apart from appeal to a higher law the very idea of an innocent party will be controlled by the overriding notion of how to justify a given war. For example, in a racial or ethnic war or even in a more conventional war between states that is expected to run for generations, there is no clear sense in which, say, bearing children, the future warriors of an enemy power, can be irresistably discounted as the activities of noncombatants. What is true of women and children in this regard is true, *a fortiori*, of factory workers, Red Cross personnel, priests, and the like.

Constraints on attacking this or that fraction of an enemy population depend at least on the clarity with which a distinctly professionalized army may be specified: Talk about the people's militia, treat every infant as a budding soldier, organize the nation's farmers as fighting soldiers, and you will have blurred the very basis on which the older distinctions between combatants and noncombatants were drawn. At any rate, in the face of novel forms of war and the apparently sincere rejection of restraints, that in more conventional wars were thought to bind the behavior of combatants, it is difficult to see that the old constraints can be merely assumed to be fair.[5]

This kind of argument is quite common but suffers from a too literal reading of war solidarity propaganda. In fact, it is not difficult to distinguish in any actual historical war whole classes of people who cannot, save in the inflamed world of the propagandist, be said to be combatants in any sense that would make them the object of attack. There will, as with every interesting distinction, be borderline cases. The criterion will be something like this: generally speaking, classes of people engaged in occupations that they would perform whether or not a war were taking place, or services rendered to combatants both in war and out, are considered immune from direct attack or targeting. This would exempt, for example, farmers and teachers (since education and food are necessities in and out of war) but not merchant sailors transporting war materials or railway drivers in charge of munitions trains. In other words, the soldiers who are now eating and studying would be doing these things even if they were not soldiers. We attack only those who are attacking us and who are supplying them with the means (guns/ammunition) for such attacks.

Much of the contemporary effort to undermine the combatant/noncombatant distinction comes from advocates of various forms of irregular warfare such as terrorism and insurgency. Consider the comment of George Habbash of the Popular Front for the Liberation of Palestine: "In the age of the revolution of peoples oppressed by the world imperialist system there can be no geographical or political boundaries or moral limits to the operations of the people's camp. In today's world no one is 'innocent' and no one is a 'neutral.' "[6]

Anyone who has seen the faces of civilians caught in the coils of the many wars of our century cannot but reject this kind of effort to characterize them as combatants. They are victims of what is to them usually a completely meaningless cataclysm equivalent to a natural disaster. This description is accurate even if they in a general way "support" their government. For given the power and technological means available to modern states, we cannot but expect the average person to support the political order of which he is a member. In any event, the terrorist argument on this matter is advanced with total hypocrisy, not as Margolis contends with "apparently sincere rejection of restraints." In the aftermath of the U.S. raid on Libya in April 1986, the television networks endlessly replayed scenes of wounded civilians in hospital. Muammar Qaddafi and his supporters around the world decried the civilian casualties as murderous attacks on innocent people. Similar reactions take place after each Israeli raid on PLO camps in Lebanon. One really can't have it both ways. Either we accept Habbash's dictum that there is no distinction between combatants and noncombatants, in which case there can be no objection to U.S. and Israeli raids on *those* grounds, or we don't, in which case the terrorist tactics of the PLO will have to be rejected. Either there is a distinction between legitimate and illegitimate targets or there is not. In condemning those who kill their own women and children, they are tacitly admitting that the distinction does obtain.

The major problem here is not the difficulty in delineating classes of people who merit immunity but in determining what constitutes a direct attack upon them. Despite the fact that the Libyan raid was directed at military targets and that civilian damage was unintended, there was widespread unease and accusations of "state terrorism" from many quarters. So obviously very great care has to be taken not only to practice discrimination and proportionality but to be seen to practice them. It is clearly not enough to initiate combats merely intending not to harm noncombatants; soldiers must be prepared to put themselves at some risk to avoid risking civilian casualties. While there is no formula for this, we clearly expect, and justice requires, that special care be taken if soldiers are to escape culpability for noncombatant deaths.

There are two lines of argument defending noncombatant immunity— moral and prudential. The first is put succinctly by Michael Walzer:

The rule (noncombatant immunity) can also be defended because of the intrinsic value it attaches to human personality. It requires that we pay attention to what men and women are actually doing, that we regard and treat them as responsible agents. So we fight soldiers, who are armed and trained and committed to fight us (whether or not they are actually engaged in combat). But we do not fight civilians who, whatever their hopes for our destruction, are not engaged in bringing it about. Obviously this defense is challenged by the claim, frequently made, that there are no noncombatants in modern war. This claim is certainly exaggerated (small children are always, one might say eternally, noncombatants) but I am inclined to say it is false unless stated very modestly indeed. In modern war there are fewer noncombatants than ever before. This minimal claim follows from the conventional recognition that munitions workers are at least partial combatants subject to attack in their factories (though not in their homes)—for modern war requires a very large industrial plant. But there remain vast numbers of people who are not engaged in any activity properly called warmaking. In the words of G.E.M. Anscombe, they "are not fighting and not engaged in supplying those who are with the means of fighting." Intentional attacks upon them do not seem to be properly called combat.

Such attacks victimize and exploit innocent people, turning them into means to an end which, it must be stressed again, they were not opposing in any military way, though they may have opposed it in other ways when they were alive. In the bombing of cities, civilians are effectively claimed as hostages by the enemy and like more conventional hostages are degraded from moral agents to human pawns even before they are murdered.[7]

The second line of argument supporting noncombatant immunity is prudential. An examination of actual historical instances of the violation of the rule of noncombatant immunity reveals a pattern. The decision to directly attack noncombatants, whether in the saturation bombings of World War II, strategies of massive nuclear retaliation, or the more familiar "terrorism" of the PLO and the IRA, always begins with a consequentialist justification that direct attacks upon noncombatants will produce net beneficial moral consequences. A good example of this is Robert Taber's discussion of the Moroccan insurgency.

The ultimate cost was nevertheless far lighter than it would have been, the terror more merciful (if that is the word) than any campaign of what we choose to call *conventional war*.

The reason is clear. In Morocco, as in Israel and Ireland, revolutionary warfare provided a shortcut; the pressure generated by terrorism and political agitation proved more potent than infantry divisions and aircraft.[8]

Moral questions aside, this argument is imprudent. The just war tradition carries the implication that war is a political act and, as such, must be directed to the production of rational political goals. Over the long haul of history states have discovered that the prudent way of achieving these goals of statecraft is to create a uniformed class of combatants who will resolve outstanding, and otherwise unresolvable, issues by a trial of strength. The justice and urgency of one's cause may tempt one to take "shortcuts," but the actual consequences of doing so (as opposed to the predicted outcomes of the consequentialists) tend to be uniformly imprudent. For once the shortcut is established as precedent, then nothing is easier than for one's opponents to imitate it. The kind of terrorism advocated by Taber tends to be ineffectual as a shortcut precisely because it involves direct attacks upon noncombatants, thereby creating a climate of fear and hatred that will linger on indefinitely to poison relations between the contending factions. Two of the countries Taber mentions are actually counterexamples to his thesis: Israel and Ireland. The continuing sad history of these two areas is directly connected with the practice of terrorism. The imprudent character of violations of civilian immunity is well described by Walter Laquer.

But even their [terrorist] achievements are usually problematical. By aggravating the crisis they make the solution of the problem more difficult or even impossible. For national and religious minorities are dispersed in such a way in today's world that resolving one grievance usually creates a new one. Given the complexity of the modern world, not every minority can have a state of its own. Seemingly successful terrorist operations (such as in Cyprus) have, in fact, ended in disaster insofar as they have poisoned the relations between the communities and made peaceful co-existence impossible. Recent events in Northern Ireland and the Middle East may have the same results: The longer terrorism lasts, the stronger the belief that there will be no peace until the other group is annihilated. With the progress in terrorist technology from the dagger to the means of mass destruction, the consequences seem ominous.[9]

Every political community has prudentially calculated the unacceptable cost to social cohesion of random and indiscriminate violence, and all have some prohibition of it. This is why a little judicious terrorism is not really possible, for the fear it generates and the precedent it sets will overwhelm any "moral" efficacy it may have as a shortcut. This, incidentally, reveals the poverty of a certain consequentialist model that treats human lives as identical counters in a bargaining game; it matters a great deal, morally and prudentially, whose lives we are taking and by what means.

A final point on the prudential aspects of *jus in bello*: Margolis's description of just war arguments as "genteel" reflects a common view that the just war tradition is essentially other-worldly. On the contrary, the upholders of justice in war intend to reflect the prudential concerns of modern societies and to claim that here at least there is no divergence of morality and state interest. The prudent society will necessarily seek to use force in a discriminate and proportional way. The prudent society will concern itself with the interests of those who cannot see to their own interests and will generate the concepts of combatancy and noncombatancy, for the prudent society will realize that to do otherwise will invite the opponent to respond in kind, creating an escalation of arbi-

trary, indiscriminate, and unrestrained violence, which can hardly be
in the interests of a rational statecraft.

Two general conclusions may be reached at this point. First, in a
justified war combatants fight other combatants, and this term refers to
a specially designated class of persons publicly identifiable and carrying
arms openly. The use of force in combat is directed toward incapacitation
where possible, not killing. Combatant deaths are foreseen but are compatible with the intention to incapacitate. Second, noncombatant immunity is presupposed and will be stated in categorical terms.
Noncombatant deaths may also be foreseen but will be regarded as
collateral if they occur in the context of a justified war as outlined above.
In both instances, the role of double effect articulates the relevant distinctions and shows that the critic of *jus in bello* mistakenly runs together
intention and foreknowledge.

If the principle of noncombatant immunity is now intelligible, we may
turn to the question of its status. This has been the most intensely
discussed issue in the contemporary literature. As I have indicated, the
principle is normally stated in absolute terms, but this fact has not prevented a sustained attack by consequentialists. The usual scenario is for
defenders of the principle of noncombatant immunity to begin by affirming the categorical nature of the principle by declaring an absolute
prohibition against direct attacks upon noncombatants. The critic then
points out that the consequences of such a priorism would be disastrous.
He is then likely to produce a series of now familiar examples of the
form, "Suppose a mad scientist threatened to destroy the world unless
we agree to torture a young child to death. Surely it would be grossly
immoral to refuse to comply. Only someone equally as mad as the mad
scientist would stick to principle in a case like this."

Defenders of noncombatant immunity have frequently responded in
one of two ways:

1. Sometimes they dismiss the critic by simply denying that such a situation
   could ever arise. This is the "fantastic example" rejoinder. Such cases, it is
   argued, are preposterous and are typical philosopher's fantasies bearing little
   relation to the real world.
2. Sometimes it is said that, even if such examples did occur, we need not act
   on the stark alternatives offered by the consequentialist. Further information
   about the situation would yield other alternatives for action. This is the "insufficient data" rejoinder. So, even if we were convinced that the mad scientist
   possessed a device to destroy the world, we might try other means of saving
   the world, such as assassination or capture, rather than giving in to him.

The trouble with the first of these attempts is that it tacitly admits that
if such situations came to pass they would be relevant. As for the "in-

sufficient data" reply, the critic can always reconstruct his example in such a way as to avoid resolution of the dilemma. It has been quite generally supposed, therefore, that some version of consequentialism must be triumphant here and that the principle of noncombatant immunity cannot be reasonably treated as categorical. Although a full scale treatment of consequentialism is beyond the limits of this chapter, it is necessary to say something in a general way about that perspective.

The idea that it is possible to stipulate the maximization of interests (pleasure, happiness, and so on) as *the* criterion of correct moral behavior arose, historically, as an answer to the supposed problem of the disappearance of generally agreed upon standards of objective morality. Consequentialism seeks to replace the perceived hetrogeneity of values with a maximizable standard. But such a program is, in effect, meaningless. For the injunction to measure and compute what is good in a way that would make it possible to maximize it would require that human beings have some single end toward which all their actions are inexorably directed. Alternatively, human actions and goals, so obviously varied, would have to be conceived as sharing some common factor that would allow the operation of a calculus of greater good/lesser evil. But even the most cursory of human goods should cast doubt on such a project. Human goods are such that it makes no sense to say that they are either subsumable under one heading or are commensurable in a way that would allow their maximization. This fact is usually recognized by consequentialists themselves (John Stuart Mill comes to mind) when they distinguish between "higher" and "lower" pleasures, desires, interests, and so forth.

If human life in all its many forms is a fundamental value, a good in itself, how is it possible to measure such a thing whereby one might calculate that the lives of this innocent group of people are to be sacrificed to save another (larger?) group of lives? My act of torturing a young child in order to bring about the consequences of saving the world would be a reasonable act only if it were possible to commensurate human goods in the required way. The actual consequence of harming the child is the child's death and suffering. The salvation of the world (if it happens) would be the result of another discrete act (that of the madman), which would be only one of the innumerable possible outcomes of the act of killing. As John Finnis puts it:

Now we have already seen that consequences, even to the extent that they can be "foreseen as certain," cannot be *commensurably* evaluated, which means that "net beneficial consequences" is a literally absurd general objective or criterion. It only remains to note that a man who thinks that his rational responsibility is to be always doing and pursuing good, and is satisfied by a commitment to act always for the best consequences, is a man who treats every aspect of human personality (and indeed, therefore, treats himself) as a utensil. He holds himself ready to do *anything* (and thus makes himself a tool for all those willing to threaten sufficiently bad consequences if he does not cooperate with them).[10]

The consequentialist argument applied to wartime situations generally involves some conception of "necessity" that is said to require either the overriding of rights or the superseding of rights in the name of producing overall good consequences. A typical example is provided by Alan Ryan:

If we deliberately bomb civilian targets we do not pretend that civilians are combatants in any simple fashion, but argue that this bombing will terminate hostilities more quickly and minimize all around suffering. It is hard to see how any brand of consequentialist will escape Miss Anscombe's objections. We are certainly killing the innocent . . . we are not killing them for the sake of killing them but to save the lives of other innocent people. Consequentialists, I think, grit their teeth and put up with this as the logic of total war. Miss Anscombe, and anyone who thinks like her, surely has to redescribe the situation or else she has to refuse to accept this sort of military tactics as simply wrong.[11]

The focus of the consequentialist argument in favor of killing some innocent people as a deliberate policy in order to save the lives of others and to "terminate hostilities more quickly and minimize all around suffering" has the defect of extreme abstraction. In the first place, the proposal to maximize good in this way runs up against the difficulty that there is no logical way to determine prior to one's "calculations" which of the various principles of maximized good is the correct one. Certainly there is no way on purely consequentialist grounds for preferring any particular one of the following: overall utility, average utility, maximum, or equal amounts. But until we know which principle of the distribution of good is the correct one, then the slogan "The greatest good for the greatest number" really makes no sense.

Furthermore, the claim that consequentialists must simply "grit their teeth" and accept the "logic" of total war reveals, I suspect, that what is crucial in decisions to directly attack innocent people is not the consequentialist calculus at all but a desire for a particular outcome—in this case, a shortcut to ending the war. Having decided upon this objective, one can easily ignore questions of justice to individuals and focus upon "good and bad" consequences of effecting or failing to effect the desired outcome.

Thus the calculus is forced through to provide a determinate solution (the quickest, cheapest way of getting what was first focused upon: hence the forced collectivization and liquidation of the farmers, the nuclear or firestorm bombing of the enemy's hostage civilians, the inquisitorial torture of suspects or informers, the obstruction of legal process, the abortion of unborn, and "exposure" of newly born children). Of course, by focusing on some other alternatives and on the life possibilities of the proposed victims, and so on, one can in every case find reasons to condemn the favored action on "consequentialist grounds." But in truth both sets of calculations are equally senseless. What generates the "conclusions" is always something other than the calculus: an over-powering desire, a predetermined objective, the traditions or conventions of the group.[12]

Here Finnis singles out another crucial defect in the consequentialist approach. Because moral judgments are based upon projections into the (infinite?) future of the life prospects of the parties among whom we are choosing and because none of us possesses a crystal ball, we are left in the intolerable position of grounding our judgments on preferred future scenarios at the expense of known and present goods. In short, ethics becomes mere *advocacy*.

A final historical point: it is sometimes noted that the view I have taken of the categorical nature of noncombatant immunity does not clearly surface until late in the tradition; Aquinas does not discuss these issues in the way they were later argued by other thinkers. The explanation for this lies in the rise of the all powerful modern state, claiming absolute sovereignty and embodying the Machiavellian ethos that the end justifies the means. In other words, discussion of noncombatant immunity as absolute awaited the challenge of the rise of full blown consequentialism. For Aquinas, and Christians generally, it would go without saying that direct attacks upon innocent people as a means of achieving a further good would not only be immoral but blasphemous, arrogating to human judgment the work of divine providence. Indeed, it is not entirely clear that the kind of consequentialism expressed so succinctly in *The Prince* ("In the actions of men, and especially of princes, from which there is no appeal, the end justifies the means") would even be intelligible to a thinker in the thirteenth century. The simultaneous rise of the sovereign ruler, from whose edicts there is no appeal and for whom the task of statecraft permits use of any means whatever, and the decline in belief in divine providence creates a dramatically different political climate in which previously unstated and assumed positions on the use of force now need to be articulated and defended. I would, therefore, argue that noncombatant immunity as absolute is central to the just war tradition.

The new conception of human life as a quantifiable determinant always available for sacrifice in the pursuit of some greater (usually political) good has by now become a commonplace, so deeply has it penetrated the Western psyche.

One arrives at a very different judgement, however, if human life is regarded not as a concrete, specific, essentially quantifiable object but as a good in which each person participates but which none exhausts or sums up in himself. In such a view of reality it is simply not possible to make the sort of calculation which weighs lives against each other (my life is more valuable than John's life, John's life is more valuable than Ed's and Tom's combined, etc.) and thus determines whose life shall be respected and whose sacrificed. The value of life, each human life, is incalculable, not in any merely poetic sense but simply because it is something not susceptible to calculations, measurement, weighing, and balancing.

Traditionally this point has been expressed by the statement that the end does not justify the means. This is simply a way of saying that the direct violation of any good intrinsic to the person cannot be justified by the good result which such a violation will bring about. What is extrinsic to human persons may be used for the good of persons, but what is intrinsic has a kind of sacredness and may not be violated.[13]

## NOTES

1. Bernard Brodie, *War and Politics* (New York: Macmillan, 1973), p. 376.

2. Thomas Aquinas, *Summa Theologica* (New York: Benziger Brothers, 1947–48), 2/2, Q. 64, Art. 7.

3. This is a modification of an example in A. MacIntyre, "The Idea of a Social Science," in A. MacIntyre, ed., *Against the Self-Images of the Age* (London: Duckworth, 1971), pp. 211–29.

4. There are many excellent discussions of the problem of prisoner immunity. The best is in Paul Ramsey, *The Just War: Force and Political Responsibility* (New York: Charles Scribner's Sons, 1968), pp. 397, 415. The argument that just force is to be directed only at the combatant and not the man derives from Aquinas. I follow Ramsey's interpretation throughout this discussion.

5. Joseph Margolis, *Negativities* (Columbus, OH: Merrill, 1975), p. 53.

6. *Time*, April 12, 1970, p. 32.

7. Michael Walzer, "World War II: Why Was This War Different?" in N. Cohen, ed., *War and Moral Responsibility* (Princeton: Princeton University Press, 1974), p. 95.

8. Robert Taber, *The War of the Flea* (New York: Lyle Stuart, 1969), p. 131.

9. Walter Lacquer, *Terrorism* (Boston: Little, Brown, 1977).

10. John Finnis, *Natural Law and Natural Rights* (Oxford: Oxford University Press, 1979), p. 121.

11. Alan Ryan, review of *Morality and Utility*, by Jan Narveson, *Philosophical Books* 9, no. 314 (1972), p. 46.

12. Finnis, *Natural Law and Natural Rights*, p. 117.

13. Germain Grisez and Russell Shaw, *Beyond the New Morality: The Responsibilities of Freedom* (Notre Dame, IN: University of Notre Dame Press, 1974), pp. 128–33.

# 9

## Islam and the Distinction between Combatants and Noncombatants

*John Kelsay*

### INTRODUCTION

There can be no question that the distinction between combatants and noncombatants, and the subsequent "immunity from harm" of the latter, is central to Western notions of the limitation of war. The developed form of the just war tradition, in particular, stresses this distinction as a part of its concern for justice in war (the *jus in bello*). According to Robert Phillips, the distinction rests on the "categorical prohibition of murder."[1] To put it another way, combatants and noncombatants are distinguished so that one might avoid killing the just (or the innocent) along with the unjust (or the guilty).

In this chapter, I want to suggest that the connections between the combatant/noncombatant distinction and the "categorical prohibition of murder" are not so obvious as one might think. The notion of noncombatant immunity is actually one way—the way most characteristic of just war thinking—of specifying who the just (or the innocent) are. To say it another way: the categorical prohibition of murder does not yield noncombatant immunity without attention to a number of other factors: religious and military factors, as well as moral ones. Attention to Islamic discussions of justice in war reminds one of this. Such discussions do not point to a notion of noncombatant immunity, purely and simply. But that does not mean that Islamic thought is inattentive to the concern for justice in war. Rather, it indicates that the substance of "justice" and "innocence" takes on a distinctive cast in the Islamic tradition. In short, the Islamic tradition on the limitation of war, like the Western/Christian one, involves the development of a consensus on justice in war: a

consensus that refers, in some sense, to considerations that are fundamentally moral, but which must be specified in terms of an interaction
with religious, political, and military (that is, nonmoral) factors.

I begin with an account of some classical Sunni perspectives on the
rules of war.[2] I shall argue that in a variety of ways these materials
demonstrate the interaction of moral and nonmoral factors in the development of a consensus on justice in war. This will be particularly
evident in connection with the distinction between combatants and noncombatants. As I argue, this is what one should expect: such notions as
"innocence" and "justice" need specification. And this need is fulfilled
under the influence of religious and military, as well as moral factors.

I then consider a number of examples of import for contemporary
Islam. I shall argue that these examples continue to demonstrate the
connections between moral and nonmoral factors in the development
of ideas concerning the limitation of war. Even more, I shall suggest
that there is a paucity of attention in contemporary Islamic discussions
of the *jus in bello* concerns, and that this points to the difficulty of keeping
a moral tradition "up to date" when its interaction with military and
political matters is limited. I close with some reflections on the significance of these points for the comparisons of Western and Islamic approaches to the limitation of war.

## CLASSICAL ISLAM AND THE RULES OF WAR

Classical Islamic perspectives on the rules of war make use of a number
of sources. Some of these are self-evident in the texts of the Sunni jurists,
which constitute our primary source of official Islamic teaching. The
treatise of Muhammad ibn al-Hasan al-Shaybani (d. 804 or 805), for
example, appeals to a number of *ahadith*, or reports of the words and
deeds of the Prophet. The following is one of the most suggestive for
the topic of this essay.

Whenever the Apostle of God sent forth an army or a detachment, he charged
its commander personally to fear God, the Most High, and he enjoined the
Muslims who were with him to do good [i.e., to conduct themselves properly.]
And [the Apostle said]: Fight in the name of God and in the "path of God"
[i.e., truth]. Combat [only] those who disbelieve in God. Do not cheat or commit
treachery, nor should you mutilate anyone or kill children. Whenever you meet
your polytheist enemies, invite them [first] to adopt Islam. If they do so, accept
it, and let them alone. You should then invite them to move from their territory
to the territory of the *émigrés* [Medina]. If they do so, accept it and let them
alone. Otherwise, they should be informed that they would be [treated] like the
Muslim nomads [Bedouins] [who take no part in the war] in that they are subject
to God's order as [other] Muslims, but that they will receive no share in either
the *ghanima* [spoil of war] or in the *fay'*. If they refuse [to accept Islam], then

call upon them to pay the *jizya* [poll tax]; if they do, accept it and leave them alone. If you besiege the inhabitants of a fortress or a town and they try to get you to let them surrender on the basis of God's judgment, do not do so, since you do not know what God's judgment is, but make them surrender to your judgment and then decide their case according to your own views. But if the besieged inhabitants of a fortress or a town asked you to give them a pledge [of security] in God's name or in the name of His Apostle, you should not do so, but give the pledge in your names or in the names of your fathers; for, if you should ever break it, it would be an easier matter if it were in the names of you or your fathers.[3]

In other places, al-Shaybani cites other reports that reinforce and add to this one. The following are of special interest for the topic at hand:

He [of the enemy] who has reached puberty should be killed, but he who has not should be spared.

The Apostle of God prohibited the killing of women.

The Apostle of God said: "You may kill the adults of the unbelievers, but spare their minors—the youth."

Whenever the Apostle of God sent forth a detachment he said to it: "Do not cheat or commit treachery, nor should you mutilate or kill children, women, or old men."[4]

As presented by al-Shaybani, these reports of the Prophet's example form the foundation for Islamic reasoning about the conduct of war. This is consonant with the general approach of classical Sunni jurisprudence, which was still in a developmental phase when al-Shaybani wrote. The phenomenon of devotion to the Prophet Muhammad and the sense that all Muslim behavior should be systematically, consistently scrutinized in terms of the guidance of God must be seen as a primary motivation for the development of classical Sunni thinking on war (and on other matters).

The jurists' ideas of the rules of war do not rest entirely on the example of the Prophet, however. As Abdulaziz Sachedina shows, the Sunni jurists in particular developed and presupposed a particular interpretation of the Qur'an, which may be read, at least in part, as an apologia for the conquests of the mid to late seventh century.[5] A jurist such as al-Shaybani thus presupposed the connection of Islam with an imperial state and its power—specifically, the power of the Abbasid caliphate, by whom he (like other jurists) was appointed as chief *qadi* or "judge." It was the task of scholars like al-Shaybani to make judgments concerning the religious legitimacy of the Abbasid caliph's policies; most (though not all) of the time, he was able to identify those policies as in the interests of Islam.

Finally, jurists such as al-Shaybani developed their ideas about the conduct of war in connection with military practice. Fred Donner suggests that a number of practices, including notions of who may or may not be killed in war, are taken by Muslims from the pre-Islamic culture of Arabia or from the conquered regions.[6] I presume this is true, though the present state of our knowledge is short on details. What is clear from the works of jurists like al-Shaybani is that Muslim scholars were familiar with the basics of military practice and strategic thinking as these existed during the period of imperial Islam. The jurists did not, then, develop their ideas about war in a vacuum. Their work presupposes and contributes to the development of a cultural consensus on the conduct of war: a consensus in which religious, moral, political, and military factors all have a part to play. This becomes clear if one considers their answers to several basic questions: *who* must fight?; *when*?; against *whom*?; *how* may the enemy be dealt with?; *where* does one find the enemy?; and by what *means* may military success be pursued? The first two of these questions have been dealt with in this book by Sachedina and Charles Butterworth; thus my discussion of them will be brief.[7] The last four, however, have to do with the conduct of war, and they are revealing with respect to the question of Islam and the distinction between combatants and noncombatants. I shall therefore devote somewhat more attention to them.

To begin, we ask who must fight? To a certain extent, the answer depends on what type of war is envisioned. For al-Shaybani, as for other Sunni jurists, the "normal" example is connected with the effort (*jihad*) to extend the boundaries of Islamic territory. This struggle, for which the preferred means is the spread of the Islamic message through preaching, teaching, and the like, may nevertheless take on the character of war. When it does, there is a "collective obligation" (*fard kifaya*) laid upon the community to supply the necessary manpower for a successful military action. Adult males who are able-bodied and have no debts are obligated to do their part for the sake of Islam—though this does not mean that all such males are obliged to fight. It is permissible, even exemplary, for some to sponsor others. So long as there is a full complement of men to fight, it is legitimate for some to take as their part the sponsorship of others, providing weapons, horses, and the like.[8]

If the situation changes, however, so that the aim becomes the defense of Islamic territory against enemy attacks, the nature of the obligation shifts. It is no longer *fard kifaya*, but *fard ʿayn*, an "individual obligation," in which each must do all that he can for the sake of Islam. While the focus of the obligation (adult, able-bodied males) remains the same, the distinction between "collective" and "individual" responsibilities is intended to reflect increased urgency.

*When* one fights is already suggested by the preceeding paragraphs. The Sunni jurists thought of the world as divided into two spheres: the one, *dar al-islam*, signified the territory where Islamic norms had official recognition. It was by definition the territory of peace, order, and justice—more precisely, one could say, it was the territory where the best approximation of such things existed. The other sphere, *dar al-harb*, signified the territory where the willful human tendency toward "heedlessness" (*al-jahil*) and ignorance of God prevailed. Again by definition, this was the sphere of war, disorder, and injustice. Even when these factors were mitigated, as in the case of a Christian empire or state, there was the danger of misguidance. And thus the territory of Islam—really, the world—could not be a secure place until and unless Islamic hegemony was acknowledged everywhere. To secure such hegemony was the goal of the *jihad*, or "struggle" (in the path of God). According to the Sunni jurists, war or *jihad* by means of "killing" (*qital*) is justified when a people resists or otherwise stands in opposition to the legitimate goals of Islam.[9]

In the "normal" circumstance, such resistance is indicated by a refusal to acknowledge Islamic hegemony. Muslims are to invite their enemies, first, to acknowledge Islam (i.e., to become Muslims). If this invitation is accepted, then there is no cause for war. If not, the enemies are invited to submit to Islamic hegemony by paying tribute. Again, acceptance of the invitation indicates a willingness to live under the norms of Islam. But if neither invitation is accepted, the state of war becomes actual. And, in answer to the question *against whom?* one must say: the people who refuse to submit; the people of the *dar al-harb*, individually and collectively. They have refused to acknowledge Islam, and so they become the "people of war" (*ahl al-harb*). The sole exception would be those who, while residing in the territory of war, are themselves Muslims—say, merchants traveling among the "people of war." As I shall show, these are not considered legitimate targets for direct attack by the Muslims, though their deaths may be brought about indirectly.

The notion of the "people of war" suggests collective responsibility for refusal to accept Islamic hegemony. In a sense, each member of the resistant people is an enemy of Islam. This does not mean, however, that each member is equally the object of lethal force. The Prophetic reports previously cited indicate that children, women, and others are exempt from killing in war. But it is not altogether clear how these exemptions are to be taken. Some jurists (e.g., al-Shafi'i, d. 820) distinguish between women who are polytheists and women who are Jews and Christians.[10] The former should be killed, while the latter should not. Further, the situation is complicated by the fact that even those who everyone agrees should be exempt from killing (children) are legitimate targets of other types of force—e.g., enslavement. All enemy persons may, under certain conditions, be regarded as booty for the Muslim forces.

A distinction suggested by Ibn Rushd (Averroes), here writing as a jurist, is useful in this connection.[11] He notes that there are three ways in which an enemy may be "damaged." These are with respect to property, person (i.e., life and limb), and liberty. Taking the second category first, one notes that all those among the enemy who engage the Muslims in battle are legitimate objects of force. If they are killed, there is no difficulty, which is what one would expect. However, such persons may also be killed as captives. Prisoners of war may be killed according to the discretion of the commander of the Muslims—in particular, adult males. Faced with a group of such prisoners, the commander has the discretion to decide whether they should be killed or taken as booty, according to a calculation of costs and benefits to the Muslims. He is otherwise limited only if the captives become Muslims—in which case their *person* is inviolable, although their *liberty* is not, and they are to be regarded as booty—or, if they can show they were taken under false pretenses, for example, they were in possession of a valid *aman* or "pledge of security."[12]

Women and children are in a somewhat different category. In one sense, they, along with land, stock, and other goods, are the property of the enemy males. Their being taken is thus a harm or a type of damage done to male warriors. Yet there are restrictions on what may be done to them. The first and most rigorous of these applies to children, who are not to be killed. This is a direct requirement of the Prophetic saying cited earlier. For comparative purposes, the interesting question is: is this a notion of noncombatant immunity? Perhaps, but two special features must be noted. First, insofar as children are not to be *killed*, some of the evidence suggests the reason is that they have not reached the age of refusal of Islam.[13] They are in the custody of their parents, and as nonbelievers they are subject to "damage." But their responsibility is diminished by their age (and competence). They are not therefore subject to lethal damage.

Second, the prescription against killing children is only given full force in the case of children taken captive. One can easily imagine situations in which children might become victims of the sword during a military action. The just war tradition, with its notions of noncombatant immunity, could nevertheless excuse such actions under the notion of double effect. The deaths of children would thus be described as "accidental"; the killing is unintentional, or better, coincidental to the main object of battle.[14]

Sunni jurists undertake such reasoning only in the case of Muslim children, however. Thus, in a case where a city is besieged or a ship attacked by archers, and it is known that Muslims will be killed, the notion of unavoidable yet unintentional killing appears.[15] But in the case of non-Muslim children, the Muslim forces are not responsible. "They are from them," said the Prophet upon hearing that some women and children had been killed by Muslims during a night raid.[16] That is, the deaths are not the fault of Muslims. Responsibility devolves to those who, in their decision-making capacity, have chosen to resist Islam. The need for excuses or justification exhibited in the phenomenon of double-effect reasoning does not seem to appear.

It is along these lines that we may interpret the rulings of certain jurists with respect to women, too. I have mentioned already that certain jurists could argue that, in the case of polytheists, women should be killed. I should note here that such jurists have in mind the situation of captivity; in battle, they assume women may be killed. Others take a different line. Thus, al-Shaybani argues that women captives are to be taken as booty, even at cost to the Muslims. In one section of his treatise, al-Shaybani discusses difficulties that may emerge in the transport of human booty, and argues as follows. If the leader of the Muslims has no means to transport this booty, he should kill the males. But women and children must be spared; means must be hired to transport them to the territory of Islam. Why are women spared and men not? There is the word of the Prophet, of course, and that is actually all the reason al-Shaybani gives. But one must say that his judgment does *not* indicate a notion of noncombatant immunity *as such*. It indicates only that, in the controlled situation of captivity, women are not subject to damage that deprives them of life. Whether this is based on an estimate of probable threat (the males might become a kind of fifth column in the territory of Islam) or on a notion of diminished responsibility, as with children, is an open question.[17]

*Where* one deals with the enemy is a subset of *how* one may deal with him or her. Thus the status of enemy persons varies, as do the duties/ rights of Muslim combatants in relation to them, according to location in the territory of war or of Islam. In his discussion of booty, for example, al-Shaybani indicates that, while every free Muslim male who partici-pates in the *jihad* has a right to a share of the spoil, such rights are not to be exercised until the spoil has been returned to the *dar al-Islam* ("the place of [Islamic] security"). One reason for this is practical—all partic-ipants deserve a share; so it is best to wait until the campaign is over to make divisions.[18]

A second reason has to do with status, however. In a discussion of a married woman captive, al-Shaybani indicates that, so long as she and her husband remain together (i.e., in terms of territory), their marriage holds and no Muslim has rights to her. That is, unless one of the partners is taken to the territory of Islam before the other. Then, "the wedlock would be broken."[19] In a similar vein, booty pledged as "prime" (i.e., excepted from the general booty and belonging to whoever captures it) cannot be used or sold until it is taken to the territory of Islam.[20]

As to the *means* of war, Sunni jurists seem in general to have held the principle *vim vi repellere licit*. Thus, al-Shaybani:

[an inquirer asked] Do you believe that it is objectionable for the believers to destroy whatever towns of the territory of war that they may encounter?

[al-Shaybani answered] No. Rather do I hold that this would be commendable. For do you not think that it is in accordance with God's saying, in His Book: "Whatever palm trees you have cut down or left standing upon their roots, has been by God's permission, in order that the ungodly ones might be humiliated." So, I am in favor of whatever they did to deceive and anger the enemy.[21]

In another place, al-Shaybani discusses various modes of attack. The context is siege warfare, and al-Shaybani approves of the use of arrows, lances, flooding, burning with fire, and mangonels. This is so, even though the issue is specifically framed to indicate the presence of "slaves, women, old men, and children" in the city. Further, "even if they had among them [Muslims], there would be no harm to do all of that to them." Why?

If the Muslims stopped attacking the inhabitants of the territory of war for any of the reasons that you have stated, they would be unable to go to war at all, for there is no city in the territory of war in which there is no one at all of these you have mentioned.[22]

Are there any exceptions to this general rule? Yes, but these again point to a certain discrepancy between the Western just war tradition and the reasoning of Sunni jurists with respect to the rules of war. The first exception has to do, for example, with the killing of children—but not just any children. We are to imagine a case in which the residents of a besieged city shield themselves with Muslim children. According to al-Shaybani, "The warriors should aim at the inhabitants of the territory of war and not the Muslim children."[23] Here there is a notion of double effect, unlike the case of non-Muslim children killed during a military action.

The other exception to Shaybani's general rule has to do with the "pledge of security" (*aman*) by which a citizen of the territory of war comes under the protection of a Muslim. Under certain conditions, this provides a pledge of immunity which has temporary and positivistic status.[24]

Now, what shall we make of these various judgments? The Sunni jurists do not, it seems to me, articulate a notion of noncombatant immunity. I note, however, that the larger category of just war reasoning is actually "discrimination." Contemporary work on the genesis of non-combatant immunity suggests it is the result of a consensus reached through the interaction of a variety of elements: religious, moral, military, and political. Even so with Sunni legal thought.[25] If I may say it this way, the Qur'an recognizes, as do other religious and moral traditions, that there is a "categorical prohibition of murder." One never takes life without cause, as Sachedina notes in his chapter.[26]

But specifications of murder depend, in some sense, on the work of nonmoral factors. If murder is "unjust killing" or the "direct taking of innocent life," one must know wherein injustice or innocence lie. The formal category is insufficient. We must know what the material content of such notions is if they are to be meaningful for an exercise such as the attempt to limit war. Western thought worked these out in terms of the distinction between combatants and noncombatants—in a sense, a specification of innocence that depends on the role one plays. "Soldiers," qua soldiers, are not innocent—regardless of their subjective involvement with the war effort. "Civilians," qua civilians, are innocent—again, with little or no attention to the fact that they may be leading the cheers in favor of the war.[27] Classical Sunni jurisprudence dealt with this question in a different way. Guilt and innocence have to do with religious and political factors. How does one fit in the scheme of things, as understood from the Muslim point of view? Specifically, is one a part of a people who are in opposition to the establishment of an order of justice and peace (i.e., an Islamic order), or not? And what is one's place in that people? If one is a leader (an adult, able-bodied male), one's guilt is obvious. If one is a follower (child, woman), one's guilt may be diminished. In either case, one is liable to "damage"; the question is only what type and how. And, given the goals of Islamic hegemony, the *means* of war that are appropriate are affected. Military might is meant to serve the cause of justice. It should not be used indiscriminately, if one means by that "carelessly." Considerations of proportionality are important, since one wants to shed no more blood than is necessary. But the necessities of the war effort motivated by religious considerations allow for considerable discretion. Should women and children be killed in the pursuit of battle, it is not the fault of the Muslims. "They are from them." The leaders of the people of war are at fault for the death of their "innocents."

## RULES OF WAR IN THE CASE OF REBELLION[28]

This fact—i.e., the determination of discrimination by nonmoral, especially religious factors—is further illustrated by al-Shaybani's treatment of the rules for fighting against dissenters and rebels. His discussion of these rules begins with the citation of a report on the practice of Ali b. Abi Talib (fourth caliph after the Prophet, d. 661). Ali's precedent is especially important in this regard, since his caliphate began with and eventually was ended by the action of dissenters. According to al-Shaybani's report, Ali said in the Battle of the Camel: "Whoever flees [from us] shall not be chased, no [Muslim] prisoner of war shall be killed, no wounded in battle shall be dispatched, no enslavement [of women and children] shall be allowed, and no property [of a Muslim] shall be confiscated."[29] This precedent forms the basis for the following exchange:

> If there were two parties of believers, one of them is rebellious (party of baghi) and the other loyal (party of justice), and the former was defeated by the latter, would not the loyal party have the right to chase the fugitives [of the other party], kill their prisoners, and dispatch the wounded?
>
> He [al-Shaybani] replied: No, it should never be allowed to do so if none of the rebels has survived and no group remained with whom refuge might be taken; but if a group of them has survived with whom refuge might be taken, then their prisoners could be killed, their fugitives pursued, and their wounded dispatched.[30]

Several aspects of this exchange are of interest. In particular, note the difference in treatment of the rebels (who are Muslims) from that of the people of war. Even according to al-Shaybani's judgment, which seems less generous than that of Ali b. Abi Talib, there is a clear distinction: after the war is over, no prisoners are to be killed. Why is this the case? Because, even though the rebels are a threat to order in the territory of Islam, they remain Muslims. If such rebels are killed in a war which they have provoked, such killing is right. But there remains a certain obligation to them that is distinct from that owed to the people of war. Thus, the "loyalists" cannot impose a peace that requires the rebels to pay tribute. This is so, says al-Shaybani, "because [the rebels] are Muslims; therefore, nothing should be taken from their property, for this would amount to kharaj" (that is, "land tax," in effect, tribute).[31] Again, if a group of *dhimmis* (protected non-Muslim minorities, notably Jews and Christians) join with the rebels in fighting, the fact that the rebels remain Muslims protects the *dhimmis*.

> If the rebels sought the assistance of a group of Dhimmis, who took part in the fighting along with them, do you think that [the Dhimmis' participation in the fighting] would be regarded as a violation of their agreement [with the Muslims]?
>
> [al-Shaybani replied]: No.
>
> I asked: Why?
>
> He replied: Because they were in the company of a group of Muslims.[32]

In the case of *baghis*, the cause of war is different than in the war against *dar al-harb* (alternatively, the war to expand *dar al-islam*). And thus the notion of discrimination is viewed somewhat differently. Guilt is established, not by a refusal to acknowledge the priority of Islam, but by an uprising against the established authority in the territory of Islam. After the war is over, the idea seems to be that the rebels are restored to the house of Islam.

During the conduct of fighting, however, al-Shaybani remains a proponent of *vim vi repellere licit*. One notes the following exchange (which is nearly an exact parallel to his judgment concerning appropriate means in an action against the people of war):

I asked: Would it be objectionable to you if the loyalists shot [the rebels] with arrows, inundated [their positions] with water, attacked them with manjaniqs [mangonels], and burned them with fire?

He replied: No harm in doing anything of this sort.

I asked: Would a sudden attack at night be objectionable to you?

He replied: No harm in it.[33]

In other passages, al-Shaybani takes up questions involving women who fight with the rebels; they may be killed.[34] Should such women be taken prisoner, however, they are not to be executed, but imprisoned until the fighting ends.[35] In that sense, they are treated as a non-fighting slave would be. Should a slave or freeman be fighting with the rebels, however, he would be executed, so long as the fighting continues.[36]

The rules governing the fighting of rebels thus continue to demonstrate the qualification of moral concerns for discrimination in war by nonmoral, especially religious considerations. The development of discrimination in classical Sunni thought is not fully consistent with the specification of the developed just war tradition, with its distinction between combatants and noncombatants. But it is not altogether inconsistent, either.

## THE *JUS IN BELLO* IN CONTEMPORARY ISLAM

When one turns from these classical materials to more contemporary discussions, one is first struck by the scarcity of *jus in bello* materials. Unlike the classical jurists, contemporary Muslim thinkers seem mostly interested in the *jus ad bellum*. There are a number of possible explanations for this fact. Most convincing, prima facie, is an explanation that refers to the recent history of Islam. At least since 1924, when the Caliphate was abolished, many of those most involved in planning military strategy for Muslim countries or groups have drawn heavily on traditions

that are not specifically Islamic. To put it another way, Muslims who
have been doing the most thinking about the conduct of war have not
been doing so as self-conscious developers of the tradition of Islamic
thought. The PLO provides a prime example. Until the developments
of 1988, many of the official documents that state the justification and
strategy for the "armed struggle" against Israel have spoken the language of Arab nationalism and have drawn on models of revolutionary
struggle or "people's war" exemplified in (for example) the Vietnamese
conflict or the Algerian struggle against colonialism.[37]

According to the Palestine National Assembly meeting in Cairo in
July, 1978, the enemy consists of "three interdependent forces": Israel,
Zionism, and world imperialism, of which the United States is the chief
director.[38] Israel is "the tool of the Zionist movement and a human and
geographical base for world Imperialism. It is a concentration and
jumping-off point for Imperialism in the heart of the Arab homeland,
to strike at the hopes of the Arab nation for liberation, unity, and
progress."[39]

To struggle against this enemy, by whatever means one can muster,
is just. Correspondingly, those who support the enemy or who stand
idly by incur guilt and become, in some sense, legitimate targets of
military force. Ideological considerations become the measure of the
notion of discrimination.[40]

That this is so is further indicated by statements of PLO leaders that
do indicate some considerations in accord with discrimination. For example, in his November 1974 speech to the UN, Yassir Arafat declared:

Since its inception, our revolution has not been motivated by racial or religious
factors. Its target has never been the Jew, as a person, but racist Zionism and
aggression. In this sense, ours is also a revolution for the Jew, as a human being.
We are struggling so that Jews, Christians, and Muslims may live in equality,
enjoying the same rights and assuming the same duties, free from racial or
religious discrimination . . . *We distinguish between Judaism and Zionism.* While we
maintain our opposition to the colonialist Zionist movement, we respect the
Jewish faith.[41]

The PLO's war with Israel, here as elsewhere, is defined in ideological,
even territorial terms. The just or innocent are those who do not join in
supporting Zionism in its "usurpation" of Palestinian land (and its denial
of Palestinian rights). The unjust, correspondingly, are those who are
active in support of Zionism, including citizens of imperialist powers
who do not distance themselves from their nation's policy. According
to the 1968 National Assembly, the method of armed resistance best
suited to the interests of the Palestinians is a protracted war that will
expose Zionism and "its complicity with world imperialism," and will

"point out the damage and complications [Zionism] causes to the interests and security of many countries, and the threat it constitutes to world peace."[42]

What one might like (even, from classical Islamic tradition, expect) is to see a greater attention to the question of degrees of guilt on the part of the citizens of Israel and the "imperialist" powers. Should children, for example, be counted as guilty? The closest one comes to such attention is the willingness of Palestinian spokespersons to foreswear military actions outside the territory of Palestine. There is a recognition here of the difficulties of "guilt by association" and a specification that the war is really about usurpation of territory. Correspondingly, the Palestinian leadership's unwillingness to foreswear military operations inside the borders of Israel points once again to the criterion by which guilt is established: those who indicate support for Zionism by dwelling in the territory of Palestine become legitimate targets for military action. And as to children, one sometimes hears Palestinians argue that Israeli children are "placed" in the land by supporters of Zionism. In a manner reminiscent of the example of the Prophet Muhammad, Palestinian activists thus argue that such children become targets, not through their own doing, but through the action of others. Their deaths are unfortunate, but do not indicate Palestinian guilt. Rather, the guilt is upon those who placed the children in the land.[43]

In more explicitly Islamic materials, two types of writing have been predominant in modern discussions of *jihad*: one is apologetic and seeks to indicate to the world that Islam is not a "religion of the sword." The other is revolutionary and seeks to indicate the justice of Islamic struggle against Imperialism. In either case, one finds only the most tenuous discussion of the conduct of war, the obvious reason being that one is not dealing with treatises written by people like al-Shaybani, who were, at least at times, actually engaged in questions of policy.

My example of apologetic literature is Mahmud Shaltut's *The Koran and Fighting*.[44] Shaltut's treatise, first published in 1948, illustrates the thought of a formidable Sunni scholar, eventually the Shaykh al-Azhar, the leading spokesman for "establishment Islam" in Egypt. His purpose in writing is to illumine the relation between Islam and warfare, a topic which he says

is of practical importance in our times, as wars are being fought all over the world, engaging everybody's attention. Moreover, it has a theoretical significance, as many adherents of other religions constantly take up this subject with a view to discredit Islam. Therefore, people would do well to learn the Koranic rules with regard to fighting, its causes and its ends, and so come to recognize the wisdom of the Koran in this respect: its desire for peace and its aversion against bloodshed and killing for the sake of the vanities of the world and out of sheer greediness and lust.[45]

According to Shaltut, the mission of Muhammad, expressed in the Qur'an, is as "a bringer of good tidings and as a warner."[46] The Qur'an summons humanity to submit to God; this is "natural" to humanity, though it is difficult for those "who do not reflect." True submission is a matter of the heart; it cannot be forced. Thus the Qur'anic dictum: "No compulsion in religion" (2:256). Therefore, fighting cannot be a part of the Islamic mission.

The Qur'an does of course contain verses on fighting. But according to Shaltut, these deal with the defense of the Islamic community. "Permission is granted to those who [have] fought because they have suffered wrong; verily to help them Allah is able. Who have been expelled from their dwellings without justification, except that they say: "Our Lord is Allah." (22:39–41) All justified war is defensive, according to Shaltut. There is no hint in the Qur'an of a justification of "conversion by force."

Thus far, Shaltut has dealt with the *jus ad bellum*. But what of the *jus in bello*? Here we find much less. According to Shaltut, the Qur'an strengthens the morale of the nation for fighting. It deals, in other words, with "factors that may lead to cowardice and weakness" and encourages self-sacrifice for the defense of the Islamic community.[47] Further, the Qur'an gives advice on the preparation of the material power necessary to war. God has said: "We formerly sent Our messengers with the Evidences, and We sent down with them the Book and the Balance, that the people might dispense justice; and We sent down Iron, in which there is violent force and also uses for the People, and (We did so also) in order that Allah might know who would help Him and His messengers in the unseen; verily Allah is strong, sublime" (57:25). For Shaltut, the mention of iron is crucial; iron encourages the development of industry, especially for the sake of defense.[48]

Finally, the Qur'an deals with certain aspects of the practice of warfare, for example, exemptions from military service, the necessity of declarations of war, army discipline, and the like. Only one heading (out of fourteen) deals with the issue of interest to this chapter. Discussing prisoners of war, Shaltut quotes Qur'an 8:67: "It is not for a prophet to have prisoners so as to cause havoc in the land," and comments:

When the Imam has caused havoc in the land and when the taking of captives has been allowed to him, he may choose between liberating them out of kindness without any ransom or compensation and taking ransom from them, which may consist of property or men. The choice must be made on the basis of what he sees as the common interest. "So when you meet those who have disbelieved, let there be slaughter until when you have made havoc of them, bind them fast, then liberate them out of kindness or in return for ransom." (Qur'an 47:4)[49]

With respect to the *jus in bello*, Shaltut's treatise is unsatisfying. Yet the preoccupation of the text with the *jus ad bellum* fits with his purpose. It also, I suggest, suits his political standing in the Egyptian state. The Shaykh al-Azhar is required to play a certain role in Egypt; that role involves setting forth the general rules governing the use of force in Islam. It does not involve a serious engagement with the particulars of military strategy, such as al-Shaybani's treatise exhibits.

My example of a revolutionary treatise is also from Egypt. The tract entitled *Al-Faridah al-Ghai'bah*, advertised as the "Creed of Sadat's Assassins," is a fascinating text in many respects.[50] Its greatest importance lies in its argument for the necessity of fighting in pursuit of an Islamic state and in its refusal to accept any "in between" solutions to the problem of forming an Islamic polity. Those rulers who attempt to implement a "mixed regime," in which laws derived from Islamic and non-Islamic sources form an amalgam of norms, are apostates and should be killed. Similarly, those who support these rulers in their apostacy should be killed. The point of fighting is the formation of an Islamic polity, which ought to be universal.

Again, the preoccupation of the text is with the *jus ad bellum*. Two sections (out of 140) deal with issues of discrimination in war. In the first, the author cites two versions of the *hadith* in which the Prophet, informed of the deaths of women and children during a night raid, says "They are from them." The author comments: "This means: when they [Muslim soldiers] do not do it on purpose without need for it (it is allowed to kill these dependents)."[51]

The second section cites two *hadith* reports in which the Prophet forbids the killing of women, children, and old men. The author comments simply: "The previous Tradition . . . concerning the permissibility of killing dependents does not contradict this Tradition inasmuch as the situation in each Tradition is different from the other."[52]

We may explain the relative lack of development of this point in one of two ways: either the author is uninterested in the *jus in bello*, or he is not actively engaged with military affairs in such a way that the kind of cases that would lead to a fuller development of *jus in bello* considerations are presented to him. I think we must opt for the latter. It is typical of much twentieth-century Islamic thought that it is not involved with considerations of statecraft. The planning and implementation of military strategy, as other aspects of political life, have by and large not been the province of Islamic thinkers in the last two centuries. Islamic thought has been either in the position of providing legitimacy, and perhaps general guidance to a leadership which has generally been authoritarian and more concerned with modernization than Islamization; or it has been in the position of opposing such leadership—in Bruce Lawrence's terms, it has been a language of resistance.[53]

## THE WAR BETWEEN IRAN AND IRAQ

It is only very recently that this factor has begun to change. The Islamic Republic of Iran is in some sense attempting to implement Islamic norms in all phases of social and political life. At least, that is its stated aim. And while a book like Shaul Bakhash's *Reign of the Ayatollahs* demonstrates that finding consensus on the implementation of "Islamic economics" and "Islamic land reform" is rather difficult, we have no reason to doubt the commitment of Iran's leadership to the development of an Islamic state.[54] That being the case, we might expect that the war with Iraq would lead Iran's leaders to the formulation of some significant judgments concerning the conduct of war, including considerations of discrimination. In fact, the very thorough analysis by Shahram Chubin and Charles Tripp in *Iran and Iraq at War* does show an increasing engagement by Islamic thinkers with the actual conduct of modern war.[55] Such analysis also shows, however, the way that nonmoral factors enter into thinking about the issues involved in the *jus in bello*. This seems particularly clear when the speeches and statements of Iranian leaders are compared with those on the Iraqi side.

Chubin and Tripp begin by noting that the war was defined by Iranian leaders, especially the Ayatollah Khomeini, in Islamic terms.

You are fighting to protect Islam, and he [Saddam Hussein] is fighting to destroy Islam. . . . There is absolutely no question of peace or compromise and we shall never have any discussions with them; because they are corrupt and perpetrators of corruption.

The damage caused by this criminal is irreparable unless he withdraws his forces, leaves Iraq and then abandons his corrupt government; he must leave the Iraqi people to decide their own fate. *It is not a question of a fight between one government and another; it is a question of an invasion by an Iraqi non-Muslim Baʿthist against an Islamic country: and this is a rebellion by blasphemy against Islam.*[56]

Those who criticize us say: Why do you not compromise with these corrupt powers? It is because they see things through human eyes and analyse these things with a natural viewpoint. They do not know the views of God and how the prophets dealt with oppressors or else they know but pretend to be blind and deaf. To compromise with oppressors is to oppress. That is contrary to the views of all the prophets.[57]

By contrast, Saddam Hussein seems to have viewed the conflict as a "sovereigns' war," in which a brief conflict would serve to show his strength as a leader. The point was to discourage Khomeini (viewed as just another authoritarian leader) from acting on rhetoric suggestive of a "revolution without borders." This view was quite mistaken; as Saddam Hussein learned this, the Iraqi war effort was redefined in terms of the survival of the Iraqi state, symbolized by the rule of Saddam Hussein. And since the official Iraqi ideology was Baʿthist, the war could also be depicted as a defense of Arab nationalism against the "Persian enemy." What began as a limited war became a war to prevent Iran from occupying Iraq.

These diverse definitions of the war had an impact on its conduct. The Iranian emphasis on self-sacrifice, the development of the Revolutionary Guards (Pasdaran) as a special military force alongside of (and often superior to) the regular army, the use of "human wave" tactics—all received ample publicity in the Western press. The following statements are typical of the thinking of Iran's leadership: "The nation that comes out ready to be martyred will not be intimidated by the threat of martyrdom."[58] Or again, "Victory is not achieved by swords, it can only be achieved by blood. . . . It is achieved by the strength of faith."[59]

Perhaps less appreciated is the extent to which the Iranian leadership seems to have thought of their endeavor as a variation on the theme of a "people's war," by which they meant a war involving the entire nation in a protracted struggle against an enemy whose military power exceeded their own. Defense Minister Fakhuri argued that the war was a struggle "between right and wrong"; unlike a "war between two armies in the classical sense," it would not be a "short-term and local war," but a "people's war" which would last for years.[60] According to the commander of the Revolutionary Guards, the relevant models for such a struggle were Vietnam and Algeria.[61]

There is an important twist in all this, however. Iran's version of the "people's war" was to be Islamic. Indeed, one leader spoke of "doing away with conventional warfare methods" in favor of "Islamic warfare."[62] For the most part, this seems to have meant a war fought by those with Islamic motives. According to Chubin and Tripp, Iranian war planning was "concerned less with outcomes than with processes; less with gaining victory than with affirming certain values and commitments."[63] At various times, speakers in the Majlis commented that it would be better to lose half the territory of Iran than to fight in a way not consonant with Islamic values.

Of specific interest to this essay is some material on the restraint of war. The Iranian leadership distinguished between Saddam Hussein, his partisans (members of the Baʿth), and the Iraqi people. Iran viewed the Iraqis as oppressed people; the leadership thought that the collapse

of Saddam Hussein's regime would follow Iranian resistance to his invasion of its territory. The people of Iraq would bring this about, encouraged by Iran's willingness to defend Islam. Eventually, Iraq would
follow the Iranian path and establish an Islamic government. According
to Rafsanjani: "We think that in the future, when an Islamic or people's
government is set up in Iraq . . . that will be more useful for the people
of Iraq who remain."[64]

The point is that the war was not to be a war against the Iraqis. It
was a war against the Ba'thist regime, with Saddam Hussein as its
symbol. According to Khomeini, the Iranians "think of Islam and wish
to act according to Islamic teachings." Thus, the military should "do
nothing to harm the cities which have no defence. . . . Our hands are
tied, because we do not wish the ordinary people, the innocent people,
to be hurt."[65] In his 1982 speech honoring the Revolutionary Guards,
Khomeini recalled the initial strikes of the Iranian air force into Iraq. He
noted that they destroyed numerous military targets, and said they could
have done far more damage "were it not for their Islamic commitment
and their desire to protect the innocent and their fear of destroying
property belonging to the brotherly Iraqi nation—a fact which still in-
hibits them."[66]

Iran held this view into 1984. Chubin and Tripp argue that such statements were not simply rhetorical: "In practice, Iran's sensitivity on the
matter of casualties was more pronounced when it came to those of Iraq
than when it concerned its own."[67] In this respect, it is interesting to
note the conclusions of the UN Security Council's report on "Prisoners
of War in Iran and Iraq."[68] While the mission dispatched by the Secretary
General did not entirely clear Iran of accusations that POWS had been
physically abused in certain settings, the characteristic Iranian offense
against the Third Geneva Convention was held to be certain types of
"ideological abuse." Prisoners were divided into "loyalists" (to the Iraqi
regime) and "believers" (who indicated their support for an Islamic
polity). The latter were given certain special favors, which seems to have
created an atmosphere of tension in part responsible for the disturbance
at Gorgan in October 1984. If this is accurate, it follows from the Iranian
sense that the Iraqi people would be open to "liberation" from the
oppressive regime of Saddam Hussein, and from the notion that Iran
should encourage this openness.

Eventually, Iran seems to have dropped this positive view of the Iraqi
people. The Iraqis did not rush to overthrow Saddam Hussein or the
Ba'th. Chubin and Tripp suggest this was less due to Iraqi nationalist
sentiment than to factors intrinsic to the Shi'i population in Iraq: small,
poor, unorganized; its chief characteristic was inertia.

Chubin and Tripp think the Iranian realization that there would be
no quick and stealthy uprising by the Iraqi populace contributed to the

decision to shell Basra in February 1984. In this interpretation, the shelling would symbolize a growing conviction that the Iraqi people must be held responsible for their continued support of Saddam Hussein. However, the same authors note that Iran's attacks on Iraqi cities (eventually the Iranians fired Scud missiles on Baghdad, too) generally followed Iraqi attacks on Iranian cities. Iran did not resort to chemical weapons, as did Iraq, nor did it carry on a "tanker war" to the same extent as Iraq. In general, the judgment of Chubin and Tripp is that "Iran's policy was to *respond* to Iraq's attacks at sea or on the cities to show that it was capable of doing so, and in order not to relinquish its right to do so or to acquiesce in Iraq's unilateral aims."[69]

By contrast, Iraq's war strategy seems to have been dictated by the calculus of military necessity. In the early phase of the war, when the conflict was defined by Saddam Hussein as a "sovereigns' war," the plan was for Iraqi forces to demonstrate their capacity to occupy territory. After the Iranians indicated that they were quite willing to respond with force, the Iraqi troops were ordered to capture the city of Khorramshahr, which they did—"reducing it largely to rubble in the process"—and then they laid siege to Abadan.[70] According to the Iraqi president, this constituted the military defeat of Iran and should have led to Iran's recognition of Iraq's rights.

This was not to be the case. Iran's military readiness was greater than the Iraqi leadership expected, so that the "sovereigns' war" quickly became a war of survival. Iran would be forced to listen to the "logic of force," said the minister of foreign affairs.[71] That logic quickly led to the conclusion that attacks on the civilian population were necessary in order to cut support for the Khomeini regime.

The rulers of Iran cannot go on with the war without the earnest backing, in word and deed, of their supporters. Therefore, the need to influence the relationship between the rulers of Iran and their supporters, by creating divergence between them on the question of war and peace, is of paramount importance.[72]

To a certain extent, this "divergence" involved the use of chemical weapons on Iranian troops. The Iraqi high command broadcast a warning to these troops to the effect that Iraq had "modern weapons [which] will be used for the first time in war," and which had "not been used in previous attacks for humanitarian and ethical reasons. . . . If you execute the orders of Khomeini's regime . . . your death will be certain because this time we will use a weapon that will destroy any moving creature on the fronts."[73] Eventually, the UN would issue a condemnation of Iraq for the use of such weapons, though Iraq continued to deny using them, at least officially.

In the meantime, other aspects of the Iraqi attempt to create the aforementioned "divergence" involved attacks on Iranian cities. In 1984, these attacks provoked the Iranian bombardment of Basra and Baghdad, leading to an agreement to stop the "war of the cities." In 1985, 1986, and 1987, this agreement was repeatedly broken and restored. In 1987, Iraq bombed Qom, apparently in an attempt to hit a target that would not only involve harm to the civilian population, but also encourage opposition to the war among Iranian religious specialists. During such episodes, Iran repeatedly made known its grievances to the UN Security Council, and Iraq repeatedly denied that its air forces had struck anything but military targets.[74]

More than anything else, Iraq's behavior bears witness to the definition its leaders gave to the war. A "sovereigns' war" is limited in its objectives and its expenditure of the sovereigns' military capacity. It need not be limited by considerations of discrimination and the like, save as those serve the political interests of the sovereign. A "war of survival" knows even fewer limits. It is a war to save the nation, and in that case, anything is justified—unless it draws such vigorous reprisals that the "nation" (Saddam Hussein and the Ba'th) are threatened. Chubin and Tripp note that by 1985, the Iraqi President had redefined victory:

Iraq is now fighting only to prevent Iran from occupying Iraq. Technically speaking, the war may also end by one side achieving a military victory and occupying the land of the other. However, only the first alternative is realistic—one spoiling the aim of the other. When one side fails to achieve its goals through war, it means defeat.[75]

According to Hussein, "Victory for us is to defend ourselves until the other side gives up."[76] Perhaps this explains the Iraqi sense that the 1988 cease-fire indicates victory.

## CONCLUSION

One might go on to discuss other examples. But my point, I think, is established. If we want to understand the Islamic tradition of thought on limiting war, we shall have to recall that cultural traditions on war, peace, and the conduct of statecraft are not purely "moral" traditions. The Islamic approach to these issues reflects the moral concern that the just and the unjust, or the innocent and the guilty, not be equally subject to the damage of war. In that respect, its concerns are analogous to those of the just war tradition. But the content of justice and injustice, guilt and innocence are specified by nonmoral factors: religious, political, and military. I think this is true for the just war tradition as well.

In addition, one cannot underestimate the importance of a real engagement with statecraft, including military strategy, for the formulation of a developed teaching on the conduct of war. Classical Islamic jurists were in rather a different position from most of their modern counterparts in this regard. No doubt, we shall know more about the meaning of "Islamic warfare" as more studies are made of Iranian discussions of the "imposed war" with Iraq. In the meantime, I think we shall have to recognize that a specifically Islamic contribution to the rules governing the conduct of modern war is still very much in process.

## NOTES

1. Robert Philips, "Combatancy, Noncombatancy, and Noncombatant Immunity in Just War Tradition" in this volume.

2. As will become clear, I use "classical" in two senses: first, with respect to the "classical period" of Islamic development—i.e., the period of the Abbasid caliphate (750–1258), during which the great patterns of Islamic piety, religious thought, and social order emerge and come to maturity; second, in connection with the idea of "classic" texts, figures, or frameworks that have an enduring, though not always decisive authority within the Islamic tradition. A more complete account of such texts would include discussion of the works of the Twelver Shi'i jurists. As Abdulaziz Sachedina shows in his chapter, "The Development of *Jihad* in Islamic Revelation and History," there are significant differences between the Sunni and Shi'i jurists, particularly with respect to the *jus ad bellum*. At this point, my own studies indicate that such differences do not extend to the *jus in bello*. See and compare A. Querry, *Droit Musulman. Recueil de lois concernant les Musulmans schyites*, 2 vols. (Paris: Imprimerie Nationale, 1871–72), which is a translation of al-Muhaqqiq al-Hilli, *Shara'i al-Islam fi Masa'il al-Halal wa al-Haram*.

3. From the translation of al-Shaybani's *Kitab al-Siyar* by Majid Khadduri, published as *The Islamic Law of Nations* (Baltimore: Johns Hopkins University Press, 1966). The report constitutes section 1 of Khadduri's translation. In this essay all quotations from al-Shaybani are taken from Khadduri's translation, and citations will be given according to the section numbers rather than by page. Khadduri's introduction contains helpful material about Islamic law in general, and about al-Shaybani's place as a disciple of Abu Hanifa (d. 767). Note that *fay'* (untranslated in the citation), like *ghanima*, indicates booty. The distinctions between the two categories are disputed. See Khadduri's introduction, pp. 48–49.

4. Ibid., sections 28, 29, 30, 47.

5. Sachedina, "The Development of *Jihad*."

6. Frederick Donner, "The Sources of Islamic Conceptions of War," in *Just War and Jihad: Historical and Theoretical Perspectives on War and Peace in Western and Islamic Traditions*, ed. John Kelsay and James Turner Johnson (Westport, CT: Greenwood Press, 1991).

7. Sachedina, "The Development of *Jihad*"; Charles Butterworth, "Al-Fârâbî's Statecraft: War and the Well-Ordered Regime," in this volume. See also John Kelsay, "Religion, Morality, and the Governance of War: The Case of Classical

218 Combatancy, Noncombatancy, and Noncombatant Immunity

Islam," forthcoming in *Journal of Religious Ethics*. Portions of that essay are excerpted here.

8. Compare al-Shaybani, sections 21–25, in Khadduri, *The Islamic Law of Nations*.

9. On these points, Sachedina's chapter becomes especially important.

10. This according to Ibn Rushd. See the translation of the chapter on *jihad* from his Bidayat al-Mujtahid in R. Peters, *Jihad in Mediaeval and Modern Islam* (Leiden, Netherlands: E. J. Brill, 1977), esp. pp. 15–17.

11. Ibid., p. 11ff.

12. Besides Ibn Rushd, *Bidayat al-Mujtahid*, compare al-Shaybani, sections 94 and following; also Ibn Taymiyya, *Siyasah al-Shari'a*, trans. as *Public and Private Law in Islam* by Omar A. Farrukh (Beirut: Khayat's, 1966), pp. 140–43.

13. See al-Shaybani, sections 28, 30. Compare his discussion of the question of whether minor children brought into the territory of Islam as prisoners of war who then die are entitled to the Muslim funeral prayer (408ff).

14. See, among others, James F. Childress, *Moral Responsibility in Conflicts* (Baton Rouge and London: Louisiana State University Press, 1982); also Michael Walzer, *Just and Unjust Wars* (New York: Basic Bopoks, 1977), 138–59.

15. See al-Shaybani, sections 117–23.

16. *Sahih Muslim*, trans. as "The Book of Jihad and Expedition," report no. 4321, by 'Abdul Hamid Siddiqi (Lahore: Sh. Muhammad Ashraf, 1981). See also al-Shaybani, sections 112–13.

17. al-Shaybani, sections 72–81.

18. al-Shaybani, section 71.

19. al-Shaybani, sections 242–57.

20. al-Shaybani, section 336ff.

21. al-Shaybani, sections 88–89.

22. al-Shaybani, section 117.

23. al-Shaybani, section 119.

24. For further discussion, see Kelsay, "Religion, Morality, and the Governance of War."

25. See, especially, James Turner Johnson, *Just War Tradition and the Restraint of War* (Princeton and Guilford, Surrey: Princeton University Press, 1981).

26. Sachedina, "The Development of *Jihad*."

27. I am grateful to my colleague Terrence Tilley, whose article "The Principle of Innocents' Immunity," *Horizons*, 15, no. 1 (1988), p. 43–63 helped me to sharpen this point. I should note that just war thinking can qualify the distinction between soldiers and civilians in this way: "civilians," in the fullest sense, are those whose work or function supports the soldier qua person—i.e., it provides for the soldier's needs as a human being, rather than as a military actor. See Childress, *Moral Responsibility in Conflicts*, and also Walzer, *Just and Unjust War*.

28. For a more complete treatment on this topic, see Khaled Abou El Fadl, "*Ahkam al-Bughat:* Irregular Warfare and the Law of Rebellion in Islam," in this volume.

29. al-Shaybani, section 1372.

30. al-Shaybani, sections 1373–74.

31. al-Shaybani, section 1394.

32. al-Shaybani, section 1401–4.

33. al-Shaybani, section 1417ff.
34. al-Shaybani, section 1444.
35. al-Shaybani, section 1379–80.
36. al-Shaybani, section 1381–86.
37. See the selection in Yehuda Lukacs, ed., *Documents on the Israeli-Palestinian Conflict, 1967–83* (Cambridge: Cambridge University Press, 1984). In light of comments by participants in the USIP Conference Series, for which this chapter was first drafted, I think it important to state that I am treating the ideas of the PLO as one example of a trend in contemporary Islamic cultural discussion of war. I do not intend my discussion as a comment on the current moves by the PLO leadership in relation to the peace process in the Middle East.
38. Ibid., p. 144.
39. Article 22 of the Palestine National Covenant, 1968, in ibid., p. 142.
40. At this point, it seems appropriate to comment on the statement by George Habash that Robert Phillips cites in his chapter "Combatancy, Noncombatancy, and Noncombatant Immunity." I follow Phillips's argument that the architects of a "people's war" (or a "total war") can hardly object to the killing of some of their people on the grounds of noncombatant immunity. But I think the point of such objections is actually that the U.S. and Israeli forces commit such acts in the service of a cause that is by definition unjust. The fact that women and children are killed simply magnifies this perception.
41. Lukacs, *Documents*, p. 174. Emphasis added.
42. Ibid., p. 145.
43. This point was made during the USIP Conference Series by Professor David Little, who had recently conducted a series of interviews in Israel and the occupied territories.
44. Translated by R. Peters in *Jihad in Mediaeval and Modern Islam*.
45. Ibid., p. 27.
46. Ibid., p. 28.
47. Ibid., p. 58.
48. Ibid., p. 60ff.
49. Ibid., p. 65.
50. Translated as *The Neglected Duty* by Johannes J. G. Jansen (New York: Macmillan, 1986).
51. Section 121 of the text as translated by Jansen.
52. Jansen, *Neglected Duty*, section 122.
53. Bruce B. Lawrence, "Holy War (*Jihad*) in Islamic Religion and Nation-State Ideologies," in *Just War and Jihad*, ed. John Kelsay and James Turner Johnson, *supra* note 6.
54. Shaul Bakhash, *Reign of the Ayatollahs* (New York: Basic Books, 1984).
55. Shahram Chubin and Charles Tripp, *Iran and Iraq at War* (London: I. B. Tauris and Company, Ltd., 1988). The discussion which follows is largely a summary of Chubin and Tripp's argument, especially their chapters three and four. Most of the quotations below are originally from FBIS or BBC/SWB sources; I simply cite the page numbers from Chubin and Tripp.
56. Ibid., p. 38. Emphasis added.
57. Ibid.
58. Ibid., p. 40.

59. Ibid.

60. Ibid., p. 42.

61. Ibid.

62. Ibid., p. 43.

63. Ibid., p. 46.

64. Ibid., p. 50.

65. Ibid.

66. Ibid.

67. Ibid.

68. U.N. Security Council, Document S/16962, "Prisoners of War in Iran and Iraq."

69. Chubin and Tripp, p. 51.

70. Ibid., p. 55.

71. Ibid.

72. Ibid., p. 60.

73. Ibid., p. 61.

74. For a sample of such exchanges, see the Security Council's Official Records, Supplement for April-June, 1986.

75. Chubin and Tripp, p. 67.

76. Ibid.

# Select Bibliography

Abd al-Qadir, Awda. *al-Tashr' al-Jinai al-Islami*, vol. 1. Beirut: Dar al-Kitab al-Arabi, n.d.

Abd al-Rahman, Omar. *Kalimat Haq*. Cairo: Dar al-itisam, n.d. al-Ramli. *Nihayat al-Muhtaj*, vol. 7. Cairo: Mustafa al Halabi, 1967.

Abedi, Mehdi, and Gary Legenhausen, eds. *Jihad and Shahadat: Struggle and Martyrdom in Islam*. Houston: Institute for Research and Islamic Studies, 1986.

Abou El Fadl, Medhat. "Jarimat al-Baghy fi al-fiqh al-Islami." April-May-June *al-Mohami* 69 (April-May-June 1982), p. 79.

Akehurst, Michael. *A Modern Introduction to International Law*. London: George Allen and Unwin, 1984.

al-Ansari, Abu Yihya. *Asna al-Matalib fi Sharh Raud al-Talib*, vol. 3. Cairo: al-Mayminyah.

Anscombe, G.E.M. *Ethics, Religion, and Politics*. Minneapolis: University of Minnesota Press, 1981.

Aquinas, St. Thomas. *The Political Ideas of St. Thomas Aquinas*. Ed. Dino Bigongiari. New York: Hafner Press, 1974.

———. *Summa Theologiae*, vol. 35. Ed. Thomas R. Heath. London: Blackfriars, 1972.

———. *Summa Theologiae*, vol. 38. Ed. Thomas R. Heath. London: Blackfriars, 1975.

———. *Summa Theologica*. New York: Benziger Brothers, 1947–48.

———, "Whether It Is Always Sinful to Wage War." *Summa Theologiae*, 2/2, Q. 5, A. 14.

Arberry, A. J. *The Koran Interpreted*. New York: Macmillan, 1967.

St. Augustine. "Reply to Faustus the Manichean." In *A Select Library of the Nicene and Post-Nicene Fathers*. Ed. Philip Schaff. Grand Rapids, MI: Wm. B. Eerdmans, 1956.

Averroes (Abû al-Walîd Muhammad Ibn Rushd). *Averroes' Middle Commentary on Aristotle's Poetics*. Trans. Charles E. Butterworth. Princeton, NJ: Princeton University Press, 1986.

Bainton, Roland. "Congregationalism: From the Just War to the Crusade in the Puritan Revolution." *The Andover Newton Theological School Bulletin* 35, no. 3 (April 1943), pp. 1–20.

al-Bayhaqi. *al-Sunan al-Kubra*, vol. 8. India: Daʿerat al Maʾaref, 1304 Hijra.

Brodie, Bernard. *War and Politics*. New York: Macmillan, 1973.

Bromwich, David. *A Choice of Inheritance: Self and Community from Edmund Burke to Robert Frost*. Cambridge, MA: Harvard University Press, 1989.

al-Buhuti. *Kashaf al-Qina an Matn al-Ina*, vol. 6. Riyad: Maktabat al-Nasr al-Hadithah, n.d.

Calvin, John. *Institutes of the Christian Religion*. Ed. John T. McNeill. Philadelphia: Westminster Press, 1960.

Camus, Albert. *The Rebel*. Trans. Anthony Bower. New York: Alfred A. Knopf, 1954.

Childress, James F. "Just-War Criteria." In *War or Peace?* ed. Thomas A. Shannon. Maryknoll, NY: Orbis Books, 1982.

———. *Moral Responsibility in Conflicts*. Baton Rouge: Louisiana State University Press, 1982.

———. "Some Reflections on Violence and Nonviolence." *Philosophical Papers* 7, no. 1 (May 1978), pp. 1–14.

Childress, James F., and John Macquarrie, eds. *The Westminster Dictionary of Christian Ethics*, 2d ed. Philadelphia: Westminster Press, 1986.

Congregation for the Doctrine of the Faith. *Instruction on Christian Freedom and Liberation*. Washington, DC: United States Catholic Conference, 1986.

al-Dardir. *al-Sharh al-Saghir*, vol. 4. Cairo: Dar al-Maʾarif, 1972.

al-Dasuqi. *Hashiyat al-Dasuqi ala al-Sharh al-Kabir*, vol. 4. n.p.: Dar ihya al Kitab al-Arabi, n.d.

Davis, G. Scott. "Warcraft and the Fragility of Virtue." *Soundings* 70, no. 4 (Winter, 1987), pp. 475–94.

Ellacuria, Ignacio. *Freedom Made Flesh*. Trans. John Drury. Maryknoll, NY: Orbis Books, 1976.

Eppstein, John. *The Catholic Tradition of the Law of Nations*. Washington, DC: Catholic Association for International Peace, 1935.

al-Fârâbî, Abû Nasr Muhammad. *Al-Farabi on the Perfect State, Abû Nasr al-Fârâbî's Mabâdi Arâ Ahl al-Madîna al-Fâdila*. Ed. and trans. Richard Walzer. Oxford: Clarendon Press, 1985. The work is known, more accurately, as *Mabâdi Arâ Ahl al-Madînah al-Fâdilah* (Principles of the opinions of the people of the virtuous city).

———. *The Fusûl al-Madanî, Aphorisms of the Statesman, of al-Fârâbî*. Ed. and trans. D. M. Dunlop. Cambridge: Cambridge University Press, 1961.

———. *Fusûl Muntazaʾah (Selected aphorisms)*. Ed. Fauzi M. Najjar. Beirut: Dar el-Machreq, 1971.

———. *Ihsâ al-ʿUlûm (The enumeration of the sciences)*. Ed. ʾUthmân Amîn. Cairo: Dâr al-Fikr al-ʿArabî, 1949.

———. *Kitâb al-Millah wa Nusûs Ukhrâ (The book of religion and other texts)*. Ed. Muhsin Mahdi. Beirut: Dar el-Machreq, 1968.

————. *Kitâb al-Siyâsah al-Madanniyah*. Ed. Fauzi M. Najjar. Beirut: Imprimerie Catholique, 1964.

Ferrari, Robert. "Political Crime." *Columbia Law Review* 20 (1920), pp. 311–13.

Finnis, John. *Natural Law and Natural Rights*. Oxford: Oxford University Press, 1979.

Fotion, Nicholas, and Gerard Elfstrom. *Military Ethics: Guidelines for Peace and War*. Boston: Routledge and Kegan Paul, 1986.

al-Ghazali, Hamid. *Ihya ulum al-Din*, vol. 1. Beirut: Dar al-Ma'aref, n.d., pp. 306–12.

Goldziher, Ignaz. *Muslim Studies*. Ed. S. M. Stern. London: George Allen & Unwin, 1971.

Gray, J. Glenn. *The Warriors: Reflections on Men in Battle*. New York: Harper & Row, 1970.

Grisez, Germain, and Russell Shaw. *Beyond the New Morality: The Responsibilities of Freedom*. Notre Dame, IN: University of Notre Dame Press, 1974.

Grotius, Hugo. *De Jure Belli ac Pacis, Libri Tres*. Trans. Francis W. Kelsey. Oxford: Clarendon Press, 1925.

Gunnemann, Jon P. *The Moral Meaning of Revolution*. New Haven, CT: Yale University Press, 1979.

————. "Revolution." In *The Westminster Dictionary of Christian Ethics*, 2d ed., ed. James F. Childress and John Macquarrie. Philadelphia: Westminster Press, 1986.

Gutiérrez, Gustavo. *The Power of the Poor in History*. Trans. Robert R. Barr. Maryknoll, NY: Orbis Books, 1983.

Halperin, Morton H. *Limited War in the Nuclear Age*. New York: John Wiley & Sons, 1963.

Harman, Gilbert. "Relativistic Ethics: Morality as Politics." In *Midwest Studies in Philosophy*. Vol. 3, *Studies in Ethics*, ed. P. French, T. Vehling, and H. Wettstein. Minneapolis: University of Minnesota Press, 1980, pp. 109–21.

Harris, John. "The Marxist Conception of Violence." *Philosophy and Public Affairs* 3, no. 2 (Winter 1974), pp. 192–220.

Hartigan, Richard Shelly. *The Forgotten Victim: A History of the Civilian*. Chicago: Precedent Publishing, 1982.

————. *Lieber's Code and the Law of War*. Chicago: Precedent Publishing, 1983.

Hauerwas, Stanley. *Against the Nations: War and Survival in a Liberal Society*. San Francisco: Winston Press, 1985.

Heath, Thomas R. "Appendix 2." In *Summa Theologiae*, vol. 35, St. Thomas Aquinas. London: Blackfriars, 1972.

Hollenbach, David. *Nuclear Ethics: A Christian Moral Argument*. New York and Ramsey, NJ: Paulist Press, 1983.

Holmes, Arthur F., ed. *War and Christian Ethics*. Grand Rapids, MI: Baker Book House, 1975.

Howeidi, Fahmi. *Al-Qur'an wa al-Sultan*. Cairo: Dal al-Shuruq, 1981.

Ibn Abidin, Muhammad Amin. *Hashiyat Radd al-Muhtar*, vol. 4. Cairo: al-Halabi, 1966.

Ibn Hajar al-Asqallani. *Fath al-Bari*, vol. 13. Beirut: Dar al-Ma'aref, n.d.

Ibn Hajar, al-Haythami. *Tuhfat al-Muhtai*, vol. 3. Damascus: Dar al-fikr, n.d.

Ibn Hazm, Abu Muhammad. *al-Muhala*, vol. 11. Beirut: al-Maktab al-Trujari, n.d.

Ibn al-Humam. *Sharh Fath al Ghadir*, vol. 4. Cairo: al-Matba'a al-Qabra, 1316 Hijra.

Ibn Jama'a. *Tahir al-Ahkam fi Tadbir ahl al-Islam*. Qatar: al-Shu'uon al-Diniyah, 1985.

Ibn Manzûr, Muhammad ibn Makram. *Lîsân al-'Arab*. 15 vols. Beirut: Dâr Sâdir, n.d.

Ibn Muflih al-Maqdisi. *al-Mubd'i fi Sharh al-Mughni*, vol. 9. Damascus: al-Maktab al-Islami, 1979.

Ibn Qudamah al-Maqdisi. *al-Mughni*, vol. 8. Cairo: Maktabat al-Qahira, 1969.

Ibn Taymiyya, Taqi al-Din. *Minhaj al-Sunna*, vol. 2. Beirut: al-Maktabah al-il-miyah, n.d.

———. *al-Siyasa al-Shariya*. Beirut: Dal al-Afaq, 1983.

———. *Siyasah al-Shari'a*. Trans. by Omar A. Farrukh as *Public and Private Law in Islam*. Beirut: Khayat's, 1966.

al-Jamal. *Hashiyat al-Jamal*, vol. 5. Cairo: al-Maktaba al-Tujariya al-Kubra, n.d.

Jansen, Johannes J. G., trans. *The Neglected Duty*. New York: Macmillan, 1986.

al-Jaziri, Abd al-Rahman. *Kitab al-fiqh ala al-Mazahib al-Arba'ah*, vol. 5. Beirut: Dar Ihya al-Turath al-Arabi, 1st printing.

Johnson, James Turner. *Can Modern War Be Just?* New Haven, CT: Yale University Press, 1984.

———. "Historical Roots and Sources of the Just War Tradition in Western Culture." In *Just War and Jihad: Historical and Theoretical Perspectives on War and Peace in Western and Islamic Traditions*, eds. John Kelsay and James Turner Johnson. Westport, CT: Greenwood Press, 1991.

———. *Ideology, Reason, and the Limitation of War: Religious and Secular Concepts, 1200–1740*. Princeton, NJ: Princeton University Press, 1975.

———. *Just War Tradition and the Restraint of War: a Moral and Historical Inquiry*. Princeton, NJ: Princeton University Press, 1981.

———. "Morality and Force in Statecraft: Paul Ramsey and the Just War Tradition." In *Love and Society: Essays in the Ethics of Paul Ramsey*, ed. James Johnson and David Smith. Missoula, MT: Scholars Press, 1974, pp. 93–114.

———. *The Quest for Peace: Three Moral Traditions in Western Cultural History*. Princeton, NJ: Princeton University Press, 1987.

Joint Services Conference on Professional Ethics. *Moral Obligation and the Military*. Washington, DC: National Defense University Press, 1988.

al-Juwayni. *Fadaih al-Batiniyya*. Qatar: Matba'at Nahdat Misr, 1401.

al-Kasani. *Kitab Bada'i al-Sanai*, vol. 7. Beirut: Dar al-Kitab al-Arabi, 1973.

Kelsay, John. "Religion, Morality, and the Governance of War: The Case of Classical Islam." Forthcoming in *Journal of Religious Ethics*.

Khadduri, Majid. *The Islamic Law of Nations*. From the translation of al-Shaybani's *Kitab al-Siyar*. Baltimore: Johns Hopkins University Press, 1966.

———. *War and Peace in the Law of Islam*. Baltimore: Johns Hopkins University Press, 1979.

Khaled, Shawqi. *Muhakamat Fir'aun*. Cairo: Sina Lil Nashr, 1986.

al-Kharashi. *al-Sharh al-Saghir ala Khalil*. Printed with al-Adawi, *Hashiyat al-Adawi*, vol. 7. Cairo: al-Matba's al-Kubra, 1317.

Kirchheimer, Otto. *Political Justice*. Princeton, NJ: Princeton University Press, 1961.

Kohlberg, Etan. "The Development of the Imami Shiʿi Doctrine of Jihad." *Zeitschrift der Deutschen Morgenlandischen Gesellschaft* 126 (1976), pp. 69–78.

Kraemer, Joel L. "Apostates, Rebels and Brigands." *Israel Oriental Studies* 10 (1980), pp. 34–73.

———. "The *Jihad* of the *Falâsifa*." *Jerusalem Studies in Arabic and Islam* 10 (1987), pp. 288–324.

Lackey, Douglas P. *The Ethics of War and Peace*. Englewood Cliffs, NJ: Prentice Hall, 1988.

Lacqueur, Walter. *Terrorism*. Boston: Little, Brown, 1977.

Lacqueur, Walter, ed. *The Terrorism Reader*. Philadelphia: Temple University Press, 1978.

Lambton, Ann. *State and Government in Medieval Islam*. Oxford: Oxford University Press, 1981.

Lammers, Stephen E. "Area Bombing in World War II: The Argument of Michael Walzer." *The Journal of Religious Ethics* 11, no. 1 (Spring 1983), pp. 96–113.

Langan, John P. "Violence and Injustice in Society: Recent Catholic Teaching." *Theological Studies* 46 (1985), pp. 685–99.

Lerner, Ralph, and Muhsin Mahdi, eds. *Medieval Political Philosophy: A Sourcebook*. Free Press of Glencoe, 1963.

Little, David. "Some Justifications for Violence in the Puritan Revolution." *Harvard Theological Review* 65 (1972), pp. 577–89.

Little, David, and Sumner B. Twiss, Jr. *Comparative Religious Ethics: A New Method*. San Francisco: Harper & Row, 1978.

Locke, John. *Two Treatises of Government*. Ed. Peter Laslett. New York: Cambridge University Press, 1965.

Lukacs, Yehuda, ed. *Documents on the Israeli-Palestinian Conflict, 1967–83*. Cambridge: Cambridge University Press, 1984.

Lukes, Steven. "Marxism and Dirty Hands." *Social Philosophy & Policy* 3, no. 2 (Spring 1986), pp. 204–23.

MacIntyre, Alasdair. *After Virtue*. Notre Dame, IN: University of Notre Dame Press, 1981.

———. "Epistemological Crises, Dramatic Narrative and the Philosophy of Science." *The Monist* 60, no. 4 (1977), pp. 453–72.

———. "The Idea of a Social Science." In *Against the Self-Images of the Age*. London: Duckworth, 1971, pp. 211–29.

Mahdi, Muhsin. "Science, Philosophy, and Religion in Alfarabi's *Enumeration of the Sciences*." In *The Cultural Context of Medieval Learning*, ed. J. E. Murdoch and E. D. Sylla. Dordrecht, Netherlands: D. Reidel, 1975.

Malik ibn Anas. *al-Mudawwana al-Kubra*, vol. 2. Baghdad: al-Muthanna Library, 1323 Hijra.

Margolis, Joseph. *Negativities*. Columbus, OH: Merrill, 1975.

Markus, R. A. "Saint Augustine's Views on the 'Just War.' " In *The Church and War*, ed. W. J. Sheils. Oxford: Basil Blackwell, 1983, pp. 1–13.

Marx, Karl. "The German Ideology: Part I." In *The Marx-Engels Reader*, ed. Robert
    C. Tucker. New York: W. W. Norton, 1972, pp. 110–64.
al-Mawaaq. *al-Taj wa al-iklil*, vol. 6. Beirut: Dar al-Kitab, n.d.
McHardy, A. K. "The English Clergy and the Hundred Years War." In *The
    Church and War*, ed. W. J. Sheils. Oxford: Basil Blackwell, 1983, pp. 171–
    78.
al-Munziri, Hafiz. *Mukhtasar Sahih Muslim*. Kuwait: al-Dar al Kuwaitiyah, 1966.
National Conference of Catholic Bishops. Ad Hoc Committee on War and Peace.
    *The Challenge of Peace: God's Promise and Our Response*. Washington, DC:
    United States Catholic Conference, 1983.
al-Nawawi. *al-Majmu Sharh al-Muhazab*, vol. 17. Cairo: al-Imam, n.d.
———. *Minhaj al-Talibin*, vol. 3. Batavia: Imprimerie du Gouvernement, 1884.
O'Brien, William V. *The Conduct of Just and Limited War*. New York: Praeger
    Publishers, 1981.
Overton, Richard. "An Appeal from the Commons to the Free People." In
    *Puritanism and Liberty, Being the Army Debates (1645–1649)*, ed. A.S.P.
    Woodhouse. London: J. M. Dent and Sons, 1938, pp. 323–34.
Papadotas, Pierre A. "Le delit politique: Contribution a l'etude des crimes contre
    l'etat." These no. 507, Librarie E. Droz, Geneve, 1954, First part, p. 2
    quoted in B. L. Ingraham and Kazuhiko Tokoro, "Political Crime in the
    United States and Japan: A Comparative Study." *Issues in Criminology* 4,
    no. 2 (1969).
Peters, R. *Jihad in Medieval and Modern Islam*. Leiden, Netherlands: E. J. Brill,
    1977.
Porter, J. M., ed. *Luther: Selected Political Writings*. Philadelphia: Fortress Press,
    1974.
Potter, Ralph B., Jr. "The Moral Logic of War." *McCormick Quarterly* 23 (1970),
    pp. 203–33.
Querry, A. *Droit Musulman. Recueil de lois concernant les Musulmans schyites*. 2
    vols. Paris: Imprimerie Nationale, trans. of al-Muhaqqiq al-Hilli, *Shara'i
    al-Islam fi Masa'il al-Halal wa al-Haram*.
Ramsey, Paul. *Basic Christian Ethics*. New York: Charles Scribner's Sons, 1950.
———. *The Just War: Force and Political Responsibility*. New York: Charles Scrib-
    ner's Sons, 1968.
———. *Speak Up for Just War or Pacifism*. University Park, PA: Pennsylvania State
    University Press, 1988.
———. *War and the Christian Conscience: How Shall Modern War Be Conducted Justly?*
    Durham, NC: Duke University Press, 1961.
Rasmussen, Larry L. *Dietrich Bonhoeffer: Reality and Resistance*. New York: Abing-
    don Press, 1972.
Regout, Robert. *La doctrine de la guerre juste de saint Augustin à nos jours d'après
    les théologiens et les canonistes catholiques*. Paris: A. Pedone, 1934.
Russett, Bruce. *The Prisoners of Insecurity*. San Francisco: Freeman, 1983.
Ryan, Alan. Review of *Morality and Utility* by Jan Narveson. *Philosophical Books*
    9, no. 314 (1972), p. 46.
Sachedina, Abdulaziz A. "Freedom of Conscience and Religion in the Qur'an."
    In *Human Rights and the Conflict of Cultures*, coauthored with David Little

and John Kelsay. Columbia: University of South Carolina Press, 1988, pp. 58–62.

———. *The Just Ruler in Shiʿite Islam*. New York: Oxford University Press, 1980.

al-Samarqandi. *Tuhfat al-Fuqaha*, vol. 3. Damascus: Dar al-Fikr, n.d.

Sanad, Najati. *Nazariyat al-Jarima al-Sayasiya fi al-Islam*. Cairo: Top Guy, n.d.

al-Sarakhsi, Muhammad. *Kitab al-Mabsut*, vol. 9. Cairo: al-Saʾadah, 1324 Hijra.

al-Sawi. *Bulghat al-Salik ila Arab al-Masalek*, vol. 3. Cairo: Dar Ihʾya al-Kutub al-Arabiyah, 1978.

Schacht, Joseph. "Islamic Religious Law." In *The Legacy of Islam*, 2d ed., ed. Joseph Schacht with C. E. Bosworth. Oxford: Oxford University Press, 1974.

———. "Law and Justice." In *The Cambridge History of Islam*, vol. 2B, P. M. Holt, A.K.S. Lambton, and B. Lewis. Cambridge: Cambridge University Press, (1970), pp. 539–68.

al-Shafiʿi, Muhammad ibn Idris. *al-Umm*, vol. 4. Cairo: Kitab al-Shaʿab, n.d.

al-Shaybani, see Khadduri, Majid.

Siddiqi, ʿAbdul Hamid, trans. "The Book of Jihad and Expedition," report no. 4321. In *Sahih Muslim*. Lahore: Sh Muhammad Ashraf, 1981.

al-Tabari, Abu Jaʾfar. *Kitab Ikhtilaf al-fugahaʾ*. Ed. Joseph Schact. Leiden, Netherlands: E. J. Brill, 1933.

———. *Tarikh al-Tabari*, vol. 4. Beirut: Iz al-Din, 1987.

Taber, Robert. *The War of the Flea*. New York: Lyle Stuart, 1969.

Tilley, Terrence. "The Principle of Innocents' Immunity." *Horizons* 15, no. 1 (1988), pp. 43–63.

Tucker, Robert. *The Just War*. Baltimore: The Johns Hopkins University Press, 1960.

Verkamp, Bernard J. "Moral Treatment of Returning Warriors in the Early Middle Ages." *Journal of Religious Ethics* 16, no. 2 (Fall 1988), pp. 223–49.

Victoria, Franciscus de [Francisco de Vitoria]. *De Indis Noviter Inventis* and *De Jure Belli*. In *The Spanish Origin of International Law: Francisco de Vitoria and His Law of Nations*. Ed. James Brown Scott. Oxford: Clarendon Press, 1934.

Wakin, Malham M., Kenneth H. Wenker, and James Kempf. *Military Ethics*. Washington, DC: National Defense University Press, 1987.

Walters, LeRoy Brandt, Jr. "Five Classic Just-War Theories: A Study in the Thought of Thomas Aquinas, Victoria, Suarez, Gentili, and Grotius." Ph.D. diss., Yale University, 1971.

Walzer, Michael. *Just and Unjust Wars*. New York: Basic Books, 1977.

———. *The Revolution of the Saints: A Study in the Origins of Radical Politics*. Cambridge, MA: Harvard University Press, 1965.

———. "World War II: Why Was this War Different?" In *War and Moral Responsibility*, ed. N. Cohen. Princeton, NJ: Princeton University Press, 1974.

Watt, W. Montgomery. *Islamic Political Thought*. Edinburgh: Edinburgh University Press, 1968.

———. "The Significance of the Theory of Jihad." In *Akten des VII. Kongresses fur Arabistik und Islam Wissenschaft*. Gottingen, FRG: 1974, n.n. p. 393.

Wilkinson, Paul. "The Laws of War and Terrorism." In *The Morality of Terrorism: Religious and Secular Justifications*, ed. David C. Rapoport and Yonah Alexander. New York: Pergamon Press, 1982.

Ya'la, Abu. *Al-Ahkam al-Sultaniyah*. Beirut: Dar al-Kutub al-ilimiyah, 1985.
Yoder, John Howard. *The Original Revolution*. Scottdale, PA: Herald Press, 1971.
al-Zuhayri, Wahba. *al-fiqh al-Islami wa adilatuh*, vol. 6. Damascus: Dar al-Fikr,
    1984.

# Index

# About the Editors and Contributors

KHALED ABOU EL FADL received his J.D. from the University of Pennsylvania in 1989 and subsequently held a clerkship with the Supreme Court of the State of Arizona. The author of several articles in Arabic on the relation between international law and Islamic law, he is currently a graduate student in Islamic Studies at Princeton University.

CHARLES E. BUTTERWORTH is Professor of Government and Politics at the University of Maryland, College Park, where he specializes in Islamic political thought. His published works include *Philosophy, Ethics, and Virtuous Rule: A Study of Averroes' Commentary on Plato's "Republic"* (1986) and nine critical editions and translations of works by Averroes, as well as numerous articles.

COURTNEY S. CAMPBELL, Editor of *The Hastings Center Report*, previously taught at the University of Virginia, where he received his doctorate in 1988. He is currently working on a book based on his Ph.D. dissertation, to be entitled *The Moral Reality of Revolution*.

JAMES TURNER JOHNSON is Professor of Religion, Associate of the Graduate Faculty of Political Science, and University Director of International Programs at Rutgers—The State University of New Jersey. He has written extensively on the historical development of just war tradition and its contemporary use. Previous books include *Just War Tra-*

*dition and the Restraint of War* (1981), *Can Modern War Be Just?* (1984), and *The Quest for Peace* (1987).

JOHN KELSAY is Assistant Professor of Religion at The Florida State University. He is a religious ethicist who has specialized in comparative issues between Christian and Islamic traditions. Previous publications include *Human Rights and the Conflict of Cultures* (1988), coauthored with David Little and Abdulaziz A. Sachedina, and "Religion, Morality, and the Governance of War: The Case of Classical Islam" in *The Journal of Religious Ethics* (Fall, 1990).

STEPHEN E. LAMMERS is Professor of Religion at Lafayette College. Coauthor of two books on medical ethics, his published works on Christian tradition on war include "Roman Catholic Social Ethics and Pacifism" in Thomas Shannon, ed., *War or Peace: The Search for New Answers* (1980), and "Area Bombing in World War II: The Argument of Michael Walzer" in *The Journal of Religious Ethics* (Spring, 1983).

ROBERT L. PHILLIPS is Professor of Philosophy at The University of Connecticut at Hartford. He writes widely on contemporary issues of morality, politics, and military affairs. His works include *War and Justice* (1984), and numerous articles and essays.

ABDULAZIZ A. SACHEDINA is Professor of Religion at the University of Virginia, where he specializes in Islamic Studies. His books include *Islamic Messianism* (1980), *Human Rights and the Conflict of Cultures* (1988), coauthored with David Little and John Kelsay, and *The Just Ruler in Twelver Shi'ism* (1988).

TAMARA SONN is Director of the International Studies Program at St. John Fisher College and has also taught at the University of Rochester and at Temple University in Islamic Studies. Her work focuses on contemporary issues of politics and ethics in Islamic societies and includes *The Search for Political Legitimacy in Islam* (1989).

JEFFREY STOUT is Professor of Religion at Princeton University, where he specializes in religious ethics in the western traditions. His books include *The Flight from Authority: Religion, Morality, and the Quest for Autonomy* (1987), and *Ethics after Babel: The Language of Morals and Their Discontents* (1988).